Kropotkin

Reviewing the Classical Anarchist Tradition

Ruth Kinna

EDINBURGH
University Press

Edinburgh University Press Ltd
The Tun – Holyrood Road
12 (2f) Jackson's Entry
Edinburgh EH8 8PJ
www.euppublishing.com

First published in hardback by Edinburgh University Press 2016

Typeset in 11/13 Adobe Sabon by
IDSUK (DataConnection) Ltd, and
printed and bound in Great Britain by
CPI Group (UK) Ltd, Croydon CR0 4YY

A CIP record for this book is available from the British Library

ISBN 978 0 7486 4229 8 (hardback)
ISBN 978 1 4744 2837 8 (paperback)
ISBN 978 1 4744 1041 0 (webready PDF)
ISBN 978 1 4744 0501 0 (epub)

Contents

Acknowledgements

I would like to thank Edinburgh University Press (EUP) for supporting this project, particularly James Dale who first talked to me about the book and Nicola Ramsey and Michelle Houston who took the project over. The number of editors involved is a measure of the time it has taken to complete the writing and I'm extremely grateful to colleagues at EUP for their patience and willingness to agree two extensions for the delivery of the manuscript. It has been a pleasure working with everyone involved.

I owe particular thanks to a number of colleagues: Constance Bantman for generously sharing her research notes on the Grave-Kropotkin correspondence. I'm grateful to Dominique Miething for kindly letting me read his doctoral research on Nietzscheanism and anarchism and to Kristian Williams who corresponded with me about Wilde, Kropotkin and prisons. Süreyyya Evren played a central part in developing ideas about the anarchist canon and George Woodcock's *Anarchism, A History of Libertarian Ideas and Movements*. Bert Altena has been a fantastic critical friend for a number of years, pushing me to answer difficult questions about Kropotkin's nationalism and his response to the First World War. He has also helpfully drawn my attention to archival material relevant to that debate. I've benefited enormously from Saul Newman's research, especially his work on Stirner and anarchist utopianism. He will likely dispute the treatment of egoism and interpretation of the classical tradition as it is presented here, but I'm grateful to him for opening up my eyes to a philosophy that is too easily dismissed and sidelined in anarchist histories. Carl Levy's tireless organisation of a series of anarchist history workshops at Goldsmiths, University of London encouraged me to think about Kropotkin's science and his understanding of colonialism and to clarify my ideas about his conception of the state. Carl has also offered words of support when it seemed as if the project was stalling. Peter Ryley has shared ideas about Kropotkin and his comments on the manuscript helped me think about the coherence of Kropotkin's anti-militarism. I'm grateful to Nathan Fretwell for his feedback on the draft material and, in particular, for his insights on Stirner.

As well as reading some of the manuscript, Alex Prichard has talked me through a number of debates in international relations theory and nineteenth-century geo-politics, has been a brilliant guide to Proudhon and shared ideas about republicanism and anarchism that have contributed to the formulation of some of the arguments about slavery and freedom set out here.

Hugs to Frances and Michel, who entrusted Georg and Christa's copy of the *Paroles d'un Révolté* to my care – a wonderful, treasured gift – and to Robert, Andrew, Pam and David who are always even dearer to me than Kropotkin.

Introduction

Peter Kropotkin has an unenviable reputation for being one of the foremost anarchist thinkers of the nineteenth century. Keeping company with Pierre-Joseph Proudhon, famous for adopting the epithet 'anarchist' to describe his political views and Mikhail Bakunin, Marx's fiercest foe, he is also often said to be the most accessible anarchist. There are a number of reasons for this: he left a substantial body of work that gives a good account of his conception of anarchism; he published a substantial part of this work in English; and perhaps above all, he took a leading role in the propagation of anarchist ideas and exercised a profound influence on nineteenth- and twentieth-century activist movements. Pre-eminence in a political tradition is not typically disadvantageous to an individual, except where the tradition itself is outlawed. Kropotkin's reputation as one of anarchism's central figures and canonical writers is unenviable nevertheless, not just because his work has attracted sustained attention from critics and protagonists within and outside the anarchist movement, but also because he has assumed a representative status as an anarchist of a particular type. Probably more than any other anarchist, Kropotkin defines classical anarchism.

The primary aim of this book is to rescue Kropotkin from the framework of classical anarchism and highlight aspects of his political thought that have been lost as a result of the interest that his science has generated, particularly the theory of mutual aid. The chapters situate his thought in the context of late nineteenth-century debates and show how he helped shape anarchism as a distinctive politics that was quite different to the philosophy ascribed to him. Like his friend Élisée Reclus, Kropotkin was part of a European movement that, as Marie Fleming argues, 'developed in response to specific social-economic grievances in given historical circumstances'.[1] Kropotkin contributed enthusiastically to the formation of an anarchist tradition and even endorsed Paul Eltzbacher's dispassionate, analytical study *Anarchism: Seven Exponents of the Anarchist Philosophy*.[2] However, his understanding of anarchism was more fluid and open than Eltzbacher's and instead of seeking to define a set of characteristic core concepts, Kropotkin identified anarchism with a tradition of political thought and a set of political practices. By presenting an analysis of Kropotkin's work that does not treat the science of mutual aid as the key to this anarchism, the discussion shows how he understood this tradition and located himself within it.

A second aim of this book is to explain Kropotkin's politics. As well as being regarded as one of the key theorists of classical anarchism, Kropotkin is remembered for his controversial decision to support the Entente powers against Germany. This choice is often described as a betrayal of principle that reflects his virulent Germanophobia, on the one hand, and potent Russian nationalism on the other. I argue that Kropotkin's alignment, and his subsequent defence of constitutionalism in Russia in 1917, is explicable in terms of his anarchism and that his consistent application of principle exposes some important differences within anarchism about internationalism and the idea of the state. These differences support very different ideas about the nature of solidarity and anti-militarism, for example, as well as competing conceptions of class. The analysis builds on the existing political biographies and studies of Kropotkin's political thought to contextualise Kropotkin's thought and provides a textual analysis of published and unpublished work to offer an interpretation that highlights the revolutionary impetus and political thrust of his writing.

This study has been motivated by a number of concerns. One is to counter the marginalisation of Kropotkin's anarchism in radical political theory, just when space for more sustained reflection seems to be available. Anarchists are notable by their absence in mainstream histories of ideas and have found only a place on the fringe in most histories of socialist thought. Post-anarchist critique of classical anarchism, albeit sympathetic, risks sidelining a set of ideas that were certainly significant in their time and that continue to resonate in a range of political and cultural movements. The point of hovering over Kropotkin's work for a while is not to elicit lessons for twenty-first century action or produce an authoritative ideal-type against which 'real' anarchists may benchmark their affinity. The point is to shed light on a set of ideas that have been badly misread and distorted and to challenge what is rapidly becoming a casual dismissal of a rich body of work as naive, incoherent and outmoded.

A second objective for this study is to test the exclusionary casting of anarchism. One result of classical anarchist critique has been to reinstate thinkers typically neglected in the canon, notably Gustav Landauer and Max Stirner, by introducing a philosophical or epistemological test on what counts as usefully anarchist. This move not only prioritises an approach to anarchist theory that is contestable, it has also contributed to the politicisation of anarchism, placing a particular current of libertarianism at the heart of anarchist politics. The result has been to encourage a debate about anarchism's ideological boundaries. Michael Schmidt and Lucien van der Walt's construction of the broad anarchist tradition is one response.[3] Linking anarchism tightly to an idea of class struggle, they narrow the anarchist tradition by excluding from it key figures in the nineteenth-century movement, including Proudhon, Stirner and Tolstoy. These oppositional frameworks code Kropotkin's anarchism very differently. By turns he is pulled between determinism and essentialism on the one hand, and proletarian conflict and anti-individualism on the other. My reading suggests that Kropotkin's political thought muddied these divisions. Ernst Zenker, one of the early analysts of anarchist ideas, was right to identify Kropotkin as an anarcho-communist and he correctly highlighted the tension between this current of anarchist thought and the individualism of anarchists like Benjamin Tucker. Yet in the nineteenth and early twentieth century these schools did not describe neat or discrete positions, whatever claims their advocates sometimes expressed to the contrary.

It would be wrong to argue that classical anarchism is exhausted by Kropotkin's thought or that it is identical with the anarchist canon. Classical anarchism is linked to a set of writers who espoused a particular philosophy and politics and Kropotkin is prominent among them. However, the special place he occupies in the canon as a classical anarchist is explained by the emergence of post-anarchist understandings of anarchist historical traditions. The idea of classical anarchism that post-anarchists have institutionalised owes a lot to the critique of science that Kropotkin apparently models, now appearing in discussions of anarchism with little reflection or contestation. Contemporary analysts offer rival evaluations of the classical tradition but hardly disagree about the politics it describes. Classical anarchism describes a workerist, class-based ideology committed to collective revolutionary action and communism. Historians show that movement politics was a lot more complex and rich than these categorisations suggestion. Still, the category remains. And the risk of this packaging of classical anarchism is that it becomes a barrier to the excavation of anarchist thought. What is the point of probing the history of anarchist ideas when we already know what particular categories of anarchists believed?

Post-anarchists are not solely responsible for this mainstreaming of classical anarchism. While the current theorisation of classical anarchism is distinctively post-anarchist, the construction of the tradition, and Kropotkin's place within it, has its roots in post-war anarchist historiography. The first two chapters of the book (forming Part 1) outline some of the main currents in this literature in order to demonstrate how Kropotkin attained his representative status as classical anarchist and what this story tells us about orthodox interpretations of his thought and the principles of the classical tradition.

Since the politics that classical anarchism describes de-contests concepts in particular ways, typically abstracting key ideas from selected texts, disputing the claims advanced by Kropotkin's critics involves giving ground to frameworks of analysis that are questionable. Instead of attempting to show how Kropotkin's core concepts or theoretical principles deviate from prevailing interpretations, I instead provide an alternative reading of his thought. This account draws out the dominant themes of his anarchism by examining the ways in which his concerns about the anarchist movement shaped his political theory and uses this analysis to consider how his critical engagements with other currents of ideas, notably Nietzscheanism and Marxism, brought him into relation with other leading anarchists: Bakunin, Proudhon, Malatesta, Reclus and Stirner.

The discussion is structured by the trajectory of Kropotkin's career and is organised in two parts. The first (Chapters 3 and 4) discusses Kropotkin's relationship to Russia and the ways in which his involvement with the intellectual, cultural and revolutionary movements influenced his thinking, mediating his understanding of the European contexts in which he found himself. Chapter 3 examines Kropotkin's account of nihilism, looking at his appreciation of Russian literature and his assessment of the Russian women's movement, and Chapter 4 shows how his opposition to Tsarism and his training as a geographer combined to shape his understanding of the state. I draw out Kropotkin's approach to science, his conception of the state and a model of the international order at the end of this section.

The second part (Chapters 5 and 6) is framed by Kropotkin's analysis of the history of the French Revolution and his identification of the tasks facing nineteenth-century revolutionaries. Kropotkin's concerns about the political direction of nineteenth-century European revolutionary movements reflected his diagnosis of the failures of the French Revolution and Chapter 5 considers how these shaped his ideas of anarchy and anarchism, looking at his critique of Marxism, his defence of anarchist-communism and his development of evolutionary anarchist ethics. In the final chapter, I look at the ways in which Kropotkin hoped to stimulate anarchist change through revolutionary action, in part drawing back to some of his early ideas of revolt, but looking, too, at the priority he attached to syndicalist organisation and direct action. The chapter charts the failure of the revolutionary strategy Kropotkin pursued and shows how this affected his decision to back the Entente powers in 1914. In the conclusion to this section, I assess Malatesta's critique of Kropotkin's science, as reductive, deterministic and mechanistic, and show how an alternative reading of his anarchism explains the political choices that he made in 1914 and 1917. The assessment is not designed to show that the meta-theoretical claims advanced by contemporary political theorists have no purchase, only that their application to Kropotkin is faulty and that the substantive critiques of Kropotkin's political thought that are derived from them are questionable.

Part 1 Portrait of the Anarchist as an Old Man

Out with the Old, in with the New

Pinning down precisely what classical anarchism means is a tricky task. Richard Day associates classical anarchism with writers often regarded as canonical: Godwin, Proudhon and Bakunin as well as Kropotkin.[1] To take another example, Paul McLaughlin argues that William Godwin, Pierre-Joseph Proudhon and Max Stirner were its key intellectual influences. Benjamin Tucker and Leo Tolstoy are sometimes described as classical anarchists but tend to have bit parts in the anarchist canon. On the other hand, Emma Goldman, whose exclusion from the canon is notorious, tends to be grouped with Gustav Landauer and sometimes Stirner, as pre-post-anarchists. Day, unusually, defends Kropotkin as the first post-anarchist to emerge from the canon. Inclusion in the canon does not lead to the automatic conferral of classical status. Similarly, it is possible to be put in the box marked classical without having a clearly canonical standing.

That Kropotkin is a canonical thinker is uncontentious. He was identified in Eltzbacher's study[2] and, some fifty years later, in George Woodcock's *Anarchism*, a book that has played a key role in the canon's construction.[3] Although Eltzbacher believed that it was only possible to gain an intimate knowledge of anarchism by the investigation of 'less notable' teachings as well as by the 'most prominent', Kropotkin emerged as one of seven sages of anarchism and a key referent for the construction of anarchist ideology.[4] A recent poll confirmed his top ranking in the anarchist canon.[5] Significantly, when compared to the other sages,[6] he often appears as the least anarchic. In Woodcock's words, Kropotkin gave 'the doctrine a concreteness and a relevance to everyday existence that it rarely shows in the writings of Godwin, Proudhon, or Bakunin'.[7]

Kropotkin's identification as a classical thinker undoubtedly owes something to his inclusion in the canon but the classification also touches on understandings of anarchist traditions and the history of the anarchist movement that are not always explicit. As well as referring to a theoretical canon, classical anarchism sometimes also refers to a unifying idea, variously described as a theory of 'structural renewal',[8] 'the dream of society without the state'[9] and scepticism towards authority.[10] For some it describes a historical rather than a theoretical tradition;

for others it is a construct.[11] Classical anarchism has been described in attitudinal terms, although there is little agreement about the attitudes it expresses: it is as easily classified as essentially utopian as it is deeply anti-utopian.

In an effort to navigate a way through these different understandings and approaches, this chapter presents a historiography of anarchism to illustrate the ways in which assessments of Kropotkin's work have helped shape and articulate the classical idea. The argument is that the representational position that Kropotkin has assumed as a classical anarchist rests on a set of interrelated ideas about science. Kropotkin is a particularly good vehicle for these arguments because his work contains a wealth of scientific tropes.

Kropotkin, Science and Mutual Aid

Kropotkin found a place in the anarchist canon because of the sustained contribution he made to anarchist thought. The significance of this contribution was acknowledged during his lifetime, as the canon began to take shape, and it was based in part on his advocacy of communism and, in the other part, on his exposition of the theory of mutual aid. Ernst Zenker's 1897 overview of anarchism, described by James Martin as 'the first study of a general nature which showed an understanding of the scope of the source material of anarchism',[12] devoted a chapter to 'Kropotkin and his school'. Zenker identified him as 'the father of "Anarchist Communism"', a current that was 'directly opposed both to the collectivist and evolutionist Anarchism of Proudhon and to the other philosophic and individual Anarchism of Stirner' – the other two thinkers Zenker thought worthy of a chapter.[13] The obituary for Kropotkin published in *The Times* made the same point, distinguishing his 'school' from 'Collectivist and Individual Anarchism'. In addition, the paper noted, Kropotkin was responsible for sketching an anarchist theory of social action that extended the insights of the zoologist Karl Kessler and rivalled Herbert Spencer's thesis of competition. This was a reference to Kropotkin's theory of mutual aid.

> To Kropotkin the greatest social law was the law of mutual help: and one of his most famous books 'Mutual Help', [*sic*.] was written to defend the theory which he shares with Kessler, in opposition to Spencer – that for progressive development of a species the law of mutual help is far more important than the law of the struggle for existence.[14]

These two ideas continue to resonate in the literature. Mukherjee and Ramaswamy note that in *Mutual Aid* Kropotkin 'outlined the philosophy of Anarcho-Communism'.[15] Peter Marshall's better known work advances a similar claim. The theory of mutual aid, he argues, 'forms the cornerstone of Kropotkin's philosophy'.[16] Both Dugatkin's and Purchase's detailed studies of Kropotkin's anarchism also take mutual aid as the central point for their discussions.[17]

The spotlight on mutual aid has a double significance for Kropotkin's standing as a canonical theorist. As well as providing the interpretative lens for the analysis of his political thought, the theory of mutual aid validates his anarchism by appealing to Kropotkin's credentials as a scientist.

The scientific value of mutual aid has long been a matter of debate. At least three positions can be abstracted from the exchanges. The first is a sceptical view and it was advanced by two of Kropotkin's comrades, Max Nettlau and Errico Malatesta. Nettlau acknowledged Kropotkin's 'scientific ardour' but was not convinced that his anarchism was rightly described as science. His unwillingness to treat Kropotkin's work in this way stemmed from his sense that Kropotkin used his wealth of accumulated knowledge to defend an entrenched position, not to reflect critically on his findings. Nettlau found Kropotkin's anarchism rigid, a characteristic he thought unscientific. Comparing Kropotkin's work to Élisée Reclus's, Nettlau described it as 'harder, less tolerant, more disposed to be practical; that of Reclus seems to be wider, wonderfully tolerant, uncompromising as well, based on a more humanitarian basis'. Kropotkin, he argued, was unwilling to subject his ideas to 'general scientific discussion'.[18] Malatesta arrived at similar conclusions, although from a different starting point. His view was that Kropotkin felt guilty because he was able to 'develop his mind and attain to moral and intellectual eminence whilst the great masses of the toilers stagnate in misery and ignorance'.[19] He hinted at Kropotkin's divorce from practical, everyday politics and his tendency towards reduction and simplification. Science, Malatesta argued, overwhelmed Kropotkin's social revolutionary instincts and resulted in a narrowing of his political vision. Like Nettlau, however, he remained unconvinced that Kropotkin's anarchism was genuinely scientific:

> I have no special competence to be able to pass judgment on Kropotkin as a scientist. I know that in his younger days he had rendered remarkable services to geography and to geology; I appreciate the great value of his book 'Mutual Aid' ... It seems, however, to me that he lacked something to make him a real man of science; the capacity to forget his desires and preconceptions in order to observe the facts with an impassive objectivity. He seemed to me to be rather what I should call a poet of science. He might have been able to arrive at new truths by intuitive genius, but

others would have had to verify these truths; men with less genius or no genius at all, but better gifted with what is called the scientific spirit. Kropotkin was too passionate to be an exact observer.[20]

The trend in recent years has been to reverse these judgments and to endorse the claim made in *The Times*'s obituary, namely that mutual aid provided 'the anarchist theory with a scientific foundation'.[21] This second approach takes the conception of biological evolution sketched in *Mutual Aid* as the centrepiece of Kropotkin's anarchism. It places special weight on Kropotkin's claim – made against Social Darwinists like Spencer – that cooperation is as potent a factor as competitive struggle in determining species fitness. Many root the science of mutual aid in the academic rigour of the research process. More often than not, the argument involves tracking the genesis of mutual aid to Kropotkin's expeditions in Siberia and the academic work he produced on his return to St Petersburg. Dugatkin's view is that the theory of mutual aid 'came to him' at the start of his Siberian expeditions – as early as 1862, well before Kropotkin decided that he was an anarchist and some forty years before the publication of the book *Mutual Aid*. Brian Morris also traces the foundations of Kropotkin's anarchist philosophy to this period. It was after he undertook his 'zoological, ethnographic and geographical research in Siberia', Morris argues, that Kropotkin 'became aware that reciprocal relations and "mutual aid" were significant aspects of biological existence, as well as of social life'.[22] Kropotkin's geographical work tends to get lost in these accounts of his science. As James Scott Keltie, the Secretary to the Royal Geographical Association, noted, Kropotkin made his chief contribution to science as a physical geographer, presenting new hypotheses about the orography of Central Northern Asia and glaciation in Finland.[23] The political projects he pursued with Élisée Reclus are also downplayed. Adding a different twist to the story of *Mutual Aid*'s genesis, Federico Ferretti shows that Kropotkin's work emerged from his collaboration with Reclus and Léon Metchnikoff, another anarchist geographer, in the 1880s.[24]

Other accounts concentrate on the significance of Kropotkin's findings. Encouraged by Stephen Jay Gould's endorsement of Kropotkin's work and his conception of science as a socially rooted activity, Iain McKay argues that the arguments presented in the theory of mutual aid have been confirmed by modern biology and that the idea of scientific objectivity assumed by critics like Malatesta is philosophically flawed.[25] Pablo Servigne softens these claims: Kropotkin's scientific knowledge was limited and he presented mutual aid as a factor in evolution without understanding evolutionary science, just as Darwin posited the idea of variability and natural section with no knowledge of genetics. Yet subsequent research supports his hypotheses.[26]

The third position steps between these two views and, instead of seeking to defend the integrity of Kropotkin's science, it draws on what Malatesta called the poetry of Kropotkin's science to evaluate his anarchism. This was George Woodcock's approach. 'Kropotkin ... might have claimed ... that his contribution to the anarchist tradition was the application of a scientific approach to its practical problems', he argued, but like Nettlau and Malatesta, Woodcock was not persuaded. Kropotkin, he argued, lacked 'true scientific objectivity. His approach ... was as much intuitive as intellectual, and his compassionate emotion always overcame his cold reasoning.'[27] Yet whereas Nettlau and Malatesta regretted Kropotkin's turn to science, Woodcock did not. Crediting Kropotkin with 'the humanization of anarchism' he argued that his deployment of the language of science in support of this project made his anarchism all the more compelling.[28] Kropotkin's reputation for science was more important than his actual accomplishments as a scientist and it was this aspect of his work that Woodcock canonised, establishing the parameters of classical anarchism in the process.

Kropotkin and Bakunin: Heroes and Villains of Anarchism

A gap of just over fifty years separated Eltzbacher's book from Woodcock's but both men shared a common aim, namely, to demythologise anarchism. For Eltzbacher, this meant knowing 'Anarchism scientifically', penetrating 'the essence of a movement that dares to question what is undoubted and to deny what is venerable'.[29] Woodcock understood the project in slightly different terms. His purpose was to clear away the confusions arising from anarchism's etymological association with violence, chaos and disorder.[30] The tone had already been set in *Anarchy or Chaos*, published in 1944. Woodcock's opening statement declared that anarchism 'is not a creed of terror and destruction, or social chaos and turmoil, of perpetual war between the individuals within society. On the contrary, it is the opposite to all these.'[31] Woodcock later dismissed the book as 'a jejune manual of anarchist tenets'.[32] However, his concern to divorce anarchism from its reputation for violence remained a constant theme in his writings on anarchism.

Eltzbacher's project was reasonably successful in its own terms, although until recently his work was largely forgotten. He isolated one principle common to all anarchists. The 'negation of the State', he argued, was anarchism's essential, unifying feature. Many anarchists would contest Eltzbacher's claim. Anti-statism is controversial as an ideological marker because it appears to endorse a rights-based political theory that sits uncomfortably with class analysis and because it fails to establish clear boundaries between anarchist anti-capitalism and individualism.[33] Kropotkin, however, identified anti-statism as a core principle of anarchism and it is still regarded as a kind of anarchist minimum. Moreover, the anarchist canon continues to be populated with reference to it.[34]

Woodcock failed to alter popular misconceptions about anarchism, as mainstream reporting of protest actions illustrates, even though his introduction to the topic was widely read. Nevertheless, his attempt to do so helped to cement a particular view of the anarchist canon and the classic thinkers that it embraced. It also helped to establish the idea that anarchism developed in waves: the first wave stretching from Proudhon's publication of *What is Property?* in 1840 to the crushing of the Spanish Revolution in 1939 and the second wave starting in the mid-1960s. Kropotkin's reputation as 'a savant' was always central to his desire to defend the integrity of anarchist thought against its reputation for violence. In *Anarchy or Chaos* Woodcock described Kropotkin as 'the most influential and competent' of anarchists who used his 'natural studies' to bear on the analysis of social and economic problems to 'prove the scientific validity of anarchism as a social method'.[35] Kropotkin defied the kind of anarchism that Woodcock wanted to consign to the past.

The scholarship that Woodcock found in Kropotkin's work has inspired a rich vein of anarchist thinking. Colin Ward famously described his classic *Anarchy in Action* as 'an extended, updating footnote to Kropotkin's *Mutual Aid*'.[36] Carissa Honeywell and Matthew Adams have separately examined Kropotkin's influence on other leading post-war British anarchists, notably Herbert Read and Alex Comfort.[37] Yet for all the positive engagements with politics and social policy that Kropotkin's work has inspired, his reputation for scientific rigour has also encouraged a misleading idea of historical and theoretical fracture in anarchism. Woodcock's coupling of science and non-violence was critical to this reading.

Kropotkin's particular value to anarchism is most starkly illustrated by the contrast he strikes with Bakunin. In Woodcock's work, this became pronounced in *Anarchism*. In the earlier work, *Anarchy or Chaos*, Bakunin was painted as a 'great revolutionary hero and orator of anarchism'.[38] Woodcock judged him to be the man who did more to shape anarchist doctrines than anyone else, outshining even Godwin and Proudhon. With the publication of *Anarchism* (1962) the tone changed.[39] Bakunin was described as 'monumentally eccentric, a rebel who in almost every act seemed to express the most forceful aspects of anarchy'.[40]

Bakunin's casting as the villainous anti-hero of anarchism in popular and scholarly literatures has been highlighted by Robert Cutler.[41]

Maurice Paléologue's 1938 sketch provides a good summary of that familiar picture of the cigar-smoking gargantuan. With a large heard, clear blue eyes, short nose and luxuriant, wild hair Bakunin was an iconic figure, by turns charismatic, sectarian, fanatical and arrogant.[42] Bakunin's anarchism, as untamed and chaotic as his personality, was utopian, dictatorial and disordered.

The very different portrait of Kropotkin on which the comparison rests is equally familiar in anarchist literatures.[43] Adoring portraits were published during his lifetime. Anna Strunsky's 'earnest address' captures the mood of the reporting that followed in the wake of Kropotkin's visits to America. 'A scientist, humanitarian and of royal birth, Kropotkin is a genius of the age; not only does his colossal intellect cause him to stand in bold relief, but his personality is one of indescribable and unduplicated power.'[44] After his death, most of the tributes followed this pattern. Those who remembered him remarked on his 'Christlike devotion to the cause of the down-trodden'[45] and describe him as 'the epitome of mildness, the incarnation of humaneness', 'tender ... modest ... gentle'.[46] The 'conventional Kropotkin', Nicholas Walter observed,

> is the one described in Oscar Wilde's crazy phrase about 'a man with the soul of a beautiful white Christ that seems coming out of Russia' or more soberly in Herbert Read's introduction to his anthology ... 'Kropotkin, gentle and gracious, infinitely kind and nobly wise'.[47]

Some otherwise sympathetic commentators have found the eulogising off-putting; even Woodcock declared himself discontent with the 'impression of Kropotkin as a saint.[48] Nevertheless, this flawless image of Kropotkin has seeped into commentaries on anarchism.[49] Even before Woodcock cemented the image, Alexander Grey judged Kropotkin 'free from the mouth-foaming of Bakunin; the violence tinged with insanity, of the Nihilists'.[50] Writing in the 1950s G. D. H. Cole painted a similar picture. Even when Kropotkin was 'most indignant or furious', he argued, he 'remained an essentially loveable person, and there was in him not the smallest trace of that streak of insanity that is continually showing in Bakunin's work'.[51]

Although it is tempting to dismiss them, these testimonials have become part and parcel of a wider interpretative debate. Woodcock was not the only writer to deploy these portraits as literary devices to highlight a theoretical tension or incompatibility between Bakunin's and Kropotkin's anarchism. In George Lichtheim's account, Kropotkin 'dropped the dictatorial approach ... Bakunin's anti-Semitism, his Panslavism ... his childish fondness for armed banditry and the cult of violence and destruction that went with it'.[52] Woodcock compared

Kropotkin's 'mildness of nature and outlook' to Bakunin's 'bohemian energy'. Bakunin's famous cry, 'the passion for destruction is a creative passion, too', which appeared in *The Reaction in Germany*, was emblematic of his anarchism, representing an aspect of his philosophy that would never substantially change.[53] Kropotkin, on the other hand, 'preferred the open forum of discussion to the romantic darkness of conspiracy'. The 'destructive vision of blood and fire that so luridly illuminated Bakunin's thoughts did not attract him'.[54] Paul Avrich also used the two anarchist portraits to distinguish Kropotkinian anarchism from the taint of unreasoning Bakuninism.

> Although Kropotkin embraced some of the principle tenets of the Bakuninist creed, from the moment he took up the torch of anarchism it burned with a gentler flame. Kropotkin's nature was singularly mild and benevolent. He lacked completely Bakunin's violent temperament, titanic urge to destroy, and irrepressible will to dominate; nor did he possess Bakunin's anti-Semitic streak or display the hints of derangement that sometimes appeared in Bakunin's works and actions. With his courtly manner and high qualities of character and intellect Kropotkin was the very picture of reasonableness. His scientific training and optimistic outlook gave to anarchist theory a constructive aspect which stood in sharp contrast with the spirit of blind negation that permeated Bakunin's works.[55]

The special value of the comparison was that it offered a way of challenging the popular image of the anarchist as terrorist, one of the myths that most bothered Woodcock. This was a reputation that anarchism earned initially through its open support of revolution and was reinforced by the anarchists' association with nihilism and, in Bakunin's case, by his association with Sergei Nechaev.[56] However problematic the concept of terrorism is, its application to anarchism is historically grounded. In the nineteenth century, the charge was laid against anarchists in general. The policy of propaganda by the deed caused special concern. In 1881 *The Times* described the policy as a 'not very obscure incitement to wholesale assassination'.[57] But anarchists were anyway set apart from other revolutionaries and socialists by the nature of their doctrine as well as by the means they adopted. They were no ordinary revolutionaries, the American academic Richard Ely warned. Uninterested in 'universal suffrage and annual elections' they called for 'a general destruction of present society'.[58] Assuring his readers that the threat of the Bakuninist International was still very much alive, even seven years after its formal dissolution, he argued that anarchism presaged 'a tragedy of world-wide import, which shall make all the cruelty and terror of the French Revolution sink into utter insignificance'.[59] The Haymarket Affair of 1886, which resulted in a famous show-trial and the execution of four Chicago anarchists, was grist to this mill.[60]

Kropotkin's intimate involvement with *Le Révolté* – that *The Times* identified as the paper of the dynamiters – and his defence of the Russian populists' revolutionary campaigns meant that he was also identified as a dangerous militant. The uncompromising tone of his early writings provided critics with evidence of his willingness to entertain violence. In 1886 *The Spectator* argued that Kropotkin's project threatened 'to throw the entire civilised world into a witches' cauldron of slaughter and destruction'. Kropotkin was both a victim and apostle of the most 'mischievous', 'foolish and pernicious' fanaticism.[61] Haia Shpayer-Makov's study of Kropotkin's reception in Britain shows that the weight of opinion ran counter to this view.[62] Yet not even Kropotkin was able to alter the public image of anarchism or entirely free himself from the misgivings that followed from his association with it. Ten years after *The Spectator* reported on his extremism, Kropotkin's reputation for violence appeared to be as entrenched as the estimations of his science and his saintliness. Edith Sellers observed: 'Of no man in Europe are more diverse opinions held than of Prince Kropotkine. To one section of society he is the Red Flag personified; to another he is the Sermon on the Mount incarnate.' Kropotkin, she continued 'is dubbed, in equal good faith, St. Francis d'Assisi, Danton, and Don Quixote'.[63]

Displacing one part of the nineteenth-century account of Kropotkin on to a Bakunin–Kropotkin divide effectively airbrushes Kropotkin's image but the claims about anarchist violence that result are highly dubious. The displacement relies on an argument about Bakunin's responsibility for a wave of assassinations that occurred some fifteen years after his death. Bakunin's godlessness supported this view at the time. A survey of European press reporting on anarchism noted that 'Bakunine, the chief, though not the first of anarchistic agitators, based his contention upon materialism. "Neither God nor Master" was his cry. He rejected authority of every kind.' That someone who 'declares the liberty of man to consist solely in obedience to the laws of nature, because he recognizes them himself' would feel no qualms about killing fellow beings followed as a corollary of this wild libertariansm.[64] More recent scholarship has been more measured. But the anachronistic claim that Bakunin was the 'indirect inspiration' for anarchist terrorism survives largely intact.[65] Peter Marshall acknowledges the messiness of the discussion. Bakunin, he argues, 'was against systematic terror', yet 'more than any other anarchist thinker' he 'is responsible for the violent and menacing shadow of violence'. Bakunin, in Marshall's view, 'contributed to the sinister side of anarchism which has attracted disturbed and criminal elements, individuals who delight more in ille-gality and conspiracy than in building and creating'.[66] Confronting this political reality, Marshall introduced Bakunin as 'The Fanatic of Freedom' and Kropotkin as 'The Revolutionary Evolutionist', just as Woodcock had earlier chosen to dissect Bakunin under the rubric of 'The Destructive Urge' and designated Kropotkin as 'The Explorer'. Both thereby distanced themselves from the sort of anarchist politics they believed flawed and outdated. In her historical study of anarchists in Victorian London Hermia Oliver was less cautious and mapped the violence–non-violence dichotomy to a second action–theory divide. Her assessment of the 'contribution made by late-nineteenth-century anarchism to left-wing social and political thinking' made creative use of Henry Seymour's essay 'The two anarchisms'.[67] Seymour, a nine-teenth-century contemporary of Kropotkin, presented his discussion to distinguish his brand of individualism from anarcho-communism. The essay included the claim that the latter necessarily entailed vio-lence, but Seymour's main concern was to defend a rights-based theory of anarchism that would make 'the producers the proprietors' against communism.[68] Oliver altered the tenor of Seymour's argument to high-light the pointlessness of Bakuninist terrorism and its legacy, which she identified in direct action:

> This kind of anarchism incurred so much detestation that it became neces-sary to adopt the word 'libertarian' instead. But present-day anarchists who believe in 'direct action' are still Bakuninist revolutionaries ... Kropotkin as a philosopher rather than as a revolutionary made a lasting contribution by laying the foundations of the ecological movement.[69]

The conclusions that Oliver drew about Kropotkin's non-revolutionary philosophy of anarchism seem particularly problematic in the light of the anarchist movement's actual history and Kropotkin's role within it. At the same time, her conflation of revolution and violence in direct action was not so unusual in the mid-twentieth century when the resur-gence of anarchism in Western Europe gave a new impetus to those who wanted to define their own anarchist politics against the anarchism of the past. In anarchism's so-called second wave, Kropotkin emerged as an advocate of 'new' anarchism. Bakuninism was consigned to anarchism's historical past.

Kropotkin and New Anarchism

In the 1960s and 1970s a sanitised version of Kropotkin's writing was brought into the service of 'new' anarchism. New anarchism was a catch-all term. It was applied in an effort to describe the character of the politics being expressed by protest movements, just as post-anarchism is now used to describe the horizontalism of global justice movements. New anarchism meant different things to different writers, but it importantly pointed to a shift in anarchist thinking. Kathy Ferguson identified the newness of anarchism in its existentialist turn.[70] Herbert Read contrasted old 'political' with new 'humane' anarchism.[71] An abiding theme in a significant current of new anarchist writing was the principle of evolutionary change and the commitment to gradual, piecemeal strategies that challenged the state by chipping away at its authority. New anarchism, David Stafford argued, was about 'permanent protest' or what Herbert Read called pragmatic action.[72] And the value of action was estimated by the extent to which it moved society in an anarchist direction, not in proportion to the intensity of the struggle vested in it. In new anarchism, too, opposition to the state was understood primarily in counter-cultural terms. David Stafford observed how fondly new anarchists quoted Landauer's remark that the state was 'a condition' or 'relationship between human beings', which 'we destroy by behaving differently'.[73] Inspired by this conception, new anarchists rooted the practice of anarchism in the behaviours of everyday life or, as Read put it, 'in what is steadily evolving'.[74] New anarchism did not necessarily imply a rejection of structural change. Read remained firmly wedded to traditional anarchist models of organisation and advocated decentralised free federation as an anarchist ideal. But counter-cultural politics was sometimes represented in this way[75] and the trend of new anarchist thinking was to talk up the significance of changes in perceptions and patterns of individual behaviour and to downplay challenges to the institutional fabric of society. Read put the point nicely: '[I]f we can secure a revolution in the mental and emotional attitudes of men, the rest follows.'[76] A feature of this conception of change was that it did not require individuals to self-identify as anarchists. Of greater relevance to the prospects of anarchism was involvement in anarchistic behaviours: the construction of networks of mutual support and the achievement of goals that circumvented the established authorities. The role of anarchists was to help foster and encourage further social experimentation, mobilising what Giovanni Baldelli termed society's 'ethical capital'.[77] Whereas old anarchism directed anarchist energies toward the mass struggle against the state, assuming a simple polarisation between exploiters and exploited, new anarchism opened up a space for thinking about the ways in which counter-communities may be stimulated and the social conditions that made this possible.[78]

Exponents of new anarchism were inspired by a number of factors. Changes in the social and economic condition of Europe, the sexual revolution, the expansion of administrative systems and the development of new military technologies – particularly the expansion of nuclear arsenals – were the most important. These were not exclusively anarchist concerns. As Daniel Cohn-Bendit argued, anarchism was only one component of leftism, the term he coined to describe the upsurge of militancy in the period, matured through 'a historical process' and 'realized in action'.[79] And although the traditional sectarian divisions that demarcated anarchists from non-anarchists were still pronounced, the counter-cultural, anti-materialist, anti-bureaucratic and anti-war themes new anarchists probed were part of the zeitgeist.

In this ferment and placed alongside second-wave feminists, Situationists and other subversives, Kropotkin might have easily appeared as a greybeard rather than a 'hippie longhair'.[80] However, this portrait was yet to be painted and instead of dismissing Kropotkin as yesterday's man, many new anarchists latched on to the evolutionary aspects of his anarchism. As Hermia Oliver hinted, in Kropotkin new anarchists found a commitment to ecology and the roots of a new understanding of revolution.

Kropotkin's green pedigree owed much to his influence on a line of practical utopians and critics of technology. Patrick Geddes, Lewis Mumford and Ebenezer Howard are the three key exponents that Woodcock identified.[81] Geddes, 'the great Reclusian geographer'[82] credited with the phrase 'think local, act global' was well acquainted with Kropotkin. Mumford identified Kropotkin as one of the precursors of biotechnics, or organic technology, and was particularly struck by the vision of integrated agricultural and industrial living outlined in *Fields, Factories and Workshops*.[83] Woodcock detected Kropotkin's equally strong yet unacknowledged influence on Murray Bookchin's work, although this was a more contentious claim not only because Bookchin barely referred to Kropotkin in his 1970 classic *Post-Scarcity Anarchism,* but also because he was later quite critical of Kropotkin's ideas.[84] In the discussion of utopianism he presented in *The Ecology of Freedom* Bookchin professed a preference for William Morris's work and argued that neither Kropotkin nor acolytes like Howard and Mumford added very much to the original insights of Robert Owen and Charles Fourier.[85] Nevertheless, Woodcock's claims were not without foundation. Bookchin did treat Kropotkin as a forerunner of social ecology and readily acknowledged the debt he owed to Kropotkin's 'natural and social mutualism'. The theory of mutual aid was key to this estimation: Kropotkin's contribution, Bookchin argued, was his 'unique ... emphasis on the need for a reconciliation of humanity with nature, the role of mutual aid in natural and social evolution, his hatred of hierarchy, and his vision of a new technics based on decentralization and human scale'.[86]

More important than the particular influence Kropotkin exercised on the imagination of any of the new generation of anarchist writers was the idea of evolution that emerged during this period. The indeterminacy of Kropotkin's science played well to new anarchist interest in non-violence and gradualism. Somewhat detached from Social Darwinism, the theory of mutual aid usefully supported both the ecological position that humans were intimately connected with the natural world, and the sociological view that re-imagined the concept of revolution as a process of continual change, rather than a physical fight. The lesson of Kropotkin's anarchism was that morality, springing from the principle of cooperation, provided the dynamic for social transformation. Roel van Duyn saw Kropotkin as a forerunner of the Dutch Kabouter movement:

> Kropotkin interprets morality in an evolutionary context; but at the same time he insists on revolution. For him, revolutions are part of an all-embracing evolution. When the river of life is temporarily obstructed by obstacles like dictatorship or oppression, then a revolutionary breakthrough is necessary. But his concern is with the river, not with the breakthrough as such. The future is already enclosed within the present; the future is not the antithesis of the here and now. Kropotkin's insight teaches us that we have to find ways that do not, like Trotsky's, bear within them the germ of a new tyranny.[87]

The revision of revolutionary politics may be seen as a realistic response to the entrenchment of states and the obvious power-advantages that they had over critical social movements, although these asymmetries of power were hardly new. In 1895, looking back on the history of class war in the second half of the nineteenth century, Engels declared that 'the conditions of the struggle had changed fundamentally. Rebellion in the old style, street fighting with barricades, which decided the issue everywhere up to 1848, had become largely outdated'.[88] In 1947, Woodcock reached the same conclusion. There was, he argued, 'little prospect of immediate success in an insurrection'.[89] Coming to terms with this reality was not, however, a council of despair. Rather, it opened up new strategic possibilities. Indeed, new anarchists were able to meet the charge levelled against old-style revolutionaries, namely that anarchists were caught on the horns of a dilemma: either guilty of subscribing to a theory of change that lacked organisational force – as Eric Hobsbawm, for example, argued – or wedded to concept of change that was militaristic and inescapably statist. Casting the problem in precisely these terms, Woodcock rejected the revolution on the nineteenth-century model.

> There is no longer much talk of barricades and revolutionary heroism, and while 'direct action' is a phrase continually on the lips of New Radicals, it means something very near to Gandhian civil disobedience, which Old Anarchists would despise ostentatiously.[90]

This conception of revolution emphasised the value of ethical and cultural change as a route to structural transformation. It closed the perceived gap between the peaceful, harmonious ends of anarchism and the revolutionary means of social change and placed individuals at the heart of the transformative process. Bookchin called this 'intuitive anarchism' and associated it with the 'detestation of middle-class values and lifestyles'.[91] Revolution was about refusing routine, consumption and uniformity. The evolutionary aspect of Kropotkin's theory of mutual aid and the countless examples he provided of mutual-aid societies operating within the body of the state appeared to speak to this conception.

Some of Kropotkin's contemporaries may well have questioned Kropotkin's new anarchist credentials. Edward Carpenter's generally sympathetic reminiscences of Kropotkin include a commentary about his 'charming naïveté' and his propensity 'to believe that all human evil is summed up in the one fatal word "government"', suggesting that abolitionist ideas remained paramount in his thinking.[92] Woodcock's contemporaries similarly challenged his assessment of new anarchism. Nicholas Walter argued that historical anarchism had always had an evolutionary dimension and that 'new anarchism' was not particularly new in this regard.[93] Yet Woodcock's distinction and the caricature portraits of anarchism's sages proved persuasive. And in place of the individualist–communist fracture that Zenker and Seymour had identified in anarchist thought, the absorption of new anarchist ideas in the literature established Bakuninism and Kropotkinism as the major line of cleavage. Notwithstanding Edward's Carpenter's assessment of Kropotkin's naivety, William O. Reichert presented the theory of mutual aid as a worked example of Landauer's idea of the state.[94] Admittedly, not all commentators agreed that the students' movements of the 1960s had actually arrived at Kropotkinite new anarchist positions. Paul Goodman accused elements within the student movement of holding fast to Leninism, adapting 'Jesuit' ideas of 'discipline' and the 'tactics of military cadres'.[95] In 1968 Goodman argued that 'New Anarchism is in … a Bakuninist phase: the emphasis is on agitation, direct action, sometimes disruption to bring bad operations to a stop'. But this criticism reinforced the view that Kropotkin 'belonged to a more mature anarchism that did revolutionary agitation as the day's work but was already "discussing" … the possibilities of anarchist technology, ecology, pedagogy, rural life, industrial management'. Goodman's hopes for the movement's development were in the extension of Kropotkinism.[96] Similarly, while Rudolf de Jong acknowledged the complementarity of evolution and revolution in the historical tradition, he compared the Dutch Provos to the Kabouters by referring to their divergence. The Provos, he argued, attracted 'a lot of people who were only egoists or interested in the tension of police violence'. The latter had 'more "flower-power" and "love"'. His conclusion: Kabouter expressed 'friendly Kropotkinism instead of Bakuninism'.[97]

As friendly Kropotkinism captured the mood of an important current within the radical movements of the 1960s and 1970s, anarchism also attracted renewed scholarly attention. In 1969 Eric Hobsbawm believed that the 'revival of interest in anarchism' was both 'curious and … unexpected'.[98] But it was a revival nonetheless and, in addition to Hobsbawm's critical essays it resulted in an impressive stack of literature. Anarchism also attracted the sustained attention of political theorists. A new interpretative trend emerged that helped fill the philosophy of classical anarchism in a particular way. Already established as the most genial guide to anarchist theory, Kropotkin once again occupied a leading place in these evaluations.

From New Anarchism to Post-anarchism

Kropotkin has a place in the anarchist canon as a foremost advocate of anarchist communism. His reputation as a classical anarchist extends from this advocacy but equally from his standing as the scientist of anarchism. New anarchists found the interpretative value of Kropotkin's science principally in a conception of evolution. Kropotkin's evolutionary theory not only provided an answer to critics keen to identify anarchism with violence, it also served as a foundation for the articulation of a politics based on small-scale grass-roots experimentation and continual innovation. New anarchists did not use the term 'prefiguration' to describe this politics, but the conception of anarchism they offered fits this broad understanding of anarchist change.

In anarchism's third, post-anarchist, wave, usually dated to the rise of the alter-globalisation movement in the late 1990s, Kropotkin's science has been interpreted very differently. Post-anarchist readings of Kropotkin's anarchism also emphasise the centrality of science to Kropotkin's anarchism. However, in post-anarchism science becomes the byword to describe Kropotkin's political theory, providing an exemplar for classical anarchism. Kropotkin is not so much painted as a savant but one of a handful of intellectuals who fixed the politics and philosophy of anarchism. This politics is often described as teleological, based on a particular concept of human nature and linked to a form of revolutionary utopianism that promises the realisation of anarchy. Post-anarchists dissolve the distance between Bakunin and Kropotkin that new anarchists attempted to instantiate and claim the territory of prefigurative politics as their own. In doing so, post-anarchists establish a boundary between philosophical traditions that cuts across the canon: leading anarchists are placed in or abstracted from a classical tradition or classed as precursors of post-anarchism. Post-anarchist classifications have helped solidify a set of ideological and cultural boundaries between apparently historically bounded and contemporary anarchisms, for example, class-struggle anarchism and individualism, and social and lifestyle anarchism. Kropotkin is usually placed on one side of these divisions: as a representative of a classical tradition, he emerges as a scientist who believed in the necessity of class-based revolution.

Kropotkin: Theory and Practice

A central concern of new anarchists was the relationship between theory and practice. There was no question that the ideas they discussed were intimately related to anarchist movements and that the analysis of these ideas was significant precisely because of this relationship. New anarchists were not the first to highlight the interrelationship of theory and practice, movement and ideas. Even Eltzbacher – whose book Landauer criticised for prioritising 'the *word*' over the 'unspeakable mood' of anarchism[1] – formulated his aims in terms of the anarchist movement. His hope was to 'penetrate the essence of a movement' and show 'whether to meet such a movement with force'.[2]

Three major studies of Kropotkin's life and work – George Woodcock and Ivan Avakumović's *The Anarchist Prince: A Biographical Study of Peter Kropotkin*, Martin Miller's *Kropotkin* and Caroline Cahm's *Kropotkin and the Rise of Revolutionary Anarchism 1872–1886* – document Kropotkin's activism and involvement in anarchist and radical politics.[3] He was closely associated with a number of initiatives, including the advocacy of anarchist communism, which persisted until the Jura Federation adopted the principle as part of its programme and the promotion of propaganda by the deed.[4] Kropotkin was happy to be associated with anarchist communism, but in 1909 he denied that he had ever been a proponent of propaganda by the deed, which was a policy designed to educate through provocative acts. According to Kropotkin, the idea was Paul Brousse's. His approach, which he set out in the essay 'The spirit of revolt', was instead intended to initiate mass rebellion by acts of extraordinary courage or daring.[5] Nevertheless, Kropotkin was happy to participate in propagandistic actions and in 1876 he took part in one of the first acts linked to the principle, the Bern protest, in which anarchists marched under the banned red-flag. Kropotkin was also involved in other, more conspiratorial, activities. In the same year, at the behest of Malatesta and Carlo Cafiero, he considered entering into a marriage of convenience on the understanding that his would-be wife would release more funds to buy arms for a planned insurrection.[6]

Kropotkin's better known and more sustained activity was directed towards the dissemination of anarchist ideas. As Martin Miller argues, Kropotkin's 'real forte had always been "propaganda par le mot"'.[7] He was involved in the production of a number of European anarchist papers, notably *L'Avant-Garde* (1877–8), *Le Révolté* (1879–87) and *Freedom* (1886–1914) as well as Russian propaganda.[8] He delivered talks at important movement commemoration meetings, hosted gatherings at his home, gave advice to those who sought it, lectured widely, even to university students who he supposed 'might hate advanced ideas'.[9] He also maintained a correspondence with a host of activists across the world.

Kropotkin's literary contributions to anarchism have been appraised in two different ways. One argument, advanced by Marie Fleming, is that Kropotkin developed his politics as an activist. Her view is that Kropotkin felt forced to choose between his scholarship and his politics and that he was unable to treat his scholarship as an expression of and vehicle for his anarchism in the same way that Reclus did. Believing that one career precluded the other, Kropotkin felt duty bound to give up his professional vocation for the sake of anarchism. Kropotkin also encouraged this view by separating out his two careers. In his *Memoirs* he says that he only started writing columns for *Nature* and *The Times* when he arrived in England in 1881 because of his conviction that a 'socialist must always rely upon his own work for his living'.[10] On this account, scholarship was a means to an ends, and anarchism was his calling. Kropotkin perhaps overstated the extent to which he maintained the separation between these two spheres. He did manage to inject some of his scientific writings with anarchist perspectives, notably the essays that he produced in *The Nineteenth Century*'s 'Recent Science' series. Similarly, whatever status is attributed to Kropotkin's 'science', he also found ways of bringing his scholarship to bear on his anarchism.[11] After he returned to London in 1886, the two aspects of his work came together in the essays that were later collected in the books *Fields, Factories and Workshops* and *Mutual Aid*. Nevertheless, the distance between his scientific work and his radical activity was reinforced by his habit of publishing his scholarly analyses in intellectual and professional journals like *The Nineteenth Century* and the *Geographical Journal*, which were designed for educated audiences and beyond the reach of ordinary workers.

The second interpretation is that Kropotkin's theory was scholarship and that it represented his divorce from activism. Caroline Cahm opens her study with Malatesta's assessment of Kropotkin's contribution to anarchism: 'without doubt one of those who have contributed perhaps most ... to the elaboration and propagation of anarchist ideas'.[12] The ambiguity of Malatesta's judgement turns on the distinction between theory and practice that Cahm accepts. Her view is that 'Kropotkin was mainly concerned with action' before 1886 and that his 'substantial contribution' to the 'elaboration of anarchist communist ideas' came after this date.[13]

Some activists pushed this distinction further, not only to question the practical significance of theory, but also to trim down Kropotkin's standing in the anarchist movement. A strong tradition of anti-intellectualism combined with the reputation that Kropotkin enjoyed as a 'respectable' anarchist almost inevitably alienated other militants for whom anarchist theory amounted to passive, armchair reflection. As John Quail notes, British anarchists who organised within William Morris's Socialist League were suspicious of the affinity Kropotkin found with the middle-class members of the Freedom Group. Frank Kitz 'regretted that Kropotkin and other "serious people" ever had anything to do with them'.[14] Kropotkin's account of anarchism in the history of ideas was received critically in some quarters, even though he also understood anarchism broadly as 'the name given to a principle or theory of life and conduct under which society is conceived without government'.[15] Guy Aldred questioned his identification of 'Locke, the timid, and Godwin, the Whig' as the fathers of anarchism and insisted on a clear distinction between thoughts and deeds. Using action as the relevant measure to chart the history of anarchism he claimed that Richard Carlisle, the early nineteenth-century freethinker, 'whose reward for clear thinking was imprisonment', was the real father of the British movement. Godwin – one of the writers Kropotkin identified as a precursor of anarchist ideas – had no claim whatsoever since he was 'but a politician for all practical purposes' and 'a gentleman'.[16]

Aldred's distinction re-appears in some scholarly literature, but with precisely the reverse effect. Kropotkin's saintliness paves the way for his canonisation as a philosopher of anarchism whose work may be abstracted from an activist context. Woodcock and Avakumović's biography introduces the narrative of transition evident in Cahm's work and adds a strongly evaluative note to it. They argue that Kropotkin's life changed fundamentally when he settled in England in 1886. No longer a conspirator or agitator, he retreated from 'the work of day-to-day-propaganda' and became a 'retired theoretician'. The Kropotkins move in 1894 from Harrow, north of London, to Bromley, on its southern fringes, marked the cessation of the 'ephemeral' work he had been doing up to that point and the resumption of his science – 'the studies which Kropotkin regarded as necessary for providing a sound theoretical basis to his social ideas'.[17] In the same period, Olive Garnett, friend of Helen and Olive Rossetti who edited the anarchist paper *The Torch*, recorded that Kropotkin's 'delightful manners' put her in mind of 'a learned German scientist'.[18] James Hulse's sketch uses the recollection as a trope to give us an idea of the flavour of his politics and the drift of his interests:

> Prince Kropotkin was much like his friend Stepniak in temperament and manner: those who knew him could not regard him as a desperate revolutionary. He was balding, short, and stocky, and he peered at the world through tiny eye-glasses that gave him more the appearance of the quaint continental professor than of Europe's leading theoretical anarchist.[19]

Kropotkin and Political Theory

The divorce of theory from practice that Hulse's depiction encapsulates characterises a significant swathe of political theory, although the reasons for the separation are not tied up with the politics of Kropotkin's sanctification. In the political theory stimulated in the wake of anarchism's second wave, the puzzle of anarchism was the one first set by Eltzbacher: how to find sufficient coherence in the ideas of its various exponents to provide a clear picture of the doctrine. Scholarship followed one of three approaches. Historians of ideas attempted to analyse anarchism by looking at the ideas of leading exponents, their sympathetic interest almost inevitably contributing to the cementing of an anarchist canon.[20] Historical sociologists adopted a comparative approach and examined anarchist movements – typically European and North American – to develop a range of classificatory systems supporting the identification of different anarchist 'schools'.[21] Political theorists focused their attention on the construction of anarchist theory and examined conceptions of constitutive ideas, particularly authority, liberty and power.[22] Kropotkin loomed large in all of these accounts, advantaged by the availability of English-language texts. Even though the list of canonical thinkers varied, the volume of work that Kropotkin published was enough to ensure that he featured in the discussions of the history of ideas. Similarly, when it came to typologies, Kropotkin re-emerged – as Zenker had argued – as the father of anarcho-communism. His presence in these two realms reinforced his status as a representative of anarchist theory and, therefore, a valuable subject for theoretical analysis.

The genesis of Kropotkin's standing as the key theorist of classical anarchism can be traced to the analytical work that began to appear in the 1970s. Although a number of important works examining the relationship of anarchism to non-anarchist socialism also appeared in this period,[23] probably more attention was directed to the links between anarchism and liberal political theory, particularly after the publication of Robert Paul Wolff's seminal study of authority and autonomy, *In Defense of Anarchism*.[24]

The connection between anarchism and liberalism was established in anarchist literatures before Wolff's philosophical anarchist treatise appeared. Kropotkin's friend Rudolf Rocker described anarchism as the 'confluence' of socialism and liberalism. In 1969 Nicholas Walter offered a similar conception. Rocker's placement of anarchism in the movement of historical currents of thought established a template for later analyses. But whereas Rocker had distinguished between currents of ideas, political concepts and approaches to social theory, acknowledging the complexity of liberal and socialist doctrines, subsequent writers presented the conjunction in less nuanced ways. David Apter's distillation, which depicted anarchism as 'a socialist critique of capitalism and a liberal critique of socialism', implied a parasitical relationship with two identifiable and bounded ideological positions.[25] In other political theory the anarchists' claims tended to be stretched from a consideration of overlapping methodological positions or values (particularly in respect of the critique of state socialism) to an assumed absorption of liberal concepts. Indeed, anarchism featured in some political theory only because it poses an abstract question about political obligation, an issue that might be discussed without reference to anarchists at all.

Alan Ritter's discussion of anarchism and liberalism used Kant, Mill and utilitarianism to discuss Proudhon, Bakunin and Kropotkin's work, but failed to consider how any of these philosophies were discussed in anarchist literatures.[26] Elsewhere he drew on Gerald MacCallum's analytic of freedom to examine anarchist approaches to liberty, identifying its negative and positive components. He argued: 'Like all concepts of freedom that apply to agents, the anarchists' is a triadic relation of *subjects* who are free from *restraints* to reach objectives.'[27] On this account, anarchists and liberals conceptualised liberty in exactly the same way and just disagreed about the necessity of the state as its guarantor. Almost inevitably, this formulation put anarchism on the back foot since it pointed to a potential problem in individual–community relations that liberals believed the state resolved. Perhaps as a consequence, Ritter's attention was drawn to the inconsistency of anarchist arguments for liberty; his examination led him to doubt the strength of anarchist libertarianism and to argue that the coherence of anarchism lay in the commitment to the ethical goal of communal individuality. Nevertheless, having taken the anarchists' libertarian impulse as his starting point and highlighting the flaws in anarchist reasoning along the way, Ritter reinforced the idea that the concept of liberty was in fact a natural starting point for the analysis of anarchist ideology. This view remains powerful and is particularly associated with classical anarchism, as Simon Critchley's recent work illustrates. 'Classically – and rightly' he argues 'anarchism was always concerned with freedom and struggles for liberation'.[28]

The identification of anarchism's libertarian impulse had a particular significance for Kropotkin. Encouraging political theorists to ask questions about the ways in which anarchists expected to ground social relations in anarchy, the commitment to liberty directed attention to anarchist conceptions of reason, nature and science – the conceptual and methodological instruments which anarchists used to show how non-coercive social compliance could be achieved. Kropotkin's theory of mutual aid appeared peculiarly well-developed for these discussions. George Crowder tested his contention that anarchism was 'united by a theory of freedom – an account of the nature, value, and social conditions of human liberty' against the work of Godwin, Proudhon, Bakunin and Kropotkin.[29] But his desire to show that anarchism had a 'strong scientific ambition' led him to place a premium on Kropotkin's political theory.[30] As Crowder noted, '[t]he scientistic tendency … reaches its height in the later writers, Kropotkin in particular'.[31] Although his analytical methods were different, Crowder consciously aligned his project with Eltzbacher's.[32] However, in doing so, he presented an assessment of Kropotkin that diverged strongly from new anarchist interpretations and substantially revised the classification of anarchist political thought that it supported.

The departure from new anarchism emerged in the reinterpretation of mutual aid that political theory provided. For new anarchists the theory resonated with the peaceful evolutionary approaches to social change they championed, but his science was not central to his anarchism, at least not independently of the credence it gave to Kropotkin's capacity for original research and abstract thinking. Woodcock argued that Kropotkin claimed that his contribution to the anarchist tradition was the development of a scientific approach, but Woodcock had not been persuaded.[33] Analysis of the political theory of mutual aid pointed in a different direction. David Miller scrutinised 'Kropotkin's claim to have placed anarchism on a scientific foundation' by first describing his positivism.[34] Kropotkin believed that scientific methods could be applied to all phenomena and that it was possible to ground morality in science. Kropotkin 'appears to have had it in mind that science could (a) identify persistent moral values, in animals and different human societies; (b) explain psychologically why these values should have been adopted; (c) justify the values, by showing that adhering to them has desirable social results'.[35] Having isolated the principles of Kropotkin's scientific theory, Miller found his anarchist political theory wanting. He is 'muddled and inconsistent'.[36] In *Mutual Aid*, moreover, Miller detected a tension between Kropotkin's 'moral ideas' and his 'biologically based evolutionary theory'.[37] Kropotkin endorsed evolutionary methods, but presented an account of change that was deeply a-historical and that wrongly assumed that mutual aid was 'an immutable trait of human nature'. Because he thought that history could be understood as a struggle between solidarity and subjection he ended up offering an idea of change that was not only 'anti-evolutionary' but contradictory. Miller noted: '[W]e may want to ask why Kropotkin should have thought (as he did) that an anarchist-communist society would shortly be evolved from the breakdown of capitalism, given that human nature is essentially unchanging.' The answer he gave, that mutual aid is 'progressively more refined over the course of history', pointed to the comforting but teleological conclusion that 'anarchy is the final outcome of history'.[38] Miller referred to Malatesta's critique of Kropotkin's fatalism to support this reading.

These themes were developed in Crowder's treatment of Kropotkin's science. Crowder qualified Miller's interpretation, but similarly presented Kropotkin as a Comtean positivist who used modern evolutionary science to outline his ethical and political theory.[39] Like Miller, Crowder was critical of Kropotkin's science and argued that it contained a fundamental flaw that epitomised the anarchist predicament. The basis of his claim was the suggestion that the principle of mutual aid, which Kropotkin treated as 'the *dominant* factor of evolution', was only another example of a classical anarchist commitment to natural law.

> If mutual aid is really dominant, then why does selfishness show no sign of dying out? In what sense is evolution tending in the direction of mutual aid when the modern age is so patently ... pervaded by the pursuit of self-interest? He would reply that while mutual aid is becoming more widespread, at the same time it is weakening in intensity. Why? Because of the baleful influence of the State, which has grown in power since the Middle Ages. But this returns us to the sort of difficulty encountered with Bakunin, the question of the relation between human misconduct and the operation of a descriptive law of nature. How is it that such a law could be disrupted or violated or affected in any way by the institutions or actions of man?[40]

Kropotkin's turn to science was problematic for two reasons. First, it highlighted the redundancy of natural law theory and, second, by serving as its proxy it also illuminated the bankruptcy of anarchism. The conformity with nature that anarchists looked for was both denied by modern science, which instead indicated a world of 'divergence and fragmentation', and by sociology. Michel Foucault's critique of science, Crowder argued, exploded Kropotkin's anarchism by showing how science had only reinforced state power by legitimising 'standards of "normal" behaviour' and sustaining 'more comprehensive forms of social control'.[41] The failures of Kropotkin's science thus pinpointed a general failure of nineteenth-century anarchism, namely, that it lacked a persuasive philosophical foundation.[42]

Crowder's conclusions about the shortcomings of anarchism formed the basis of the revised classification of anarchism. Banding his selection of Eltzbacher's sages together in a single group blurred the differences between Bakunin and Kropotkin that Woodcock had sought to establish, and gave classical anarchism a distinctive and novel political and philosophical content. Whereas Woodcock had associated 'classic anarchism' with class struggle, insurrectionism and terror, Crowder linked classical anarchism to an Enlightenment tradition of political theorising, rationalism, positivism and, as he argues below, a principle of anti-statism defined as a primary commitment to liberty:

> In the writings of [Kropotkin's] immediate successors and of the more recent proponents the conclusions of the nineteenth-century theorists are preserved largely intact. It remains the distinctive claim of these writers that the State necessarily does more evil than good; that in particular the State is a destroyer of freedom, which is, if not absolutely inviolable, at least inviolable prima facie; and that in the absence of the State, non-coercive but stable forms of social organization will arise through agreement, co-operation and solidarity.[43]

Although he acknowledged that anarchism had a twentieth-century existence, Crowder firmly situated anarchist ideas in a nineteenth-century theoretical past. Ironically, given his divergence from new anarchist interpretations, his argument dovetailed with a historical assessment of anarchism's redundancy that Woodcock had helped institute and that was revived by a second generation of new anarchists in the late twentieth century. The important difference between this generation of post-anarchists and the new anarchists of Woodcock's generation was that they accepted the critique of science that Miller and Crowder advanced but sought to detach anarchist ethics from its outmoded Enlightenment principles in order to rescue anarchism and show its relevance to contemporary political practice.

Classical Anarchism in Contemporary Anarchist Theory

Reviewing *Anarchism* for the journal *Anarchy* in 1963, Nicholas Walter noted that Woodcock painted anarchism as a failed movement, 'an anachronistic and amateurish protest against the way the Industrial Revolution and state socialism were going rather than a genuine challenge to either of them'.[44] The moment of truth came in 1939 when the Spanish rebels marched into Barcelona to end the anarchist revolution. Objecting strongly to this account, Walter thought it ironic that the book's appearance coincided with anarchism's revival. He agreed with Woodcock that the campaigns of the 1960s did 'not belong to the territory of classical anarchism' but, unlike him, Walter believed that 'there is no doubt that we belong to them'.[45] Like Woodcock, Walter believed that the 1960s revival expressed something new, but unlike Woodcock, he argued that it was possible to find continuities between these movements.

For Woodcock, new anarchism departed from nineteenth-century traditions in two ways. As well as expressing an evolutionary, green, non-violent politics, it operated in a different political realm. The passing of old anarchism, he argued in his 1968 essay 'Anarchism revisited', marked the passing of a movement. New anarchism was 'not the historical anarchist movement resurrected. It was something quite different, a new manifestation of the idea.'[46] In the prologue to *Anarchism*, written in 1973, he repeated this claim. The revival of anarchism coincided with the emergence of a radical student and youth movement: anarchism reappeared within this but only as an idea.

Some of the flaws in Woodcock's account of anarchism's supposed death have been exposed by historians of non-European movements and of a host of late nineteenth and twentieth-century literary, artistic and avant garde groups whose members either identified as anarchist or showed strong affinities with anarchism. Transnational, postcolonial and cultural histories of anarchism paint a very different picture of anarchist activity and the continuities and discontinuities of anarchist thinking to the one sketched by Woodcock. The familiar waves of European anarchism are complicated by surges in activity elsewhere in the world – Latin America, China and Africa – and by the incorporation of anarchist ideas in anti-racist, anti-colonial resistance campaigns. Woodcock's separation of the libertarian impulse from the historical anarchist movement's past and his suggestion that anarchism can be imagined as a form of libertarian thinking has also been challenged. Two separate strands of contemporary analysis, one focused on movement politics and the other on the anarchist political theory, reassert the link between movements and ideas. In both, however, classical anarchism is positioned as an abstract that has little relevance to contemporary radical politics.

Although the rise of the global anti-capitalist movement at the end of the 1990s was widely acknowledged to mark anarchism's revival – its third wave – there is some debate about the extent to which this wave altered the character of anarchism or just its emphasis. Gabriel Kuhn leans toward transformation. 'The contemporary anarchist movement is only partially inspired by historical anarchism.' Recent sources of inspiration, he continues, 'are the anti-bourgeois protest movements of the late 1960s, various social movements of the past decades ... a strong sense of anti-authoritarian organizing ... and post-colonial Third World movements such as the Zapatistas or the Landless Workers Movement in Brazil'.[47]

Uri Gordon notes the same influences active on currents within anarchism but argues that these coexist with others. The distinction between 'small-a' and 'big-A' groups describes the principal division, although Gordon is cautious about overplaying its significance for activist organising. What he calls the 'new school' or 'small-a' anarchists take their lead from the radicalism of 1960s movements. The 'threads which would weave together to form a new wave of anarchism', he notes, came from 'radical feminist, ecological, anti-racist and queer struggles' of the 1960s.[48] In contrast, 'so-called capital-A anarchists work more closely within the traditional political culture of the anarchist movement established before the Second World War'.[49]

On both accounts, the turning point for new anarchism is located in the 1960s, as Woodcock contended, but the reverberations of the shift for the conception of classical anarchism are quite different to those he portrayed. Not only is the transformation of anarchism linked to the influence of protest movements rather than to anarchism's internal revision, the process of change is also re-described. From the perspective of the third wave, anarchism appears to have remained wedded to a set of ideas that had their roots in the first wave; the influence of 1960s radicalism was felt only thirty years later. The ideas that animated the historical movements that Woodcock declared dead in 1939 lingered on, even beyond 1968. And the libertarian spirit was not unhooked from the anarchist movement's historical past, as Woodcock had suggested.

Gordon's discussion of small-a and big-A cultures challenges Woodcock's account of anarchism's political history and links the resurgence of anarchism in the 1990s to a turn in anarchist thinking. Gordon resists using small and big-A distinctions to describe this turn, even while recognising the unwillingness of some activists to accept anarchism as a political identifier and a tendency to treat it as a foil to elaborate an alternative libertarian politics. Such an approach 'invites talk of a movement that is "broadly anarchist" or "inspired by" anarchism – which reifies anarchism and expects "really" anarchist movements to conform to some pre-conceived ideal type'.[50] Indeed, the turn he has in mind is precisely a move from this way of thinking. It may be described as a change from doctrine to plurality or ideology to politics. In theoretical terms, Gordon argues, the anarchism that emerged in the 1990s from the fusion of 1960s radicalism is distinguished by its resistance to domination rather than rejection of state power, a commitment to prefigurative change as opposed to a faith in revolutionary rupture and the embrace of 'present-tense' utopianism in favour of blueprint planning.[51] Consistent with his recognition of the interrelationships between small-a and big-A anarchist cultures, Gordon acknowledges that elements of new anarchist thinking were active in the historical past when doctrine dominated. He nominates Rudolf Rocker as an old anarchist who expressed ideas that resound with new anarchist thinking. Kropotkin, however, is placed on the other side of the divide. Specifically, Kropotkin inspired the idea

> that a revolution in social, economic and political conditions would encourage an essentially different patterning of human behaviour – either because it would now be able to flower freely under nurturing conditions, or because revolution would remove all hindrances to the development of human beings' cooperative/egalitarian/benevolent side.[52]

It is difficult to judge how far Kropotkin's position in the anarchist canon informs Gordon's judgement. In post-anarchist theory, in contrast, the critique of Kropotkin's canonical 'classical anarchism' is explicit.

Post-anarchism is not only one of the most significant currents to emerge within contemporary anarchist thought in recent years, it also has 'evident affinities' with small-a anarchist movement politics.[53] Indeed, post-anarchist analysis of anarchism's canonical figures has both reinforced the theory–practice divide that Woodcock's *Anarchism* promoted and crystallised the idea of a classical anarchist tradition by re-ordering the canon according to its new theoretical markers.

As Gabriel Kuhn notes, the affinity between post-anarchism and small-a anarchist cultures turns on the rejection of meta-narratives, associated with old-style anarchism. One of the strong claims advanced by leading post-anarchist writers is that the anti-capitalist and anti-war movements that exploded on to the political scene in the 1990s exposed the inadequacy of anarchist political thought. Although he referred to anarchism as a 'political philosophy and activist tradition', Saul Newman reflected on the ways in which 'anarchism as a philosophy is … in need of rethinking'. His suggestion that there was scope for the convergence of theory and practice assumed the existence of their separation in classical anarchism.[54] Gabriel Kuhn helpfully sums up post-anarchism's broad position: " 'traditional anarchism," while an important ethical and political guide, has theoretically been embedded in the "naturalistic" and "essentialist" philosophy of the nineteenth century and its many epistemological shortcomings'.[55] Post-anarchist theoretical revision not only injects new life into worn out ideology but in setting out an approach to anarchist political theory that chimes with movement activism, it also contributes to resistance struggles.

Newman's identification of the space between theory and practice resonated with Woodcock's analysis, yet instead of trying to demonstrate the continuing relevance of ideas within the libertarian tradition by detaching them from exhausted movements, as Woodcock had sought to do, Newman used the complexity and plurality of the protest movement as a call for theoretical revision. Similarly, whereas Woodcock claimed that libertarian thought was compatible with new forms of radical practice, Newman argued that established anarchist traditions were not up to the mark. Not only had social movements altered the face of anarchist movement activism, Newman believed that anarchism lagged behind developments in contemporary philosophy. As a critique of Marxism, anarchism remained inspirational, but as philosophy capable of providing critical insight into contemporary politics, it had been overtaken by postmodern and poststructuralist thinking.

> The central contribution of anarchism to radical political thought lies in its rejection of the state and all authoritarian forms of politics, its critique of Marxism, and its commitment to a libertarian and egalitarian ethos. In particular, the innovativeness of anarchism lies in its theorization of political power – namely the power of the state – as an autonomous field of power relations and a specific site of political struggles that was analytically separate from, and not determined by, the capitalist economy or class relations ... However, the theoretical innovativeness of anarchism today is, at the same time, limited by the humanist and positivist framework in which it was originally conceived.[56]

Newman's critique of anarchism's rootedness in Enlightenment traditions echoed Crowder's; Crowder was a source for *From Bakunin to Lacan*, his first book. Like Crowder, Newman identified the essence of classical anarchism in a particular conception of liberty. The principle of autonomy at the heart of the classical project, he argued, was 'based on the idea of the true, essential self, which has moral authenticity as its ultimate goal'. Post-anarchism, in contrast, offered a view of authenticity as 'an ongoing process', not 'an end goal'.[57]

Anarchism was still wedded to many of these outworn ideas, Newman argued. Contemporary advocates included Noam Chomsky, John Zerzan and Murray Bookchin. Delving further back into the past, he identified Bakunin and Kropotkin as key exponents of the tradition. These historical writers were products of the Enlightenment, wedded to a naive conception of human goodness, reason and progress, who subscribed to the possibility of social harmony as an achievable, revolutionary goal.[58] Science, too, was an essential component of the classical anarchist vision. In Kropotkin's case, science assumes a significance that Woodcock willingly exploited, but always disputed. Lewis Call remarked, 'Kropotkin – himself a geographer and biologist of some repute – could conceive of anarchism only in purely scientific terms. His political philosophy and his scientific viewpoint were one and the same.'[59] Newman similarly turned his attention to the theory of mutual aid.

> This epistemological framework is apparent in a number of central aspects of anarchist theory. For instance, while anarchists like Bakunin warned of the dangers of allowing life to be dictated to by scientists, both he and Kropotkin still saw society as an objective reality whose workings could be observed scientifically, particularly through the methodology of the natural sciences. Central here is the notion that socialism and the liberation of humanity have a materialist and scientific basis: there was a rational logic at work in society and history, a logic that was only intelligible through science ... For Kropotkin, this rational social logic could be found in a natural sociability that he observed in humans and animals – a 'permanent instinct' toward cooperation, which he believed could provide the foundation for a new ethics of mutual aid, and a new conception of justice and morality. Further, anarchism relies on an essentialist understanding of human nature as largely benign and cooperative. Indeed, for classical anarchists, the social revolution and the creation of a free society would allow man's immanent humanity and rationality finally to be realized.[60]

Newman's post-anarchist branding of a range of nineteenth- and twentieth-century writers with the classical badge reinforced the idea that it described an identifiable philosophical position. The suggestion that the some anarchists, neglected in the historical canon, may be abstracted from classical anarchism and treated as precursors of post-anarchism further underlined its theoretical coherence. Just as Gordon picks out Rocker as a historical anarchist in tune with contemporary new activism, Newman selects Stirner as a pre-post-anarchist. Both also select Landauer, demonstrating an enthusiasm for Landauer's description of the state as a social relationship that is as pronounced as the appreciations David Stafford observed among new anarchists in the 1960s. Unlike those new anarchists, however, Gordon and Newman would likely recoil from the suggestion that this conception may be linked to 'friendly Kropotkininsm'.

Post-anarchist theory has contributed to the recasting of classical anarchism as a form of naive revolutionism – echoing Woodcock's critique of Bakuninism but extending it to include Kropotkin. This strange dialectical twist of recent political theory highlights the extent to which the difference between first- and second-generation new anarchists has turned on a disagreement about what may have died in anarchism's past, not a dispute about its death or the necessity for its rebirth. Having served as a touchstone for new anarchist ideas in the 1960s, Kropotkin has become a victim of post-anarchist review. But while the ethical and political space that Woodcock believed separated old Bakuninism and new Kropotkinism has collapsed, Kropotkin persistently appears as the bearer of a classical tradition. Not even recent sympathetic evaluations of Kropotkin's politics have effectively challenged this view. On the contrary, they have tended to ground classical anarchism in a commitment to class struggle and revolution, introducing another dimension to the story of Kropotkin's canonisation.

Kropotkin and Class Struggle

The important issue on which Kropotkin's protagonists and critics converge is in their advocacy for prefigurative change. Benjamin Franks defines this concept in terms of a relationship between ends and means and a rejection of both consequentialism, the idea that the outcomes of actions are the proper measures of rightness, and deontology, which considers the justness of actions in terms of duty, or conformity with established norms or laws.[61] Prefiguration, Franks argues, steers anarchists towards virtue ethics, a position that grounds morality in character or behaviour and the intentions of actors. In addition, Franks associates prefiguration with what he terms 'pragmatic ethics'. This means that anarchists reject instrumentalism, or the idea that 'the success of a plan is determined by its efficiency in meeting the objectives'.[62] Franks associates instrumentalism with Max Weber but Machiavellianism and Nechaevism are also examples. In contrast, anarchism embodies 'the forms of social relation that actors wish to see develop'.[63] Prefiguration also describes a wide range of political strategies, from the rejection of parliamentary politics and vanguardism to the expression of new social relationships and ways of living. The practices that prefiguration promotes are quite different, but however it is fleshed out, the everyday behaviours and choices that individuals adopt are central to anarchist actions.[64]

Kropotkin's reputation as an exponent of prefiguration can be explained by the ease with which his work is malleable to contrary conceptions. Cast as the hero to Bakunin's villain, a champion of evolutionary as opposed to revolutionary change, Kropotkin becomes an advocate of micro-political experimentation. Treated as a classical anarchist aligned with Bakunin, he stands out as a rebel who pushed the construction of anarchist organisations and alterative systems in the body of the state. The first conception of prefiguration brings Woodcockian new anarchism into a close but unhappy alignment with small-a anarchism and post-anarchist practice. The second reveals another fault line in contemporary anarchism that divides individualists from class struggle anarchists or, following Bookchin's misleading classification, lifestyle from social anarchists.

Colin Ward occupies a key role in bridging the gap between friendly Kropotkinian new anarchism and small-a anarchist experimentation. Ward presented a reading of mutual aid that stressed the persistence of anarchist behaviours. As Carissa Honeywell notes, his view was that 'anarchism was in keeping with existing tendencies within nature and society'. In *Anarchy in Action* Ward argued that 'individuals were naturally co-operative and that current societies and institutions, however authoritarian, capitalist and individualist, survived only because of the real subterranean forces of mutual aid and voluntary association'. Ward, she continues,

> did not focus on revolutionary organization but emphasized the ongoing state of struggle between authoritarian and libertarian tendencies. His emphasis ... was such that he effectively wrote out any notion of climactic revolution ... in favour of an emphasis on the piecemeal activity of co-operative groups.[65]

Ward's conception of change not only dovetailed with non-violent 1960s activism, it also looked forward to the experimental nowtopianism of the 1990s. Indeed, Ward's openness to Hakim Bey's temporary autonomous zones (TAZ) underlined the continuities of thought between these two waves of activism.[66]

In acknowledging Kropotkin's influence on his work, Ward not only helped bind Kropotkin to the evolutionism of the 1960s, he cleared the path for the rediscovery of mutual aid as a principle of contemporary politics. Matthew Wilson shows how social movement activists and post-anarchists converge on a particular model of prefigurative practice constructed around DIY activism, autonomous politics and experimentation in TAZ inspired by Wardian action.[67] Wilbert and White suggest that Ward and Kropotkin anticipated 'the critique of grand narratives and "totalising theory"' long before it 'was mounted by the likes of Lyotard and Foucault'. They argue that Ward's writings 'present anarchism as a constant subjective desire that appears in social life characterised by creative forms of self-organization and expression, a libertarian current that, following Kropotkin, he sees as always in competition with the forces of authoritarianism'.[68]

Newman rejects the suggestion that Kropotkin offered a prefigurative conception of change on this model. He contrasts 'micro-political' understanding' with 'scientific utopianism'. The first is post-anarchist; the second is anarchist.[69] While this judgement is rooted in a contentious account of historical anarchism, his reluctance to acknowledge the overlaps between mutual aid and contemporary utopianism may also be explained by the strength of the sympathetic opposition to this interpretation of Kropotkin's work. For responding to critiques of classical anarchism, leading exponents of class-struggle anarchism have sought to detach Kropotkin from this kind of experimentation and reassert his standing as a revolutionary, promoting principles of old anarchism that Woodcock rejected.

For Lucien van der Walt and Michael Schmidt class-struggle anarchism is a politics about the 'struggle by the working class and peasantry' who 'constitute the great majority of humanity'. It is designed to 'fundamentally change society' through self-emancipation, not by elite deliverance. It does not equate to 'crude workerism'.[70] Nor does class-struggle anarchism focus narrowly on economic issues. Class-struggle anarchism is internationalist, anti-imperialist, anti-militarist, anti-racist and feminist. Van der Walt and Schmidt identify Bakunin and Kropotkin as the 'towering figures' of classical anarchism, bringing Kropotkin into alignment with Bakunin, in a manner that Woodcock would not have countenanced, precisely in order to assert the continuing relevance and appeal of his revolutionary theory. Indeed, returning to Eltzbacher's seven sages, and finding his approach badly wanting, they argue that Bakunin and Kropotkin alone are legitimately regarded as anarchists.[71] Their radical trimming of Eltzbacher's canon excises Stirner, Godwin, Tolstoy, Proudhon and Tucker.

Kropotkin's credentials as a class-struggle anarchist have also been championed by Brian Morris. In some respects, Morris's general description of Kropotkin's 'essential conception of revolution' merges with the micro-political vision of prefiguration associated with Ward. Kropotkin fought for 'the replacement of state institutions based on hierarchy and coercion with voluntary relationships'.[72] Morris also invokes Landauer's understanding of the state as a social condition to exemplify Kropotkin's view. However, the idea of 'replacement' is the tell-tale sign of the distance between Morris's interpretation of Kropotkin's anarchism and the micro-conceptions that extend from Ward, certainly erecting a barrier to the possibility of convergence with Newman's post-anarchism. Morris's claim that Kropotkin shared a 'common viewpoint' with anarcho-syndicalists places further distance between the two conceptions. Morris admits that Kropotkin was not uncritical of anarcho-syndicalism, but he argues that his criticisms were insignificant in comparison to his disapproval of other anarchist currents, notably Tolstoyan anarcho-pacifism and Stirnerism. Kropotkin had no interest in 'experimental communities' or with 'autonomous colonies'.[73] For him, prefiguration was about building the structures of anarchist society in the body of capitalism, as part of a strategy of resistance and revolutionary change secured through direct action.

> Kropotkin, as an anarchist communist, tended to envisage the local commune, not the trade union, as the key unit of organization, and he sought to replace the present bourgeois order with a system of decentralized, cooperative communes ... The distinction between anarcho-syndicalism and anarchist communism is, however, more a matter of emphasis rather than a difference in kind, for both affirm the importance of class struggle and workers' control of the productive associations.[74]

The malleability of Kropotkin's work to these two different conceptions of prefiguration suggests that the politics of classical anarchism may be filled in different ways. However, since class-struggle anarchists have asserted this claim largely unchallenged and because post-anarchists have willingly given the ground, classical anarchism has tended to assume this colouring.

Murray Bookchin's confusing conflation of class-struggle anarchism with social anarchism, deployed as an antonym for lifestyle anarchism, has helped reinforce this political conception of the classical tradition. While Bookchin's dichotomy flew in the face of his early defence of personal politics and also imposed a narrowly construed politics on customary understandings of social anarchism, it successfully juxtaposed anarchist communism to individualism. As the father of class-struggle anarchism, Kropotkin was made the adversary of individualist anarchisms. Moreover, by dint of the attempts of a variety of contemporary activists and post-anarchists to rehabilitate Stirner's work in radical theory, Kropotkin was also turned into an opponent of post-anarchism, as well as Hakim Bey's post-left anarchy and Christian anarchism. Bookchin's classifications were too blunt. As Morris notes, Kropotkin indeed pitched himself against Stirner and 'he tended to see both Stirner and Nietzsche as expressing a form of extreme bourgeois individualism'.[75] But he aligned himself with Tolstoy. Yet in van der Walt and Schmidt's writing the invocation of Bookchin's slippery critique of lifestyle individualism is less a lens to read Kropotkin's rejection of Stirner than it is a platform to cement a fundamental philosophical and political rift between class-struggle anarchism and its rivals. Their reservation about Bookchin's critique of lifestyle anarchism is his willingness to bestow the A-word on those he regards as individualists. They otherwise endorse his use of the 'term "lifestyle anarchism" to refer to a range of Stirnerite currents and eccentric grouping that claim the anarchist label' and apply his term 'social anarchist' to refer exclusively to the genuine anarchism of Bakunin and Kropotkin.[76] The result of these twists and turns is that classical anarchism is tied closely with the politics of class-struggle. As a classical anarchist – its chief exponent – Kropotkin, too, is painted in these terms.

Conclusion to Part 1

The pre-eminent position that Kropotkin attained as an exponent of anarchism in anarchism's second wave explains the exhaustion of his political thought in its post-anarchist third incarnation. Kropotkin achieved canonical status as a classical anarchist. Instead of questioning the premises of this representation of his ideas, third-wave anarchists accepted it and used it against him, rejecting Kropotkin as an exponent of classical anarchism. The most important challenge to this view reverses the judgements of dominant second-wave new anarchists, reinforcing an association with a form of revolutionary politics that the third-wave activists hold at arm's length. In many ways, Kropotkin emerges as an old man: worthy but out-of-time.

George Woodcock and Ivan Avakumović's biography makes quite a lot of play about the effects of Kropotkin's maturation on his political thought. The period of his late scholarship is peppered with reminders about the deterioration of his health, his life as an invalid and the start of his 'virtual retirement'.[1] Increasing ill-health, they also note, resulted in Kropotkin's detachment from the anarchist movement, explaining his 'mitigated French patriotism', increasing 'political abstractionism' and aggressively Germanophobic turn to militarism.[2] Kropotkin aged not just in years, but in his judgments. By the time of his death in 1921, his support for the war demonstrated just how old and out of touch he had become. This impression of Kropotkin's exhaustion is reinforced by post-anarchist critiques of nineteenth-century traditions. The 'politics and ethics of classical anarchism can be understood only within a certain Enlightenment rationalist-humanist paradigm ... which supposes there to be an objective truth to social relations that is suppressed by power and yet will be revealed'.[3] Enlightenment thinking should not be abandoned, Newman argues, but it is important to recognise that aspects of 'the paradigm have broken down and are no longer sustainable'.[4]

Kropotkin's comrade Jean Grave remembered Kropotkin differently. According to Grave, despite the hardships he suffered, Kropotkin remained youthful in his outlook, a twenty year-old all his life.[5] Class-struggle anarchists find a similar youthfulness in his political legacy. But the success of the label leaves them swimming against the tide. The development of classical anarchism as a shorthand to describe nineteenth-century anarchist thought formalises the time-worn character of the leading ideas it is said to describe.

The tag 'classical anarchism' is not only an obstacle to the study of Kropotkin's ideas; it is a distorting lens for movement histories. Classical anarchism introduces a set of ideological and philosophical markers into a complex history. In different ways anarchism emerges as an ideological position, framed by a set of theoretical concepts and methodological assumptions, rigorously applied. How far does Kropotkin's work bear out these interpretations? In the following chapters, I want to suggest that the classical stereotypes do not stand up to scrutiny and that the ideas of classical anarchism's leading representative diverge both in content and form from those that have been attributed to him.

Part 2 Coming Out of Russia

Introduction to Part 2

(A Beautiful White Christ) Coming Out of Russia

Nicholas Walter's irritation with Wilde's tribute to Kropotkin stemmed from the symbolism that attached to Kropotkin's goodness and the purity of his vision. Yet for all its extravagance, Wilde's phrase is richly suggestive. Woodcock and Avakumović use Wilde's accolade as a chapter heading, reduced to 'White Jesus'. Kropotkin's nobility is trumpeted and the idea of his removal from Russia is subsumed by his virtues. Read differently, Wilde's handle rightly directs attention to the character of Kropotkin's politics when he came out of Russia in 1876.

The Chaikovskii Circle (also known as, for example, the Circle of Tchaikovsky and Circle of Chaikovtsy), which Kropotkin joined in 1872, is often said to have had a lasting influence on his politics. Drawing on the warm recollection of the Circle that Kropotkin gives in his memoirs, Caroline Cahm describes its influence as 'formative' and adds that 'the idealism of the Chaikovskists continued to influence him long after he left Russia – especially in his view of revolutionary action'.[1] Drawing on a wealth of Russian sources, Martin Miller's study details Kropotkin's participation in the Circle and also considers how his manifesto, *Must We Occupy Ourselves with an Examination of the Ideal of a Future System?*, contributed both to the politics of the wider revolutionary movement and the development of his own political ideas.[2] Miller describes Kropotkin as a budding Bakuninist.[3] Departing from this account, Cahm emphasises how Kropotkin was affected by the Chaikovskists' personal virtues and impressed by the constitutional principles of the group. According to Kropotkin, these principles were adopted 'in opposition to the methods of Nechayev'. The Chaikovskists had decided, 'quite correctly, that a morally developed individuality must be the foundation of every organization, whatever political character it may take afterward and whatever programme of action it may adopt in the course of future events'.[4] The Circle operated on the basis of trust, openness, transparency and close friendship. Yet beyond the rejection of elite conspiracy, which Kropotkin combines with the advocacy of a Bakuninist spontaneous insurrectionary politics, the ways in which this influence marked his anarchism is difficult to discern.[5] The clue that Kropotkin gives is that the behaviours of the Chaikovskii Circle were 'characteristic of the Nihilist'.[6]

The difficulty of assessing the character of Kropotkin's politics at the point of his exile stems from the interconnections of the West European and Russian movements. The establishment of the Russian colony in Zurich and the often illegal transmission of Western ideas in the radical press, supported by the work of émigré intellectuals meant that radicals like Kropotkin were familiar with a wide range of European literatures and advanced ideas, interpreting these through the refractive lenses of Russian intellectual traditions and socio-economic conditions. If, as Miller argues, Kropotkin had absorbed Bakuninist and Proudhonist ideas before he went into exile, his socialism was likely to resemble the politics of some of the anti-authoritarian groups active in the West. Kropotkin's serial displacements compound the problem. Moving from Russia to Switzerland, France and Britain suggests an episodic development of ideas that militates against the analysis of his distinctive political culture. The usual history is that Kropotkin became a revolutionary activist in Switzerland and France and an evolutionary scientist in England. The suggestion made in recent Russian research that Kropotkin became an anarcho-reformist as a result of his assimilation of English liberalism is contestable, but exemplifies the extent to which his long period of exile in Britain has provided a crucial interpretative frame for the assessment of his ideas.[7]

It is sometimes said that in the thirty or so years that Kropotkin spent in Britain he lost his outsider status. During this period, Haia Shpayer-Makov remarked, 'his scholarly pursuits and absorption into suburban life made him appear almost an exemplary English gentleman'.[8] A New Zealand local press survey of *Who's Who* took Kropotkin's naturalisation as read, describing him as 'the Russian refugee who is practically an Englishman'.[9] Kropotkin's experience of British exile was in fact more trying than this picture of his integration suggests. Whereas he 'never considered himself an exile so long as he was on French speaking soil', Martin Miller notes, he found 'adjustment to life in England' hard. Language was a particular problem: he could read and write English, but he could not speak it when he arrived. Unable to settle when he landed in England in 1881, he described his first period in the country as 'a real exile'.[10]

In many ways Kropotkin's experience of exile was untypical. The assorted asylum seekers and political refugees who arrived in London to escape particular bouts of repression tended to maintain strong and near exclusive ties with other members of their language-groups. Kropotkin had strong personal relationships with fellow Russians but he also had connections with his family, was networked with activists and intellectuals across Europe, was lauded in London's cosmopolitan socialist scene and was well-regarded in British society. When the Liberal MP Sir Charles Dilke made the case against the introduction of the 1905 Aliens Act he argued that the measure threatened to exclude 'from this country people whom we shall afterwards be ashamed we have excluded' and invited the House of Commons to remember Kropotkin.[11]

In other ways, however, Kropotkin's émigré years resembled the exile of other political refugees. Looking at the experience of French anarchists, Constance Bantman comments that 'the anarchists were very much focused on French politics'.[12] Pietro di Paola finds similar limits to the practical internationalism of Italian anarchists and argues that 'Italian anarchist exiles' political horizons remained predominantly focused on events in Italy'.[13] Kropotkin became actively involved in British and West European political struggles, especially through his involvement with the paper *Freedom*. But he never entirely relinquished his interest in Russian affairs.

Miller argues that Kropotkin drifted from active engagement in Russian movement politics during his British exile and dates the revival of his interest in Nicholas II's accession in 1894. However, his relationship with Russia, Miller argues, was more diffuse than this direct involvement in Russian politics implies. Not only did he try to educate Western audiences about the Russian revolutionary movement and the repressive nature of the Russian regime, mounting sustained public campaigns against the Tsarist regime, he also attempted to influence the politics of the Russian movement through his promotion of anarchism in Western Europe. Kropotkin's approach was neither conventional nor, insofar as some of his Russian comrades were concerned, persuasive. The passage from the Russian edition of Kropotkin's *Memoirs* to which Miller refers indicates that Kropotkin was also aware that his comrades felt that he confronted a choice, and that he disagreed with them. Whereas they considered his decision to devote his time to West European politics to be an abandonment of the Russian revolutionary cause, Kropotkin's view was that this effort was part of a commitment to the Russian underground.

> I could never feel comfortable with the Russian view on propaganda abroad. Russian comrades considered me almost a traitor because I devoted my strength to agitation in Western Europe. But I think, on the contrary, that by working for Western Europe I also worked for Russia, perhaps more than if I had remained in Russia. All movements are conceived under the influence of Western Europe and carry the imprint of the trends of thought prevailing in Europe.[14]

Kropotkin did not outline the thinking that underpinned this theory of transnational activism clearly, but as Miller argues, Kropotkin's re-integration in the Russian anarchist movement, notably his partic-ipation in the publication of *Kheb i volia* at the turn of the century, can be explained by his anxiety about the growing strength of Marxist Social Democracy in Russia. As Kropotkin told a Jewish member of the London East End *Workers' Friend*, he was not interested in converting London Social Democrats to anarchism, but he was deeply concerned about the influence of social democracy on the workers' movement. "'[W]e are not missionaries, we are idealists,"' he is reported to have said. "'Let them be Social Democrats if they so choose, that's their busi-ness. Our field of activity is among the workers."'[15]

If Kropotkin's efforts to counter the sway of social democracy in Russia drew him back into the orbit of Russian-language propa-ganda, in the 1890s he found a second front for anarchist campaign-ing in Nietzscheanism. This critical engagement brought to the fore the influence that Russian politics, specifically nihilism, exercised on his anarchism. Kropotkin's earliest writings published in *Paroles d'un Révolté* are peppered with references to Russia and to nihilism. Yet the significance of these allusions only becomes transparent after the fact and in the light of the extensive accounts of the Russian movement that Kropotkin presents in his memoirs and his study of Russian lit-erature.[16] As well as exposing Kropotkin's worries about the direction that the West European anarchist movement appeared to be taking in the 1890s, his discussion of Nietzsche also reveals the extent to which Kropotkin came out of Russia, moulded by the Chaikovskists, immersed in nihilist politics.

Richard Morgan has recently argued that Kropotkin's scientific expe-ditions were fundamental to the later development of his anarchism. It was in Russia, Morgan argues, that Kropotkin's interest in statistics and mapping was piqued. Kropotkin's formative experience in Russia helps explain his scientific epistemology and his interest in Victorian social and natural sciences. It sheds important light on his conceptions of anarchy and revolution and, moreover, points to his innovative development of a turn-of-the-century bio-politics.[17] If, as Cahm argues, Kropotkin's admi-ration for the nihilists profoundly shaped his understanding of anarchist ethics and his conception of revolutionary commitment, Morgan's anal-ysis suggests that his immersion in nihilism tells only half of Kropotkin's political story. Accepting that it is possible to give different accounts of Kropotkin's early life and the influences acting on him, and that the choice of starting point will elicit different interpretations, the conjec-ture here is that Kropotkin adopted nihilist approaches to all areas of activity, including his approach to science. In his memoirs, Kropotkin presents a detailed account of the expeditions he conducted in Siberia and Finland in the 1860s and 1870s. He also hints at their value for the scholarly work he produced on his return. Frustratingly, he is less forthcoming about the relationship of geography to anarchism and his conception of geographical science, even though his appreciation of Reclus's work gives some indication of the broad lines of his thinking.[18] Reading Kropotkin's geography in the light of his nihilist commitments sheds light on this relationship and explains his approach to the state.

The following chapters consider how Kropotkin's émigré status and his relationship with the Russian movement stimulated and shaped his anarchism. The first looks at the inspiration he took from nihilism and the ways in which he integrated his knowledge of the movement's history to advance a critique of Nietzschean individualism. The second looks at his critiques of Tsarism and outlines his understanding of the development of the Russian state in the post-Emancipation era, and its relationship to the European state system. Kropotkin's contention that Russia's political development was intimately linked to changes in Western Europe is explained by the approach he took to the analysis of the international state system and his understanding of its impermanence and instability. Kropotkin presented an account of the state that he explored as a geographer. Taking a global perspective on the European state system enabled him to illuminate the destructive character of state organisation and lay the foundations for a scientific approach to anarchism that indicated the potential for revolutionary transformation.

Nihilism

Kropotkin began to write about Russia at length only in the late 1890s, when he published the *Memoirs of a Revolutionist* and *Ideals and Realities in Russian Literature*. During the same period, Kropotkin began working on the theory of mutual aid. As he explained in the posthumously published *Ethics*, one of his key concerns was to address the failure of nineteenth-century science to present a compelling ethical theory capable of explaining the natural origins of moral instincts and providing criteria for judgement.[1] Kropotkin turned to Darwin's theory of evolution to frame his own conception and in the early formulations of the theory of mutual aid, he looked closely at the work of T. H. Huxley, whom he associated with the popularisation of Social Darwinian doctrines. Kropotkin set out to refute Huxley's description of nature as red in tooth and claw in order to also reject Huxley's conclusions: that the basis of morality could only be found in the divine, not the natural world.

Kropotkin continued to work on the theory of mutual aid until he returned to Russia in 1917 and the arguments became very technical, resulting in the rejection of Darwin's Malthusian assumption of scarcity, a Lamarckian interpretation of Darwin and a speculative discussion of biological transmission, supporting Kropotkin's thesis that environmental adaptations could be inherited, and his claim that Darwin also adopted this view.[2] Yet Kropotkin's motivation to set out an anarchist ethical theory was political. He had already presented the substance of the historical account of ethical development that appeared in *Mutual Aid* in the 1880s. His decision to return to and elaborate this work was made in the context of his growing concerns about the hold that Nietzschean ideas seemed to be gaining within the anarchist movement. In Kropotkin's view, the negative influence of Nietzschean philosophy helped explain the disastrous turn within the anarchist movement to terrorist violence and it created a wrongful impression in the public mind about the relationship between anarchism, nihilism and violence.

When Kropotkin decided to include an account of nihilism in his autobiography, the death of his friend Stepniak (Sergey Mikhailovich Kravchinsky) in 1896 particularly prayed on his mind. As he told Georg

Brandes, Stepniak was not just a comrade, he was the very model of the courageous and just revolutionary.[3] Shortly before his death in 1896, Stepniak was unmasked as the assassin of General Mezentsev, the head of St Petersburg police. The publicity played to all the negative stereotypes of the nihilists, as well as adding to the hysteria surrounding anarchist terrorism.[4] It was easy for detractors to attack The Society of the Friends of Russian Freedom, the anti-Tsarist organisation that Stepniak had helped establish in London, for being anarchists of Ravachol's type.[5] The misinformation circulated by Tsarist spies and stoolpigeons about the character of the Russian revolutionary movement was a strong incentive for Kropotkin to present a corrective to the popular view.

In the 1890s Kropotkin used key works on Russia to defend an idea of individual rebellion that could rival Nietzsche's 'bourgeois' individualism, complementing the theoretical work he undertook in advancing the theory of mutual aid. In the process he not only described anarchist ethics, describing principles of behaviour and judgement, he also revealed the powerful influence that the Russian underground had exercised on some of his most vital early anarchist writing. Stepniak once argued that nihilists and anarchists shared a similar psychology but distinguished nihilism, which he described as a practical movement from anarchism, which he described as a 'good theory'.[6] By the time that Kropotkin came out of Russia, he had adopted a very practical conception of anarchism, but his political theory had also taken on a decidedly nihilist flavour.

Kropotkin approached nihilism as a critic of Nietzsche, but also as an interpreter of Russian literature. Nietzsche's conception of nihilism is often traced to the influence of Dostoevsky; Kropotkin gives an account that elevates Turgenev and Chernyshevsky, Dostoevsky's rival, as nihilism's creators. One of the striking features of Kropotkin's defence of nihilism is his analysis of the feminist currents within the Russian revolutionary movement. Although he did not give a full account of his impressions of this movement until the 1890s, he took the example of the nihilist women's commitment to social transformation directly into his anarchism and it infused some of his most influential writing of the 1880s.

Nietzsche, Individualism and Violence

Kropotkin made very few references to Nietzsche in his published writings, however, his scattered remarks and his private correspondence show how baleful he felt Nietzsche's influence on the anarchist movement was. In Kropotkin's posthumously published work *Ethics*, he bundles Nietzsche together with Bernard Mandeville, the author of *The Fable of the Bees*, and argues that both 'took an utterly negative and mocking attitude toward all morality, representing it as a survival of religious environment and of superstitions'.[7] In a letter discussing what he characterised as the paralysis of the French movement, Kropotkin told Nettlau that 'Nietzscheanism is one of a number of *spurious* individualisms'. It was 'bourgeois', describing 'lackyism, slavishness towards tradition, *obliteration of the individuality* of the oppressor himself, as well as among the down-trodden masses'. At root, Nietzsche's '*handsome blond beast*' was 'a slave – slave to king, prince, law and tradition – a member of the herd of oppressors, bereft of personality'.[8] In some of his allusions to Nietzsche, Kropotkin also refers to Stirner and attacks a composite type of individualism that he variously describes as egoistic, sensualist and aristocratic.[9] Neither Kropotkin's use of the amalgam, nor his denigration of Nietzschean and Stirnerite ideas as 'bourgeois', was unusual. But this dismissal was misleading to the extent that it suggested an unwillingness to subject Nietzscheanism to scrutiny. In fact, the descriptor was his final verdict on a debate about the relationship of individualism to communism that simmered in anarchist circles in the late decades of the nineteenth century and the early years of the twentieth.

The thinking that informed these debates could be very creative. Diverse ideas were weaved together to produce a range of innovative syntheses. As Max Nettlau argued with reference to the German anarchist scene, Stirner, Nietzsche, Tolstoy and Ibsen formed the melange of literary figures that animated rich discussions of social ethics. Landauer was one of the important parties to these debates.[10] Kropotkin's work was also sometimes integrated into these conversations. Indeed, Ananda Coomaraswyamy read mutual aid alongside Nietzsche to create an ideal of Western anarchism to complement the anti-colonial struggles that he was engaged with in the East.[11]

These philosophical discussions had a political significance. Arguments about the relative merits of Stirner and Nietzsche revolved around issues of abstract theory, but they were also pertinent to movement politics. To give an example: Max Baginski's critical review of *The Ego and Its Own* was designed both to dispel myths about Nietzsche's rumoured indebtedness to Stirner and to demonstrate that the freedom from slavery that Stirner had championed depended on the successful struggle for communism, which he had wrongly rejected. Baginski's message to the readers of *Mother Earth* was clear: 'I am a Communist *because* I am an Individualist'. He added, 'Individualism and Communism go hand in hand.'[12] Activists attracted by Stirner's analysis of spooks should recognise that he failed to comprehend the necessity of abolishing private property. Rather than turning inwards to their own liberation, they should therefore focus their efforts on the struggle against capitalism.

Unlike Baginski, Kropotkin was no more able to see the creative potential in Nietzsche's work than Nietzsche was willing to find the value in Kropotkin's.[13] However, his vilification of Nietzsche as a bourgeois individualist stemmed from concerns that he shared with Baginski about the ways in which philosophies shaped movements and the potential for individualism to undermine communist principles.

Kropotkin identified this threat in the behaviours of activists and he linked the influx of Nietzschean ideas into anarchism with terrorism. The association turned on the popular interpretation of Nietzsche's amoralism as an expression of anarchist freedom, but it had a number of facets that varied according to the contexts in which it was rehearsed. In the Italian movement, the argument was linked to questions of organisation. Malatesta argued that the refusal to recognise moral codes not only resulted in the justification of indiscriminate violence but also in the rejection of movement-building that was self-defeating. Individualists in turn accused Malatesta of supporting a rigid, moralised form of socialism that flew in the face of anarchist commitments to individual liberty.[14] In the French movement Nietzschean individualism was linked to terrorism and all kinds of illegalism,[15] particularly theft, and the provocations of agents provocateurs.[16]

Kropotkin's worries about Nietzschean individualism were fuelled by his assessment of the principle of propaganda by the deed that had evolved from a confrontational tactic designed to support the construction of a mass resistance movement to a policy of individual violence.[17] In the period between the assassinations of Tsar Alexander II in 1881 and Archduke Franz Ferdinand in 1914, the two milestones of political violence, anarchists were implicated or actively involved in a range of high-profile killings. These reached their peak in France in 1890–4 and in Spain in 1904–5. The victims famously included the French President Carnot (1894), Empress Elizabeth ('Sissi') of Austria (1898) and US President William McKinley (1901). There were numerous civilian casualties, too, since anarchists took to bombing public spaces. In the public mind, there was little to distinguish one *attentat* from another. For Kropotkin, however, there was a qualitative difference between the violence that led to the assassination of the Tsar and the *ravacholisme* that characterised the campaigns of the 1890s. The distinction was not rooted in the justness of the perpetrators' cause, as some liberal critics of Russian autocracy argued, but in their motivations.

Felix Volkhovsky, who with Sergei Stepniak founded the London Society of the Friends of Russian Freedom, accused Kropotkin of denying anarchist violence. When challenged, Kropotkin's default was to argue that the individuals charged with violence were not genuine anarchists.[18]

In some cases, the links to anarchism were indeed tenuous; but Kropotkin's more usual rejoinder was to explore the causes of violence rather than to denounce the actions of the perpetrators. Responding to the news of Elizabeth of Austria's assassination, Kropotkin argued that the killer, Luccheni, had been brutalised in the Italian army. Was it surprising that this killing machine had not learned to respect women?[19] The obviously pointless slaying of Elizabeth of Austria could be explained, even if it could not be excused. More often than not, anarchist violence was a response to state repression. In these cases, too, Kropotkin acknowledged the culpability of anarchists and he identified what he believed to be the drivers of the actions that explained their acts. Writing to his friend Nannie Dryhurst, in the aftermath of Paulino Pallás's attempt on the life of the captain general of Catalonia, Kropotkin warned against hasty denunciation. His general point was that 'judgments at a distance are, in fact, unjust and worthless'. He gave an example: 'Living here, abroad, I blamed the Executive Committee who, in order to blow up the Tsar, blew up 200 soldiers, killing and maiming 70 – who stood between their explosives and the Tsar.' Had he been in Russia, he continued, 'with all my personal dislike of violence, I probably would have done like to others. Only that I should have blown myself with the rest.' Turning to Pallás, Kropotkin considered the defence that his action was a response to the execution of two other anarchists. His conclusion was that revenge 'is no aim in itself', and that it was a biblical rather than an anarchist principle. Yet Pallás's was also a '*human*' act and Kropotkin argued that 'all revolts have borne and for a long time will bear that character'.

> In fact *we* who have not suffered from the prosecutions as they, the workers suffer; some, who in our houses seclude ourselves from cry and disgust of human sufferings, *we are no judges* for those who live in the midst of all this hell of suffering. The less *we* lecture them, the better. *We* have no right to do it, so long *as we have not been the pariahs which they are in Society*.

> Personally I hate those explosions, but I cannot stand as judge to condemn those who are driven to despair.

> I should not revenge a personal offence. But, seeing a child violated – should I refrain from killing on the spot the violator? Should I assist calmly at an execution of Paris prisoners by a Versailles peloton, under the applause of the merry ladies of the garrison? Should you?[20]

Woodcock described Kropotkin's reasoning as confused. However, while Kropotkin runs a number of separate ideas together his letter usefully captures some of his central ideas about violence.[21] One general point that emerges from Kropotkin's reflections on Pallás is that he stood some distance from Tolstoy, whose Christian anarchist principle of non-resistance ruled against action driven by passion, either to prevent harm or to redress the sufferings of others.[22] Second, where violence described the act of a revolutionary but was not a revolutionary act, Kropotkin was prepared to defend actions that had a social character. This was the view he adopted in the 1870s, when he and Elisée Reclus suggested to Paul Brousse that a narrow concern with the consequences of actions risked sanctioning mere sensualism on the part of the propagandists by the deed.[23] Kropotkin and Reclus were still prepared to justify violence on condition that it was driven by virtuous intentions – a genuine hatred of oppression in Kropotkin's case and a regard for progressive development in Reclus's.[24] This was the position that he reiterated in the 1890s, when he parted company with Reclus in his assessment of the rebellious character of *ravacholisme*. Kropotkin worried that Nietzschean amoralism may persuade anarchists that it was acceptable to enter into activities that were purely self-aggrandising and that misleadingly benchmarked liberation against the preparedness to flout all and any social conventions. Holding Nietzsche indirectly responsible for the individualism that resulted in anarchist violence, Kropotkin outlined an idea of liberation to rival Nietzsche's – as he perceived it – and that was directed towards the achievement of social transformation driven by individual commitment. He took the principles for the idea he had in mind from nihilism.

Life Imitating Art

Kropotkin's autobiography and his lectures on Russian literature, published as *Ideals and Realities in Russian Literature*[25] are the main sources for his discussion of nihilism, together with an unpublished manuscript on the Russian women's movement.[26] His argument is that nihilism was first a literary phenomenon that sparked a political movement. Nihilism was not just an illustration of life imitating art, however. It also described an approach to art that was integral to the movement's ethics.

Kropotkin argued that nihilism was brought to life in two books, Turgenev's *Fathers and Sons* and Chernyshevsky's *What is to be Done?*, and that it was launched into the political realm by the literary critic Dmitri Pisarev. These books contributed to the emergence of the movement in different ways. Turgenev's book was the literary masterpiece, but Kropotkin recognised that it painted an ambivalent, if not negative, picture of the nihilist and that it was received with hostility in activist circles. Chernyshevsky's book, by contrast, was not a great work of art, but its portrait was deeply attractive and left a positive impression on the radical movement.[27] Unlike the Chernysevkians, who had reproached Turgenev for the opinions he gave to his anti-hero Bazarov,[28] Kropotkin attempted to show that Turgenev was in fact as nihilist as Chernyshevksy and that *Fathers and Sons* and *What is to be Done?* both achieved the standard of 'art for life's sake' championed by the great Belinksy.

To explain the reception of his work and Turgenev's apparent reluctance to embrace nihilism Kropotkin turned to Turgenev's 1860 lecture 'Hamlet and Don Quixote', delivered two years before the publication of *Fathers and Sons*. In it Turgenev contrasts Don Quixote, the 'archetype of self-sacrifice' to Hamlet, who he describes as the representative of 'analysis, egotism, scrutiny and ... disbelief'. Turgenev treats each as 'extreme expressions of two opposite tendencies' both found in different measure in all people.[29] In Kropotkin's account of Turgenev's essay Hamlet and Don Quixote appear as different types of actor. Individuals of Don Quixote's stripe, Kropotkin argued, bear the familiar characteristics of the utopian personality: fighting against windmills and taking 'a barber's plate for the magic helmet of Mambrin[o]' ('who of us has never made the same mistake?' Kropotkin asked). Less typically, Kropotkin also detected in Turgenev's reading of Don Quixote

> a leader of the masses, because the masses always follow those who, taking no heed of the sarcasms of the majority, or even of persecutions, march straight forward, keeping their eyes fixed upon a goal which is seen, perhaps, by no one but themselves. They search, they fall, but they rise again and find it, – and by right, too.[30]

In the Hamlet group were those who prioritised '[a]nalysis first of all, and then egotism, and therefore no faith'. This model was sceptical, 'disbelieves in Good' and, as a result, 'never will achieve anything'. Yet Hamlet 'does not disbelieve in Evil'. According to Kropotkin, Hamlet 'hates it; Evil and Deceit are his enemies; and his skepticism is not indifferentism, but only negation and doubt'. The tragedy, then, was that for characters of this type doubt 'finally consume[s] ... will'.

Returning to *Fathers and Sons*, Kropotkin argued that Turgenev was himself a version of Hamlet, and that this explained his ambivalence toward Bazarov, who was another Hamlet. Turgenev was sympathetic to nihilism. In Bazarov he 'represented his superiority admirably well, he understood the tragic character of his isolated position'. But his characterisation was 'harsh', 'merely negative'.[31] Unlike the younger generation who also saw some of themselves in Bazarov, Tugenev 'could not surround him with that tender, poetical love which he bestowed as on a sick friend, when his heroes approached the Hamlet type'.[32] He 'could not supply by intuition the lack of knowledge'[33] and failed to see that Bazarov could live as a Don Quixote, 'for a great cause'.[34] Had Turgenev 'lived a few more years', Kropotkin concluded, 'he surely would have noticed coming into the arena the new type of men of action'.[35] To support this claim, Kropotkin related a conversation with Turgenev.

> He knew ... that I was an enthusiastic admirer of his writings; and one day ... he asked me what I thought of Bazarov. I frankly replied, "Bazarov is an admirable painting of the nihilist, but one feels that you did not love him as much as you did your other heroes."

Turgenev denied the charge: ' "On the contrary, I loved him, intensely loved him ... When we get home I will show you my diary, in which I have noted how I wept when I had ended the novel with Bazarov's death." ' Kropotkin summarised:

> Turgenev certainly loved the intellectual aspect of Bazarov. He so identified himself with the Nihilist philosophy of his hero that he even kept a diary in his name, appreciating the current events from Bazarov's point of view. But I think that he admired him more than he loved him.[36]

Chernyshevsky had none of Turgenev's doubts and indeed wrote *What is to be Done?* as a Quixotic text. Pitting himself against the generation of the 40s and the aesthetics of German idealism, Chernyshevsky rejected the idea that art's role was to present a blemish-free world of beauty. For Chernyshevsky, beauty was life, and the 'beautiful is whatever man really values in life as precious and desirable'.[37] As Kropotkin puts it in *Ideals and Realities in Russian Literature*, Chernyshevsky's claim was that 'art cannot be its own aim'; 'life is superior to art'. The purpose of art was *'to explain life, to comment upon it, and to express and opinion about it'*.[38] Not uncoincidentally, Kropotkin noted that Bazarov expresses the same principle; Turgenev characterised it as a 'negation of art', and it was the one idea that, he told Kropotkin, he could not love in his creation.[39] Kropotkin was not so repulsed and, following Pisarev, who also attacked idealism, named it 'thoughtful realism'.[40]

Kropotkin described thoughtful realism as a mid-point between idealism and what he described as the enervating, anatomical realism of Zola.[41] This treatment suggested that there was no trade-off between art and reality but an interrelationship: thoughtful realism rooted art in life and give it an inspirational, elevating quality.

Kropotkin's formulation enabled him to reconcile Turgenev's apparent negativity towards nihilism with his own enthusiasm about it and show that the hostility that *Fathers and Sons* provoked among activists was based on a misunderstanding of Turgenev's position. *Fathers and Sons* and *What is to be Done?* outlined the same ideas but whereas Turgenev embraced them hesitantly, Chernyshevsky did so with gusto. Nihilism, Kropotkin concluded, had a double aspect. The nihilists were those like Chernyshevksy who promoted thoughtful realism. Because Chernyshevsky successfully captured the mood of the Russian youth and transformed doubts into dreams nihilism became manifest in a social movement. This was its second aspect. Chernyshevksky's appeal, Kropotkin argued, proved particularly powerful to women. Nihilism became a motive force for Russian feminism and this peculiarly Russian flavour set the women's movement in Russia apart from the movements in Western Europe.

Nihilism and Women's Emancipation

Franco Venturi, the historian of Russian populism, dates the rise of nihilism to 1862, when Pisarev transformed the ideas expounded in *Fathers and Sons* into a political doctrine and used them to develop Chernyshevsky's thought.[42] Because he also identified Chernyshevsky as the pivotal figure in the movement, Kropotkin argued that the years from 1858 to 1864 were the crucial dates, but acknowledged that nihilism had left a mark on the movements of the 1870s.[43] These were 'improperly called nihilist'.[44] And although he dubbed as nihilist those executed for the assassination of the Tsar in 1881, he carefully distinguished nihilism from the terrorism of 1879–81, which culminated in this killing.[45] Stepniak adopted a looser usage, deploying it in a generic sense to describe revolutionary movements in Russia and Western Europe that adopted terrorist methods – specifically dynamite.[46] In nineteenth-century Europe, popular usage followed Stepniak rather than Kropotkin, as the diffusion of the literature on nihilism dovetailed with the incidence of violent acts. Coming to Turgenev and Chernyshevsky a generation after Kropotkin, Emma Goldman remembered seeing a 'huge poster announcing the death of the Tsar, "assassinated by murderous Nihilists"' and imagining them as 'black, sinister creatures' and ferocious beasts.[47] More generally, too, as Venturi notes, nihilism 'served to express the feeling of mystery which surrounded Russian Populists and terrorists'.[48] An early Italian history (recommended to Gladstone by Madame Novikov, the so-called MP for Russia and a sworn enemy of Stepniak) used the English-term 'self-help' to describe nihilist ideas but observed that nihilism had gained a reputation for utopian impracticality, mysticism and violence.[49]

The uncertainty about the span of the movement's activity was reflected in disagreements about the movement's intellectual genesis. Some commentators included Alexander Herzen as an exponent of nihilist ideas, whereas others treated him as a precursor. Some associated nihilism with anarchism and identified Bakunin, 'the arch-conspirator', as its mastermind. Bakunin's involvement with Sergei Nechaev helped seal this reputation.[50] Fuelling suspicions about the organisational discipline and psychological fanaticism of the nihilists, Nechaev's principal work, *The Catechism of a Revolutionary* (later resurrected by the Black Panthers), provided a blueprint for revolutionary cell-structure and outlined the duties of revolutionaries in dark and chilling terms.[51] The *Catechism* came to be regarded as the ultimate expression of nihilist doctrine, although it appeared in 1869, five years after the end of the movement's flowering, according to Kropotkin's estimates.[52]

The early dating of the movement was significant for Kropotkin, not just because it divorced nihilism from terrorism but also because it provided a bridge to the women's movement. Kropotkin's claim that women actively entered into nihilism is not controversial. As Cathy Porter notes, Chernyshevsky's work was attractive both to groups of women involved in liberal philanthropy and to those who mixed in radical student circles.[53] But his sympathetic understanding of women's role in the movement ran counter to the mainstream in the 1870s and 1880s. Admittedly, public opinion was not unremittingly hostile to nihilism: Oscar Wilde's first, abortive play, *Vera; Or, The Nihilist*, which enjoyed a one-week run in New York in 1883, told the story of a romantic revolutionary, both high-minded and self-sacrificing;[54] George Kennan, the American explorer who took the trouble to travel to Russia to observe the conditions that political prisoners endured in the Siberian salt mines, described the nihilists as 'quiet, orderly, reasonable human beings' with legitimate cause.[55] Sophia Perovskaya and Vera Zasulich were often included in this rank.[56] But the complaint that the 'popular idea of a Nihilist' as a 'ferocious ruffian, ready for rapine and thirsty for blood, hating restraint and loathing the law'[57] was one-sided suggested that the prevailing view was largely negative, and public reaction to Wilde's play bore this out.[58] As far as women were concerned, moreover, nihilism created a moral panic.

Women's presumed natural political passivity fuelled some of the anxieties. 'When women ... actively and enthusiastically step forth in a revolutionary or national movement, even to the extent of sacrificing their lives, it is always a sign of a people's feelings being wrought up to the highest tension.'[59] The misogyny that typified all anti-feminist campaigns was also evident in a lot of the commentaries. An article published in France described the 'type of woman peculiar to Russia and its Nihilism' as 'ugly' not just because 'their physiognomies mirror the abominable principles they inwardly cultivate, but positively ugly'.[60] In John Baker Hopkins's *Nihilism Its Words and Deeds*, the hideousness of nihilism is represented in the figure of Mrs Ziegelbauer, a foul-mouthed, 'empty-headed', cigar-smoking 'virago and a gabbler', who eats like a pig and boasts of her distain for 'sham hair, ditto teeth, ditto ditto complexion, figure', but nonetheless patches her face with 'artificial colour'.[61]

The nihilists' sexual depravity ran through much of the popular literature. Authors of popular fiction created beautiful seductresses to emphasise the dangers of nihilist enslavement. Rarely autonomous and typically depicted as easy targets for manipulative, authoritarian nihilist men, these beauties were recruited to corrupt the moral behaviours of upstanding citizens and to lure their hapless dupes into terrorist plots.[62] Accounts of the sexual immorality of nihilist women both exposed the dangers of free love and the cold, utilitarianism of nihilist philosophy. The lesson was that nihilists, like liberals, loved liberty more than life, but unlike liberals they were also prepared to give up love for the cause. Contrasted to free love, true love was the antidote to revolutionary terror. Torn between her love for the Tsarevitch Alexis, who she is charged to assassinate, Wilde's heroine Vera takes her own life rather than sacrifice that love to revolutionary commitment.[63] The story *Within an Ace* works in a similar way. A blustering, querulous, pathetic Bakunin appears in this story bemoaning the loss of his love, Natalie Herzen, as the personal price he has paid for his dedication to the revolution.[64] Because the love of a good woman was seen as the saving of a potentially revolutionary man, the corruption of the nihilists' morals became doubly threatening. The lesson of this literature is that women's revolutionary engagement leaves men dangerously adrift because it destabilises the domestic institutions in which love inheres and sullies romance through the encouragement of perverted practice.[65]

Kropotkin also identified interpersonal relationships as a key concern for women nihilists. The tenor of his analysis is earnest but it belies the 'essential puritanism' ascribed to him by Woodcock[66] and qualifies Emma Goldman's claims about his apparent lack of interest in questions of sexual liberation, which Woodcock and Avakumović also cite and Bonnie Haaland makes a cornerstone of Goldman's critique of Kropotkin's work.[67] Kropotkin certainly avoided the prurience of the critics and rather than telling a story of corruption or manipulation, instead traced a process of radicalisation, from individual rebellion to collective action.

Kropotkin claimed that women of all classes were attracted to nihilism, but uppermost in his mind were women from the middle and upper classes. Nihilism was not a movement of peasant women. Indeed, one of Kropotkin's more baffling ideas is that women in rural Russia had already carved out an important independent economic and political role in the villages and that, unlike their privileged sisters, they had no reason to fight for social emancipation, because all they lacked was economic security.[68] The enormous burdens of work that fell to women – from housework, gardening, dairy and poultry farming to weaving and spinning were an indicator of their success: peasant women had established a sphere of activity and 'the man has no right to interfere ... *unless a brute*'. Kropotkin's other dubious claim was that these women exercised an important political role and had a strong voice in village affairs.[69]

Kropotkin described the middle-class women that nihilism attracted as the '*Highest Revoltées* against the conventional *life* in all its aspects'.[70] These women rejected crinoline and velvet, wore short 'cropped hair and blue spectacles' and preferred 'scotch plaid' to traditional overcoats.[71] Beneath these outward gestures of defiance lay a complete rejection of midle-class mores. The transformation of 'muslin girls' (Pisarev's description of women whose conception of the world did not extend 'beyond their muslin dresses'),[72] into nihilist women was driven, at first, by a thirst for knowledge and it resulted in the overhaul of domestic politics. Taking a long, rational look at family life, the nihilists rejected the frippery and coercion that conventional domesticity involved:

> Marriage without love and familiarity without friendship were repudiated. The Nihilist girl, compelled by her parents to be a doll in a doll's house, and to marry for property's sake, preferred to abandon her house and her silk dresses ... The woman who saw ... that neither love nor friendship connected any more those who were legally considered husband and wife ... preferred to break a bond which retained none of its essential features; and she often went with her children to face poverty, preferring loneliness and misery to a life which, under conventional conditions, would have given a perpetual lie to her best self.[73]

Nihilist rebellion was 'met with horror by retrogrades'. Typically, said Kropotkin, because the Russian women's movement successfully bridged the generational divisions that set fathers against sons, the critics were men.[74] However, the reactions that women encountered extended far beyond the personal slights and humiliations of the patriarchal family. Nihilist women also met considerable state repression. '*The revenge* the rulers took against the women in our country was terrible. Thousands of them after long imprisonment were dispersed in the remotest corners of the country.'[75]

Kropotkin argued that the radicalisation of women provoked a serious political crisis because the demand for and commitment to change fundamentally threatened the stability of the entire social system in ways that mere politicking could never do, not because women's engagement in politics was judged peculiar, as the critics of nihilism believed. Kropotkin appreciated the personal in the political. Yet having identified repression as a spur to radicalism, he also argued that the real power of the women's campaign came in the shift away from a politics that was focused narrowly on individual emancipation. Starting as a process of middle-class emancipation and encouraged by access to education, nihilism blossomed into a movement for social reform as women turned their campaigning zeal outwards. 'At no time did the despotic ruler so tremble as when he saw the women raising the banner of *Freedom* for *all*.' Kropotkin continued:

> There is a time in all nations when a sudden feeling rises that things cannot go on like they are. That is a radical change in mankind in the political and economical domain but also in the moral relations between individuals. And that awakening we have had in Russia in the beginning of the sixties. And it was the youth who took the liveliest part in the revolte [*sic*] against the conventional life.
>
> a) Fortune! they said I am ashimed [*sic*] to enjoy it. Each fortune is the result of injustice.
> b) Luxury! they said I dispise [*sic*] it. It is weakness it makes a slave of you.
> c) The conventional education! they said is faulse [*sic*] it is against morals and nature. The marriage which you call holy is mostly a disgraceful bargain.
> d) The criticism ment [*sic*] even to the way of dressing. The young student looked with a deep dispise [*sic*] at the smart comrades.
>
> Now could you wonder that the women who displayed such energy for their own independence should *be open* to *accept* any *advanced* ideas. In meeting young men, as comrades the highest ideas were discussed. *She finds* that the struggle for her own freedom is not yet the highest ideal. *She became* socialist.[76]

In his memoirs, Kropotkin describes how nihilism led women to socialism and how nihilist men encouraged women to enter into the struggle for emancipation, rebuking those who 'indulged in small talk' or who prided themselves on their 'womanly manners and elaborate toilette'. 'How is it', radical men would say, 'you are not ashamed to talk this nonsense and to wear that chignon of false hair?'

Kropotkin did not explain the motives that resulted in this movement from nihilism to socialism, but it seemed that the processes that drew nihilist women to socialist struggle mirrored Kropotkin's own epiphany, which he explains with reference to Stepniak's *Career of a Nihilist*. '[E]very revolutionist has a moment in his life when some circumstance, maybe unimportant in itself, has brought him to giving himself to the cause of revolution.'[77] He denied that women's revelation resulted in a new set of pressures to conform.[78] Motivated by their desires to determine their own futures women instead carved out their autonomy and independence, just as Chernyshevsky's heroine Vera does in *What is to be Done?* In an exchange about the benefits of entering into loveless marriages, Vera tells her friend Julie, who thinks of herself as a 'fallen woman':

'You call me a dreamer and ask what I want out of life. I prefer neither to dominate nor to submit. I wish neither to deceive nor to dissemble. I don't want to be concerned about other people's opinions, or strive for what others advise.'

She continues:

'I don't want to submit to anyone. I want to be free; I don't want to be obligated to anyone for anything. I don't want anyone ever to say, "You're obligated to do this for me!" I want to do only what I desire and want others to do likewise."[79]

Men, too, were also changed by the engagement with nihilism. Chernyshevsky 'taught young men to see in women a comrade and a friend – not a domestic slave'.[80] Kropotkin added, moreover, that women transformed socialism by their engagement, forging relationships with men that were mutually supportive and beneficial because they were established on equal terms. In Kropotkin's account women were neither playthings of domineering men nor the manipulative exploiters of male weakness, the two stereotypes that prevailed in popular literature. And the example of the nihilist women was one he used repeatedly in his later writings to explore ethical action.

Nietzscheanism and Liberation

In nihilism Kropotkin found a model of social transformation that was driven by individual commitment and that offered an alternative to the individualism he associated with Nietzscheanism. Nihilism articulated a forceful desire for individual liberation but it also captured the aspirations that Kropotkin attached to legitimate revolutionary action. In the absence of these aspirations, individualism collapsed into villainy, exploitation and slavery.

Kropotkin gave an illustration of the differences between nihilist and Nietzschean individualism in a discussion of sexual liberation and free love. Free love was understood in different ways, but a dominant view was that it simply pandered to a male heterosexual 'desire for the long-term sexual availability of multiple women'.[81] As Stepniak argued:

> with us the question of the emancipation of woman was not confined to the petty right of 'free love', which is nothing more than the right of selecting her master ... the important thing is to have liberty itself, leaving the question of love to individual will.[82]

Kropotkin did not use the term 'free love' but set out a similar position in a letter to George Bernard Shaw. Their relationship, typical of many that Kropotkin enjoyed, was kindled by the fluidity of radical politics that perforated ideological divisions. According to Kropotkin's daughter Sasha, Shaw was so frequent a visitor to the Kropotkin household that she felt she had 'always known' him. His fondness for her father, she recalled, was 'reinforced by their endless political disagreements'.[83] In 1903 Shaw sent him a copy of *Man and Superman*, a play received at the time as an expression of Shaw's Nietzscheanism.[84] Kropotkin was not impressed with the play, also thinking it Nietzschean. He told Alfred Marsh, who took over the editorship of *Freedom* in 1895, that he wished 'somebody would give a *good* trashing' to Shaw's main character, Jack Tanner.[85] After thanking Shaw for it, he delivered his doubly wounding reponse: 'What awful Philostines [*sic*] you, English writers, are.' Kropotkin focussed his criticism on the '[l]iberty to flirt' that he believed Shaw had awarded his 'superman' Tanner, and he compared this to the genuine partnership and commitment of nihilist relationships. Tanner, he told Shaw, 'is a typical British philistine who is awfully in touch with the fashion of to-day', happy to shock anyone who cared to listen to him by claiming 'more liberty in love-matters' but actually changing nothing. 'Nietzsche's "Blond Beast"', Kropotkin remarked 'is bourgeois enough' but 'your Jack a Superman??? It is the "Blond Beast" silvermark (not gold) changed into pennies'. Had Shaw read any Russian literature, Turgenev in particular, he might have understood that 'Deeds – not words – will produce a change in the marriage customs' and 'only in such case *when there is something more* in your British men and girls than the mere claim of more liberty in love-matters'. Shaw, Kropotkin complained, was ignorant of the way in which women had challenged conventions through nihilism, and he failed to understand the significance of the relationships that they had established, perhaps absorbing more from the vulgar literature on free love than he may have been willing to admit. In nihilism the couple '*have* something in common. They are Life-Forces';[86] each partner '*standing by* and *helping*' to increase the other's 'forces as a social actor'. The institutionalisation of these partnerships was by-the-by: for their freedom was linked to the spirit in which they were undertaken. 'Marriage in the church or before a city clerk *may* come, or may not,' Kropotkin said. 'This is irrelevant.' In its true sense, marriage was a partnership 'for common action, common *love*, common *happiness* etc.'

Sasha, whom Shaw described as 'very pretty' but with features that 'would be ridiculously ugly' on an Englishwoman, detected a general weakness in Shaw's treatment of women.[87] His 'judgment of people was usually very shrewd', she remembered, 'except where women were concerned'. The 'intricacies of the female mind – or perhaps I should say of female character – were beyond his understanding'.[88] For Kropotkin Shaw's shortcomings typified a Western attitude to women's emancipation. In his memoirs he says that he consciously decided not to call nihilist women like Chernyshevksy's Vera 'feminists', because when he thought of feminism he thought of a special group of middle class women 'desirous to get their share of the privileged positions in society and the State'.[89] Western women were suffocated by a phony, hypocritical 'morality of Tartufe'. The rich dressed their daughters as courtesans, setting limits to female aspiration and squeezing all conceptions of beauty and genuine passion from life.[90] Until this culture was challenged, there could be no liberation. In Russia, Kropotkin argued, the 'movement for women's rights went on lines different from West Europe'.[91] He further described the distinctiveness of the Russian movement by retelling a story about Turgenev's trip to the theatre with Zola and Flaubert in Paris. They watched a play about a woman who had separated from her husband and who had made her life, with her two children, with another man. Having wrongly believed the woman's lover to be their biological father, the son discovers the truth and promptly rejects him. Zola and Flaubert joined in with the rapturous applause that greeted the child's stance. Turgenev instead thought the child 'mischievous' and 'perverted'. Kropotkin agreed and believed that the difference highlighted the 'real chasm ... between the conceptions which prevailed in Russia upon marriage relations and those which prevail in France: amongst the workers as well as in the middle class'. In Russia, nihilist women achieved a quality of independence that, while supporting genuine interdependence, challenged fundamentally the priority attached to paternity.[92]

Far from challenging such deeply engrained attitudes, Nietzscheanism encouraged individual rebellion, leaving social conservatism intact. In the case of free love, Kropotkin argued, it left women open to exploitation and male domination. In contrast, nihilism was directed towards fundamental social change. Kropotkin repeatedly drew on the Russian example to ground his general ethics of revolutionary action. In the essay *Anarchist Morality* he compared the 'soundrel' who 'obeys an impulse ... seeks satisfaction of a craving' to 'one who sacrifices his whole existence to free the oppressed, and like a Russian nihilist mounts the scaffold'.[93] 'Perovskaya and her comrades', he continued, 'killed the Russian Czar. And all mankind ... recognized the right to do as they did. Why? Not because the act was generally recognized as *useful*' but because of the certainty 'that it was no youthful bravado, no palace conspiracy, no attempt to gain power. It was hatred of tyranny, even to the scorn of self, even to the death.'[94] From Kropotkin's perspective, tactical errors could always be forgiven as long as individuals acted ethically, as the nihilists exemplified. He disavowed the same actions when they were inspired by the kind of individualism for which Nietzschean amorality provided a cover.

Nihilism and Anarchism

Kropotkin's defence of nihilism was a retrospective account of a movement from which he had long been divorced, appearing ten years after he started his exile in Britain. The pervasive influence of nihilism is nonetheless detectable in Kropotkin's early anarchist writings. The most striking example is the *Appeal to the Young* written in 1880 when he was still dividing his attention evenly between Western Europe and Russia. The *Appeal* was included in Kropotkin's first collection of essays, *Paroles d'un Révolté*. It was translated into English by H. M. Hyndman, another adversary with whom he was friendly, and described by him as 'the best propagandist pamphlet that was ever penned ... a masterpiece, alike in conception and execution. Nothing ever written so completely combined the scientific with the popular, the revolutionary with the ethical.'[95] His view was echoed in *Justice*, the newspaper of Hyndman's Social Democratic Federation.

> The Appeal not only has the effect of stirring up the feelings, but the lessons sought to be inculcated are kept well in the forefront ... It glows from beginning to end, and is the best tonic for an attack of Socialist pessimism.[96]

Like the other articles he completed for *Le Révolté*, Kropotkin wrote the *Appeal* with a particular purpose, which he outlined in his autobiography: to highlight the constant flux of social systems, explode conservative myths about human development and overcome the 'cowardice of mind and will' that facilitated their perpetuation. Using 'plain and comprehensible words' he aimed to expose the causes of inequality and the sociological, political and economic phenomena that pointed to the possibility of social re-organisation.[97] The essays for *Le Révolté* were designed to 'make one feel in sympathy with the throbbing of the human heart all over the world'.[98] Kropotkin did not claim that the *Appeal* was an exercise in thoughtful realism, but the tone of the writing suggests the influence of Russian aesthetics.

The essay published in *Paroles d'un Révolté* has four chapters, subdivided into three sections in the English-language version.[99] The appeal is directed principally to men, although a short section towards the end of the essay addresses working-women.[100] Kropotkin organised his audience into one of two categories, intellectuals and working class, sorting the first into professional groups: doctors, scientists, lawyers, engineers, teachers and artists in turn. For each of the professional groups, Kropotkin sketched a scene from daily life and invited readers to consider their response. These sketches examine the ethical purposes of the disciplines that the young have studied and the ways in which prevailing social and economic inequalities distort them. Lawyers, fired by ideas of justice, discover that they must use their knowledge of the law to enforce the rights of landowners against tenants. Teachers, similarly inspired by lofty romantic ideals, discover that their love of poetry and literature finds purpose only in polishing the social skills of successive generations of exploiters and oppressors – would-be army officers and factory bosses.

Kropotkin's appeal to the working class is much shorter than the section devoted to the intellectuals and it looks at the disappointments, compromises and contradictions that daily life imposes from a perspective of disadvantage. Like middle-class intellectuals, the workers also confront a dilemma. This is also rooted in the disjuncture between the ideals and realities of everyday existence. Although the text suggests that the experience of oppression and exploitation breeds rebelliousness in the workers and that intellectuals typically lack this, Kropotkin's argument is sensitive to the power of powerlessness. The daily struggle for subsistence, combined with knowledge of the traditions of oppression, dulls the workers' innate intelligence and saps their energy, encouraging resigned passivity and slavishness. Facing the brutality of life, the worker concludes: ' "Whole generations have undergone the same lot, and I, who can alter nothing in the matter, I must submit also. Let us work on then and endeavor to live as well as we can!" '[101]

A section titled 'What you can do' and that nearly coincides with the start of the third chapter in the original French appears between these two parts. Insofar as this draws on the dilemmas faced by the intellectuals and uses them to advance a generic appeal, it is a continuation of the first. Yet by drawing the intellectuals' attention to the socialist movement, the socialist critique of inequality or 'capitalist robbery',[102] and the choice that they have in respect of the movement and its aspirations, it segues the two appeals, enabling Kropotkin to draw the intellectuals and the workers together. Individuals in both groups, Kropotkin argued, have options: to cling to their ideals or to relinquish them for the sake of a quiet life, albeit one that intellectuals will enjoy in considerably more comfort and security than the workers. They can give into hopelessness and despair and decide to do nothing about the injustices they see around them or they can enter into a struggle with the socialists and 'work for the complete transformation of society'.[103] This is precisely the choice that the workers face. However, workers and intellectuals confront different obstacles when making their decisions. For workers, making the right judgement depends on their meeting two conditions. First, they have to understand that the hardships they endure are neither inevitable nor explicable as personal failings; they result from the imposition of artificial structural constraints. Second, they must be willing to use their direct experience of injustice as a spur to rebellion. The intellectuals must also find courage and commitment to play a role in the workers' education, put Samuel Smiles aside for Friedrich Schiller and rework 'afresh' the 'fundamental principles' and 'applications' of their academic disciplines.[104] To accomplish this, they must also overcome their social prejudices and rise above the 'customary' dismissal of 'workers as a lot of brutes'.[105]

Having issued two separate appeals, Kropotkin ended with a single call, unifying intellectuals and workers through socialism. This move is reflected in the language of the text. From the early sections of the text, where he addresses 'you' intellectuals and workers, Kropotkin shifts to talking about 'us' socialists, and concludes with the use of 'we', signalling the power of socialist solidarity.[106] The first shift dissolves the social divisions between intellectuals and workers. 'Every one of you then, honest young people, men and women, peasants, laborers, artisans, and soldiers, you will understand what are your rights and you will come along with us.'[107] The second brings these activists into the socialist camp. 'Don't let anyone tell us that we – but a small band – are too weak to attain unto the magnificent end at which we aim. Count and see how many there are who suffer this injustice.' The third shows the overwhelming strength of movement solidarity:

> Ay, all of us together, we who suffer and are insulted daily, we are a multitude whom no man can number, we are the ocean that can embrace and swallow up all else. When we have but the will to do it, that very moment will justice be done: that very instant the tyrants of the earth shall bite the dust.[108]

Kropotkin's use of common-garden situations as a basis for utopian imagining was not the only way in which the *Appeal* echoed nihilist themes. The content of the argument also contained ideas that he later identified with nihilism. In the middle of the *Appeal* Kropotkin has the Western intellectuals ask Chernyshevsky's question – " '[W]hat is to be done?" '[109] A little later on, they rephrase the question: " '[W]hat shall we do?" ' – prompting Kropotkin's response: '[T]here is everything to be done'.[110] In appealing to the young, Kropotkin resurrects nihilist themes by also appealing to science, reason, the rejection of tradition and romanticism – precisely the topics that Turgenev explored in his portrayal of Bazarov. He tells his young audience that they are 'free from the superstition which your teachers have sought to force upon you; that you do not fear the devil'.[111] He relies on the power of 'reason' to combat rote learning and the 'cloudy fictions' – metaphysics – that underpin elite education. But in their actions, Kropotkin implores the young to follow the example of the nihilist who 'carried his love of sincerity even into the minutest details of everyday life'.[112] At one point in the text, Kropotkin mocks the poets, writers and painters 'who preach of liberty' and 'speak of the people with tears in their eyes' while remaining narrowly focused on their literature and art. Because they do nothing but hold fast to their pure ideals and conceptions of beauty, Kropotkin dismisses them as a 'band of hypocrites'.[113] Having consciously moved beyond the mere reporting of complaint and suffering to inject socialist critique with hope and vision, Kropotkin encourages Western intellectuals to adopt the same thoughtful realist approach:

> You poets, painters, sculptors, musicians, if you understand your true mission and the very interests of art itself, come with us. Place your pen, your pencil, your chisel, your ideas at the service of the revolution. Figure forth to us, in your eloquent style, or your impressive pictures, the heroic struggles of the people against their oppressors, fire the hearts of our youth with that glorious revolutionary enthusiasm which inflamed the soul of our ancestors. Tell women what a noble career is that of a husband who devotes his life to the great cause of social emancipation!

Show the people how hideous is their actual life, and place your hands
on the cause of its ugliness. Tell us what a rational life would be, if it
did not encounter at every step the follies and ignominies of our present
social order.[114]

Anti-Nietzschean Ethics

Kropotkin's critique of Nietzscheanism was a rejection of Nietzsche's
thought, as Kropotkin understood it. But the extent to which Nietzsche's
thought is actually inflexible to anarchist readings is a moot point.[115]
Nietzsche was concerned with the loss of the transcendent and the 'spiritual and ethico-political crisis of the West'.[116] At the end of his life Kropotkin argued that the 'end of morals cannot be "transcendental," as the
idealists desire it to be: it must be real. We must find moral satisfaction in
life and not in some form of extra-vital condition.'[117] Kropotkin rejected
the politics he associated with Nietzsche and that has since seeped into
Nietzsche's account of nihilism through Dostoevsky's critique of the
character-types depicted in Turgenev's novels.[118] Exactly what Nietzsche
took from Dostoevsky's writing remains a matter of conjecture.[119] However, the political model is one made famous in *The Devils*, a book that
fictionalised the exploits of Sergei Nechaev or, as Alexander Brückner put
it, a 'windbag' version, the 'intriguer Petrúsha' (Pyotr), who displayed
none of the 'steel-like energy and hatred of the upper classes' for which
Nechaev was famed.[120] Kropotkin sidelined Dostoevsky in nihilism's
genesis, not only bending over backwards to demonstrate Turgenev's
definitive role in shaping nihilism but also dismissing Dostoevsky's work
as a 'mixture of realism and romanticism run wild'.[121] His defence of
Chernyshevsky was made in the context of a Dostoevskian critique of
nihilist materialism, rational self-interest and the denial of compassion
and personality.[122]

Using nihilism as a model to develop anarchist ethics, Kropotkin thus
challenged conventional wisdom about nihilist doctrines. The prevailing
view was that nihilism was 'a philosophy of despair' that 'ignores, if it
does not entirely renounce, the hope of social regeneration'. For nihilists,
'the world's redemption is synonymous with the world's destruction, and
hence the extinction of social evils is sought in the annihilation of society'.[123] Critics found part of the explanation for the destructiveness of
nihilism in atheism and the rejection of moral codes. Nihilists violently
attacked both 'the laws and institutions of the country' and the 'ethical
conceptions, aesthetic aspirations, and religious convictions' that underpinned them.[124] They traced the other part to the extreme egoism of
nihilist doctrines. Nihilism was about breaking up

the actual social organisation into mere individualism, with entire independence of each separate person. They maintain that no one should be
bound by laws or even moral obligations of any kind, but that everybody
should be allowed to do exactly as he pleases.[125]

For others, nihilism was a catchall term, open to a variety of doctrines. Apart from the nihilists who 'cultivate a Philosophy of Despair,
of Disgust, and of Destruction' and those who 'profess to do away
with all State organizations, for the sake of a morbid Individualism',
there were other nihilists who, 'in a semi-revolutionary vein of Comte,
incline towards a socialist Collectivism in a rather utopian, not to say
hierarchic form'.

Focusing on the behaviours of women, Kropotkin chose to highlight
the nihilists' positive commitments and ideals. He used agnosticism
rather than atheism as his framework for analysis. Nihilists, he argued,
certainly rejected 'the hypocrisy that leads people to assume the outward
mask of a religion which they continually throw aside as useless ballast'
when it suited them. The nihilist, Kropotkin notes in his memoirs, broke
'with the superstitions of his fathers, and in his philosophical conceptions he was a positivist, an agnostic, a Spencerian evolutionist, or a
scientific materialist' and he 'declared war' on 'the conventional lies of
civilized mankind'.[126] Similarly, nihilists rejected as spurious all talk of
the devil and held church authority in low esteem. However, they were
not faithless. On the contrary, they retained 'the simple, sincere religious
belief' that Kropotkin described as 'a psychological necessity of feeling'.[127] And rather than rejecting all values, they used their hatred of
'evil' to develop an alternative set. Cool rationalism led the nihilists in
this direction; and as egoists, driven by the search for individuality and
the rejection of conventional morality, they fleshed out the concept of
evil in social critique, especially when the resistance they encountered
made the wider structural obstacles to liberation apparent.

Kropotkin believed that, far from being a philosophy of despair, nihilism was a politics of hope. In the 1890s, soon after Kropotkin presented
his history of the Russian movement, he began to work on the theory
of mutual aid, advocating an approach to ethics that was consistent
with it. In this project, he found support in the work of Albert Fouillée,
the step-father of the philosopher Jean-Marie Guyau, who Kropotkin
regarded as an unconscious exponent of anarchist ethics. Like Fouillée,
Kropotkin defended Guyau's quest to devise an ethics without obligation or sanction rooted in a conception of a moral life as one lived
intensely and vitality. Like Fouillée, moreover, he challenged what he
saw as the aristocratic and self-regarding currents in Nietzsche's work
and the conception of the will as a form of competitive power. One of

the ways in which Fouillée described the difference between Guyau's position and Nietzsche's, was to distinguish 'desire' from 'desirable'. In morals, Fouillée argued:

> We cannot ignore the fundamental notion of a deliberate and voluntary *aim*, and consequently the notion of the *desirable*. In whatever way this notion may be conceived, whether as some idea of duty or simply the ultimate satisfaction of our own nature, it cannot be entirely absorbed in the thing desired, without destroying alike morality and the object or morality. And this is what Nietzsche has done.[128]

Kropotkin's story of nihilism and the aims of the women who shaped the movement may have been written with Fouillée's understanding of the desirable in mind. Kropotkin's attempt to use nihilist women's understanding of the desirable as a model for revolutionary change did not gain traction in the history of ideas. Even in Russia a different conception of the movement prevailed and the slavishness that Nietzscheans associated with nihilism was eventually extended to anarchism. Indeed, as Robin Aizlewood argues, in the years leading up to the First World War, Nietzschean currents supported strongly gendered associations of anarchism with femininity, passivity and submissiveness.[129] Kropotkin's attempt to show that women gave nihilism its positive force and to remove women and nihilism from the association with slavishness and resentment was anti-Nietzschean in this respect.

Mapping the State

Kropotkin matched his defence of the Russian revolutionary movement with a critique of Tsarism and in the course of his exile he established a reputation as a foremost commentator on the abuses of the regime. As well as raising awareness of the corruptions and brutality of Russian autocracy, Kropotkin also promoted anarchist politics in Russia. Working from a distance, he both encouraged anti-Tsarist activism in Western Europe and articulated a radical politics in order to encourage far-reaching change in Russia. As he put it in his *Memoirs*, he returned to Russia after his first trip to the West in 1872 convinced that 'conflicts take place, not on the ground of vague aspirations, but upon definite issues; not upon secondary points ... but upon broad ideas which inspire men by the grandness of their horizon which they bring into view'.[1] In the 1870s and 1880s Kropotkin's commitments gave rise to three parallel accounts of the state. The first described the iniquities of the Tsarist regime and the social, economic and political problems that Russian revolutionaries were attempting to redress. The second was a general critique that probed ideas of class and slavery and set out the reasons why the constitutional solutions being proposed by radicals in Russia – and elsewhere – would fail to bring about the transformations that were required. The third was an examination of the dynamics of change that drew directly on his understanding of geography.

Against the State: Tsarism

In 1881 and 1882 Kropotkin wrote a series of articles explaining Russian autocracy.[2] Written for a British audience, these articles presented a case study for the theoretical critique he advanced in *Le Révolté* during the same period. Kropotkin developed his account by examining Russia's recent history, looking especially at the reforming power of the 1861 Emancipation of the serfs. His view was that Alexander II's reform was part of a liberal agenda that was never fully implemented. Tsarism lacked the necessary means to 'consolidate the reforms' and 'make them bear fruit'.[3] Writing at the turn of the century, Kropotkin argued that:

> [a]ll honour is certainly due to Alexander II for having dared to announce his intention of liberating the serfs and of reforming all the inner life of Russia, and especially for the support he gave to the granting of the land to the liberated serfs.[4]

Yet the Tsar's failure had not only stoked the fire of 'the Reactionary Party'[5] it had also put paid to the idea of constitutional reform. Change, he argued, would only come through revolutionary action and the state's destruction.

The major thesis underpinning this argument was that the emancipation served as a cover for the introduction of a new form of exploitation revealing the existence of a fundamental injustice that turned on the ownership of the land. Kropotkin acknowledged that millions of 'peasants had acquired a certain amount of personal liberty' as a result of emancipation; the change could 'certainly not be underrated by those who have themselves witnessed ... the horrors of serfdom'.[6] However, the Emancipation was far from liberation. The emancipated peasants were lured into accepting terms that suited the landowners, their former masters, and were 'freed from feudal dues and compulsory labour only by losing a considerable part of the lands they possessed and by consenting to pay a heavy indemnity which ruined them'.[7] As Paul Avrich noted, in the 'black-earth provinces of Central Russia, once the bulwark of serfdom ... "beggarly" allotments of land abounded'.[8] These areas, Kropotkin noted, were 'pompously described as the "granary of Europe"' by 'short-sighted patriots, or Slavophiles', but the reality of rural production was quite different.[9] Emancipation released vast tracts of land to the open market and it was the rich who benefited from the land-grab.[10] As Stepniak later argued: '[s]ince the Emancipation, hundreds of thousands of dessiatines have been filched from the peasantry by means of thousands of ... lawsuits, which differ from open robbery only in name'.[11] And although the state was less efficient in collecting taxes than the old taskmasters, who had given bailiffs free reign to force peasants to fulfil their obligations,[12] Kropotkin argued that the former serfs were also forced to give up a substantial proportion of their produce in taxes, having first been made to bear the costs of freedom in redemption charges. Emancipation thus replicated the systems adopted to regulate forced labour in the Siberian exile communities. Large cash advances were given to workers to start work on specially constructed farms, 'in order to put them permanently in debt, and to reduce them to a kind of perpetual serfdom'.[13]

Kropotkin measured the economic costs of the emancipation in the mortality rates. Over the period of Alexander II's reign, he argued, there had been a sharp rise from 20 per 1,000 at the start of the century to 38 per 1,000 at the time of the emancipation, reaching from 47 to 67 per 1,000 in different parts of the Empire. Modern scholarship suggests that mortality rates correlated with epidemics, notably cholera, qualifying Kropotkin's claim.[14] Kropotkin blamed poor diet and the cyclical changes in production that exposed large numbers of rural workers to starvation. The economic injustice of the post-Emancipation settlement was particularly acute in areas subject to periodic droughts. In 1867 and 1870, Kropotkin argued, the result was famine. In Southern Russia people 'literally died from starvation. Thousands and thousands of children were swept away by contagious diseases.' More than one half of the cattle owned by peasants were killed by 'epizootics, brought about by a want of food'. And the causes were economic, not environmental: famines were artificial and entirely preventable. While 'they were dying … wagons loaded with corn were running towards the ports of the Black Sea for export', Kropotkin recorded.[15]

Kropotkin considered the possibility that the economic problems created by the system of land ownership may be addressed by further constitutional and legal reform, admitting that Tsarism could assume a more or less liberal character. But he discounted this possibility, arguing that reliance on the Tsars legitimised the principle of autocracy, and that the decision to reel back on the planned political reforms exposed a paralysis at the heart of the state. The ostentatiously lavish court was dependent on a fraudulent, parasitic bureaucracy to prop it up; the St Petersburg government was trapped in its own systems of corruption and incompetence. In an effort to maintain control of the vast Empire, the autocracy gave free reign to ministers, and the Tsar blindly signed off the most draconian legislation on trust. As a consequence, the regime authorised a plethora of actions for which no-one was accountable.[16] With the administrative changes that the emancipation necessitated, governance was not improved: sleazy officialdom was expanded. 'The pillage that went on in all the ministries, especially in connection with the railways and all sorts of industrial enterprises, was really enormous.' From state-funded construction projects 'immense fortunes' were made. 'As to commercial enterprises', Kropotkin continued, 'it was openly known that none could be launched unless a specified percentage of the dividends was promised to different functionaries.'[17] Similarly, although the Emancipation had led to the introduction of *zemstva*, organs of local government on which the peasantry had a voice, these soon became 'nests of gentry' and the effect of their introduction was to enhance the control of corrupt officials and elites.[18] Kropotkin's charge was that government ministries worked against these bodies, compromising local policy initiatives, notably the introduction of primary schools. In sum, emancipation had initiated a set of economic and political changes but these had succeeded only in changing the terms of rural enslavement and the character of elite power. Kropotkin made the same point much later in 1909, characterising Russia as a terror state.[19] In 1882 this was his conclusion:

> As long as our peasants bear on their shoulders nearly all the burden of the increasing expenses of the state; as long as they remain under the management of, at least, forty different authorities, each of which is worse than a Persian satrap; as long as they are compelled to pay for their lots of land twice and thrice their value; as long as our farmers remain in the same miserable state as now; and all spirit of initiative is killed in the germ for fear of revolution – it is foolish to imagine that anything can be ameliorated in the situation of our peasantry by the sham reforms which are discussed now at St. Petersburg.[20]

Kropotkin justified his call for the abolition of Tsardom by drawing attention to its repressive, illiberal politics and the degenerate social relations it fostered. In the first case, he explained the increased despotism of the regime as a result of the emancipation's 'indefinite character'. Faced with demands to introduce more far-reaching changes, Alexander II turned against even the moderate wing of the reform movement.[21] In 1881 Kropotkin reported that the government 'refuses any liberty; it refuses to tolerate even the most humanitarian opinions'.[22] The apparatus of Tsarist repression grew in tandem with the revolutionary movement, entrenched in aggressive systems of policing and surveillance, press censorship, mass arrests, habitual use of courts martial and exiles, imprisonments and executions. Kropotkin's sympathetic portrayal of Alexander Soloviev, Alexander II's would-be regicide, and Sofia Perovskaya, his assassin, explored this dynamic in a narrative that pitched principled resistance against tyrannous violence.[23]

Turning to the social character of the regime, Kropotkin described Tsarism as a particular kind of degeneracy. One of its striking features was the callous indifference of the rich to the plight of the poor. In Russia it was not only possible to find enormous wealth alongside desperate poverty but a culture that revealed a deep revulsion for the suffering of ordinary people. Reactionaries revelled in their own achievements and happily gauged their cultural sophistication and wealth against the ignorance, misery and degradation of the poor. The idea of just deserts made the poor responsible for their own ruination, just as it legitimised the rewards that accrued to the rich. Symptomatic of this attitude was the claim that the peasantry was prone to idleness and drunkenness. As an explanation of the causes of poverty Kropotkin dismissed it as ridiculous and, presenting an elaborate calculation of vodka consumption, demonstrated that it was in fact unfounded. His counter was that Tsarism fostered a culture characterised by hypocrisy and corruption.

Committed to the overthrow of the regime, Kropotkin found the solution to the land question in the demand for national autonomy and independence. Indeed, looking beyond Russia, he argued that land ownership and nationalism were the two issues at the very core of resistance politics in Western Europe – in Ireland, England, Spain, Italy, Switzerland and parts of Germany.[24]

Aware that national politics was not 'in vogue now in Europe', he put the absence of serious discussion down to the failure of the 1848 revolutions. The shattering of nationalist illusions had destroyed the idea of independence, promoting 'the social question' in its stead.[25] Kropotkin rejected this opposition, arguing that the re-ordering of priorities was based on a confusion of the 48ers struggle for 'political independence' with the 'insurrectionary agitation' and 'autonomist tendencies' of oppressed groups who understood that economic emancipation required political freedom. Some national movements still followed the old models, dreaming of the 'ephemeral liberty which is bestowed on the people by the rule of the richer classes, whatever their nationality'. The Polish rising was a case in point. At first inspired by the 'the brave sons of Poland', Russian radicals were saddened to see 'purely nationalist elements of Poland' take 'the upper hand'.[26] It was precisely this brand of nationalism that Proudhon had also rejected.[27] In a similar spirit, Kropotkin argued that the separation of national from social issues was based on a false dichotomy.[28] Serbo-Croats, Czechs, Slovaks, Poles, Slovenes, Bosnians, Herzegovinians, Serbs and Bulgarians, Kropotkin argued, were all struggling for self-government against Turkish, Austrian and Russian rule. And, in Russia, the failure of emancipation was driving these movements on. Together 'peasants and working men' were drawing strength from the 'abolition of serfdom' to free themselves from autocracy.[29]

Kropotkin's conception of the land question as an issue of national independence was buttressed by the introduction of aggressive Russification policies. These had their origin in the doctrine of official nationality engineered by Nicholas I (1825–55) that required 'unconditional allegiance to orthodoxy and autocracy'.[30] Although it had resulted in significant censorship in Finland during Nicholas's reign,[31] it had only been pursued half-heartedly until the emancipation. Kropotkin explained the systematic implementation of official nationality as a strategic reaction to the rise of irreligious and anti-statist nihilist movements in Alexander III's period.[32] However, the structural impetus came from the changes in land ownership that the emancipation facilitated. In the Western territories, in particular, the Russian state took advantage of the emancipation in order to acquire vast areas of land. The Polish insurrection of 1863, Kropotkin noted, 'was crushed rather by the agrarian measures of the Russian Government than by its armies and scaffolds'.[33] To illustrate the process, he gave an account of the expropriation of the Loghishino estate, in Minsk, a story that Stepniak later retold.[34] Here, not only were the estates of those implicated in the Polish rising confiscated, but also the lands owned by the peasantry, which had been granted to them by Polish kings and subsequently guaranteed by the Russian Senate. First absorbed by the Crown, these vast lands were subsequently sold on very easy terms to individuals loyal to the Tsar. The peasants protested but their complaints fell on deaf ears, largely because the wheels of the Ministry of Interior were greased by the corruption of local officials, also beneficiaries of the land deals. Indeed, the peasants were jailed or exiled for their trouble. This was not an isolated event, Kropotkin argued.

> However disgusting and even incredible such an affair is – with us, in Russia, it is the commonest thing. It would be a great mistake to suppose that it represents something exceptional. Quite the same is going on throughout Russia, and every month we might produce such a story with some insignificant changes of names and of localities. In all western Russia the same 'Russification' was carried on to a large extent. The wholesale robbery of Bashkirs' lands ... is another instance on an immense scale, of the same practice ... whole important navigable rivers were appropriated in the same manner by influential persons. Almost all our so-called 'insurrections of peasants' have the same origin as the insurrection at Loghishino and they are accompanied by the same disgusting scenes of brutality and uncontrolled arbitrariness.[35]

Bringing the politics of national autonomy to bear on the realities of Russian politics, Kropotkin acknowledged that the rural distress created by the system of land distribution was also a cause of division within workers' and peasants' movements, providing a particularly fertile ground for anti-Semitism. In a speech reported in the *Newcastle Daily Chronicle*, Kropotkin argued that that religious difference was always a potential source of tension. 'As long as they had priests, rabbis, mollahs, &c., who each declared *their* religions to be the best, and condemned all those who did not share their religious opinions or belong to their way of worship', the report noted, 'the national and race divisions were certain to be greatly accentuated by differences of creeds'. But in response to a wave of widespread pogroms in 1881–2, Kropotkin rejected the inevitability of faith-based social divisions, attributing anti-Jewish rioting to 'economical causes'.[36] He put the same view, years later, to the French writer Augustin Hamon, chiding him for his 'antipathy towards the Jews'. Religion, Kropotkin told Hamon, was not a determinant of social character, unlike nationality: Jewish people were cosmopolitans, but revolutionaries were no less so.[37] Kropotkin believed that it was views like Hamon's that played into the hands of reactionaries, in Russia fuelling anti-Jewish violence in times of social distress. Indeed, failing to distinguish 'between the true exploiters and those who are but their instruments' ethnic Russians wrongly directed their fury against the impoverished, not the wealthy. Kropotkin's analysis countered the view advanced by some revolutionaries that 'the Jews had replaced the land-owners as the principal local exploiters'[38] and that popular anti-Semitism had a revolutionary flavour. And it chimed with the account of the 1871 pogroms presented by leading Jewish activists in Odessa, organised in a sister group to the Chaikovskii Circle.[39] The Odessa group acknowledged the existence of social cleavages within the Jewish community and suggested the possibility of forging class alliances across religious divides. Indeed, pushing the line that Tsarism exploited 'Christians and Jews alike', Kropotkin found some historical evidence to support such a strategy. One was the Khmelnytsky rebellion in the Ukraine (1648–57) where 'Orthodox Cossacks' exterminated 'Catholic and Orthodox proprietors and their Jewish agents with the help of Mussulman Tartars'. Another was the Pugachev risings (1773–5) where 'Orthodox peasants cruelly exterminated Orthodox proprietors with the help of Mussulman Baskirs'.[40] It was not clear from this analysis precisely how Kropotkin expected the cultural and religious tensions that anti-Semitism exposed to be resolved. But his point about cross-national class solidarity was clear. Kropotkin was convinced that the solution to the problems that the emancipation exposed would be found through a process of national liberation that placed control of the land in the hands of peasants.

While Kropotkin was sanguine about the revolutionary potential of national land movements, he also knew that anarchism had little purchase on revolutionary politics in Russia. In 1882 he identified the Jacobin Peoples' Will and the Marxist-leaning, insurrectionary Black Partition as the movement's dominant forces. The groups who embraced 'the principles of Federated Socialistic Communes' and who advocated 'liberation and federation' and the 'independence of all majority ethnographical subdivisions of the Russian Empire' were not influential.[41]

Inspired by Bakunin, Kropotkin hoped that the success of anarchist propaganda in the West would provide a fillip for federalist politics in the East.[42] Aware that his politics was out-of-step with the reforming aspirations of the Russian movements, he therefore set out the reasons why he believed that constitutional change was unable to resolve Russia's problems in a theoretical critique of the state.

Against the State: Rights and Slavery

The critique of the state that Kropotkin set out in his critique of Russia exposed the limits of constitutional reform by showing how Tsarism had concentrated power in the hands of a crooked elite, expropriated the lands of indigenous people and maintained them in a condition of desperate poverty by means of violence and, increasingly, cultural homogenisation. In the *Paroles d'un Révolté* he condensed this analysis in a general formula: political institutions reflected the nature of economic power, which was fundamental.[43] This analysis seemed to align Kropotkin with mainstream socialist opinion. Bakunin had advanced the same argument, crediting Marx with its most sophisticated scientific articulation.[44] However, Bakunin had qualified Marx's class analysis by introducing a distinction between masters and slaves into this analytical framework. Kropotkin, who said very little about Marx, followed suit.[45]

Hegel's analysis of the master–slave dialectic had undoubtedly helped introduce this framework into radical thought, and certainly helped shape Bakunin's ideas.[46] But as Susan Buck-Morss argues, the Haitian Revolution at the turn of the eighteenth century also propelled the issue of slavery to the forefront of European debates, helping to crystallise Hegel's ideas in the process.[47] Rousseau's critique of inequality was also saturated with the idea of freedom from slavery, providing another conduit into anarchism. Proudhon, Bakunin and Kropotkin were all critical of Rousseau's social contract theory, but his analysis of economic enslavement was compatible with the critiques they developed.

In *What is Property?* Proudhon juxtaposed slavery and murder to interrogate the relationship of property to theft. In Bakunin's work, the idea of slavery resolved the seeming contradiction between his fanatical love of liberty as the liberation from mastership and mental enslavement and his acknowledgement that freedom was legitimately constrained by rules that free people agreed to.[48] In Emma Goldman's work, slavery was not only a lens to analyse prostitution, but a metaphor for statism. 'Just as religion has fettered the human mind' so has 'the State enslaved his spirit'.[49] Tolstoy's critique of slavery, which resonated with American abolitionists, defined the condition as an instance of 'the ancient and universal recognition, contrary to Christian teaching, of the right of coercion by some men in regard to others'.[50]

The significance of these arguments was that slavery illustrated an idea of unfreedom that extended beyond the brutal slave systems that the abolitionists campaigned against. Tolstoy traced the origins of the 'slavery of our time' to 'three sets of laws: those about land, taxes and property'. For as long as these three pillars of exploitation and inequality remained intact, slavery would also continue. Just as Kropotkin argued in the Russian case, the legal abolition of slavery concealed a metamorphosis. Tolstoy observed: even though the 'slaver owner' was deprived of 'slave John, whom he can send to the cesspool to clear out his excrements', he had money 'to be a benefactor' to 'anyone out of hundreds of Johns ... giving him the preference and allowing him, rather than another, to climb down into the cesspool'.[51] Less graphically, Kropotkin described the 'state of freedom' championed by economists as the 'enforced contract (under threat of hunger) between master and workingman'. His view was that 'in all discussions of freedom our ideas are obscured by the surviving influence of past centuries of serfdom and religious oppression'. Not surprisingly, then, the condition of citizenship lauded by politicians, only described the position of the 'serf and a taxpayer of the State'.[52]

In the posthumously published *Ethics*, Kropotkin identified slavery with ancient Greek thought and anti-slavery with the French revolutionary free-thought, suggesting a closer alignment to Rousseau than Hegel. Moreover, using the history of ideas to distinguish democratic/anarchist from aristocratic/Nietzschean currents in nineteenth-century thought, he hinted at a classically rooted Franco–German philosophical divide.[53] In his early writings, the effect of his invocation of the master–slave relationship was to focus his analysis of economic exploitation on the nature of elite rule and the process of its cementation as opposed to the technicalities of its operation.

Kropotkin argued that the state was designed to protect the strong against the weak, the rich against the poor and the privileged against the labouring classes, contrary to its declared purposes.[54] This account reversed the narratives of contract theory and also challenged class analysis. Instead of charting a history of class struggle in which power was violently contested, driving social change, Kropotkin divided people into leaders and led and showed how power was negotiated by different constituents within the advantaged groups. His account of the state's rise subdivided the leadership into military, religious, financial and political elites and indicated that each used their separate resources to secure a shared stake in the state. Because membership of the elite was open to those who derived their power from sources other than property, oppression was usually experienced in multiple ways: in Russia, for example, through patriarchy, religious orthodoxy and anti-Semitism.

In accordance with his general finding that the political institutions of the state served the dominant class, Kropotkin described bourgeois government as a special vehicle for the protection of commercial and industrial class interests. In formal terms it excluded both the aristocracy and the people. However, Kropotkin argued that it was difficult to distinguish the arrangements that the bourgeoisie made with the aristocracy from the agreements that were struck in monarchical regimes, where the bourgeoisie had not fully asserted their economic might. In representative systems, the ruling bourgeois dealt with the old elites in a polite, considered and elevated manner. Similarly, in despotic regimes, aristocrats and commercial classes entered into power-sharing agreements: the former relinquishing the right to legislate on the condition that existing patterns of ownership would be maintained.[55] Social relations between the bourgeoisie and the workers had a wholly different character: class analysis assumed that there were different cultures of domination in which elite interests converged.

Kropotkin argued that elite power was expressed in law through the assertion of rights. Although regimes differed in important ways, liberal constitutional and despotic monarchical regimes were identical in this respect: both used rights to legitimise the powers of those who had already secured their freedoms against those who had not. And although history demonstrated that commercial and landed interests within the master class could turn on each other, as they did in the French Revolution, it also showed that rights were fundamental to the identification of their elite interests.[56] Rights regulated relationships between masters and slaves, exploiters and exploited. Slavery could hardly be alleviated by the conferral of rights because they existed only to uphold and regulate the cultures of domination that elites had secured. Kropotkin acknowledged, however, that rights also conferred significant powers and liberties and that it was legitimate for the oppressed and excluded to struggle for rights where they were otherwise made subject to the most brutal repression. Yet the manner in which these claims were made was crucial to the success of the struggles. Rights should be demanded not negotiated. If it was now impossible to flog men and women in the streets of Paris, as was still the case in Odessa, Kropotkin argued, this was because the government knew that the perpetrators would fall victim to public rage. Similarly, if there was a degree of equality between French workers and bosses, it was because previous revolutions had established the dignity of slaves and new boundaries for social interaction that masters were forced to respect.[57] The political and social rights that slaves enjoyed were measures of their ability to exert their collective will against their masters. Masters extended privileges to slaves when they were forced to do so. They did not extend the same privileges to those who acquiesced to their enslavement or to those who lacked the power to assert their will.[58]

Kropotkin's historical account of the European state's emergence reinforced the elite thesis. The story anticipated the analysis he presented in *Mutual Aid* and *The State: Its Historic Role* but instead of outlining the ways in which competitive self-interest trumped the principle of mutual aid, as he did in this later work, Kropotkin charted the loss of liberty to the rise of representative government in the European city-states during the twelfth century. He described the city-states as oases of freedom in a feudal sea. The inhabitants constituted themselves as independent bodies, organising their own defence, industry and commerce, production and exchange. Distinguishing federal from representative principles of organisation, Kropotkin argued that the city was made up of a range of units: neighbourhood associations, sections, and corporations, as well as the city as a whole. Political differences were negotiated through deliberation, not closed off by the imposition of majority rule. Art, science and philosophy flourished in this atmosphere of freedom.

Kropotkin explained the loss of liberty as a result of the inequalities that developed internally. These arose as a result of the commercial exploitation of the countryside that enabled traders within the cities to accumulate wealth through the appropriation of property. As class divisions appeared, the rich pushed for changes in governance, introducing representative institutions in which their power was enshrined. In the struggles that followed, the rich joined forces with feudal lords and through war, investment, fraud and intrigue they made the cities subservient to a new principle of imperial rule, embodied in the person of the king. The powers of the cities were centralised in the kings' hands through parliaments and church organisations that drew representatives from the elites within the cities.[59]

Kropotkin charted a parallel process in his analysis of the law: the unwritten rules that had been adopted by peoples across Europe, as a result of enjoying social life in common, became codified in ways that secured the interests of the masters and ensured compliance of newly enslaved peoples. Customary prohibitions on theft were conjoined with new obligations to pay taxes, on pain of punishment, Kropotkin observed. Most of this law regulated rights to property. Its introduction did not, therefore, suggest that law was a guarantor of order or social peace as contract theorists described, it merely indicated the success with which religious, military and political elites managed to conflate the protection of individual rights (that benefited those who had already appropriated property) with the possibility of enjoying social life in the public mind. For as long as this elision of law with order remained unchallenged, Kropotkin concluded, people would remain enslaved.[60]

Emancipation was likely to entail violence. As he told Nannie Dryhurst: '*Force* will certainly have to be used to get rid of the *force* which maintains the present.'[61] But it first involved disabusing slaves of their obedience to the law and their duty to obey those who put themselves in authority by building their capacity to put themselves on the 'wrong' side of constitutional reform. Recognising the trend towards electoral reform, Kropotkin noted the positive rebranding of monarchical and republican regimes as representative democracies. But he warned against using even reformed institutions to abolish property or any other form of domination, remembering 'poor Proudhon' when he made this point.[62] Kropotkin acknowledged that representative institutions could be more or less liberal – just as he recognised swings in the politics of Tsarism. He also acknowledged that there had been historic changes in the organisation of representative government since the rise of the state in the twelfth century. Yet this variation was only grist to his mill. That the Jacobins inaugurated a different form of government to the absolutist monarchy of Louis XVI underlined the extent to which both sets of elites adopted a consistent principle of governance: one that claimed sovereignty on behalf of individuals. Only when the enslaved rebelled against the system of representation and reclaimed their power of decision would they be able to reconstitute themselves, freely.[63] Kropotkin directed this message to Russian revolutionaries as well as to his West European audience.

Kropotkin realised that European socialist movements had a very different character to those in Russia and that the urban working class was a far more powerful force in the West than it was in the East. The difference was evident from the neglect of the land question in European socialist propaganda, which Kropotkin regretted. Yet he remained convinced that the victory of socialism in Western Europe depended on the ability of factory workers to make common cause with cultivators.[64] The land question was as significant to urban workers as it was to their rural comrades. In *Révolté* he therefore encouraged workers to help set up land leagues, familiarise themselves with the problems and attitudes of the peasantry and propagandise in villages. Reclus's *Ouvrier, Prends la Machine! Prends La Terre, Paysan!* was motivated by similar concerns and his call for the creation of workers' and peasants' alliances was inspired by the Russian example.[65] However, whereas Reclus and later Landauer referred to the concentration of capital outlined in Marx's *Capital* as a foil for their thinking about non-industrialised, anti-statist alternatives, Kropotkin sidestepped Marx to develop a geographical account of development.[66] The issue was not, as Chernyshevsky had argued, whether Russia could be turned into a socialist republic without going through the intervening 'stage' of capitalism, although Kropotkin sympathised with the politics of this view, but about the possibility of even talking about 'stages' of development.[67]

The Geography of Anti-statecraft

Woodcock and Avakumović contend that Kropotkin made three outstanding contributions to geography as a result of the research he completed in Siberia and Finland in the 1860s and 1870s. These were his theories of glaciations, desiccation and the orography of Asia.[68] Kropotkin described the expeditions in Siberia and Finland that he used to gather data for this research in his memoirs and he published a number of papers setting out his major findings.[69] However, Kropotkin's early, professional interest in geography extended beyond this research. As Federico Ferretti notes, Kropotkin remained active as a geographer, collaborating with Reclus on a number of specialist and educational projects throughout the nineteenth century.[70]

Owing to his billing as the author of *Mutual Aid* Kropotkin has sometimes featured as a theorist of cooperation in modern geopolitical debates. In anarchism's second wave the general view was that Kropotkin and Reclus argued for 'the essential unity of man and nature and the historical tendency towards co-operation' and that they found the 'explanation of spatial pattern and process' in 'balance and harmony'.[71] As Richard Peet argued in 1975, Kropotkin believed that 'a struggle between the forces ... of mutual aid and co-operation, and ... of competitiveness and human selfishness, makes up the substance of history'.[72] Brian Morris has since described Kropotkin as an ethical naturalist who combined '*humanism*, the emphasis on human agency and the recognition that human social life and culture constitute a relative autonomous realm of being' with '*naturalism*, the recognition that humans are an intrinsic part of nature'.[73] Kropotkin's rejection of Social Darwinian theory plays an important role in sustaining the view that his chief contribution to geography stems from his idea of cooperation.[74] The cooperative principle was indeed central to Kropotkin's thinking and he traced the origins of the theory of mutual aid to the geographical expeditions in Siberia.[75] But he took a broader view of geography than either this acknowledgement or his extensive accounts of these expeditions indicated. A. J. Fielding argues that geography led Kropotkin to advance an understanding of the patterning of the physical world and the relationship between the natural and human environment that supported his political ideals and an approach to the teaching of geography that tied its study to the resolution of social problems.[76] It did. The approach he shared with Reclus treated the world as 'a harmonious entity'. Geography extended beyond the description of the physical terrain to the study of relationships of people – their languages, economics and institutions, moral codes and social habits – to their environments. In Reclus's hands, Robyn Roslak argues, geography had a pronounced aesthetic dimension. In Kropotkin's work this was less well defined, but he similarly emphasised the imagery, shapes and shifts in organic life and the harmonisation of earthly forces.[77] And to realise these aims Kropotkin stretched geographical science to its limits. Geography was premised on the view 'that we are all brethren, whatever our nationality'. The role of geography was to stand against 'national self-conceit' and the 'jealousies' and 'hatreds ably nourished by people who pursue their own egotistic, personal or class interests' and create 'other feelings more worthy of humanity'.[78] The geographer's task was to 'extend knowledge of the forces of Nature, the means of utilising them, and higher forms of social life'.[79] In his *Memoirs* he recalled how his brother Alexander, adopting a too rigid interpretation of Turgenev's *Fathers and Sons*, had wrongly abandoned poetry for the sake of natural science.[80] Learning from Alexander's mistake, Kropotkin followed the subversive approach he recommended in *Appeal to the Young* and recast geography's purposes. In his hands, geography was an instrument to reveal the contingencies of history, freeing it from the analysis of what existed and hooking it up with a conception of what may be.

Kropotkin's interventions in nineteenth-century political geography debates were out of kilter with leading currents of nineteenth-century enquiry, which were statist and imperialist. Friedrich Ratzel defined the purpose of geographical analysis in terms of the extension of state power. For Ratzel the state was an aggregate organism. Geographers considered its adaption to the physical environment, measuring success by the size of settlements.[81] Adapting the Social Darwinian idea of the 'struggle for survival' he imagined a 'struggle for space', or lebensraum, introducing a concept that the Nazis would later exploit.[82] In the hands of Halford Mackinder the discipline was geared to a politics in which the world was imagined as 'a stage for competition, between races, between nations'.[83] Working within this frame, his central idea, 'the geographical pivot of history', was a spatial history of Eurasia that demonstrated the tendency towards political agglomeration. He synthesised 'an understanding of the political implications of new technology with the persistence of certain geographical patterns of political history' to explain how technological changes that benefited land as opposed to sea-powers affected states located on the periphery of the Eurasian landmass.[84] Mackinder's argument, Lucian Ashworth explains, 'had had the effect of making larger political units both possible and more dominant. The historical trend was from smaller peripheral to larger continental states.'[85] Kropotkin knew Mackinder and got on well with him: Mackinder was an admirer of Reclus's work, wrote an 'enthusiastic review of the *Nouvelle Géographie Universelle*' and invited him and Kropotkin to work on a joint publication project.[86] However, Kropotkin hotly disputed Mackinder's view of the world. As Gerry Kearns argues, he challenged the assumptions that underpinned Mackinder's particular reading of nature, environment and race in *Mutual Aid*.[87]

He set out the principles of this disagreement in the 1880s, before they met. Whereas Mackinder read geography through the lens of national sovereignty and as theatre for military action,[88] Kropotkin presented an account of historical territorialisation that complemented his critique of the state. Kropotkin's thesis did not contest the veracity of the observations that geographers like Mackinder made about nineteenth-century geopolitical trends, but added a critical spin and questioned the assumptions on which these observations were based.

The premise of Kropotkin's anti-statecraft was that the tendency towards the development of large territorial political units was detrimental to human well-being. He outlined a history of domination that, by means of conquest, targeted assassination and trickery, and drew groups of people into the orbit of controlling factions.[89] The difference between this account of the state and his critique of rights and contract was that it sketched the processes that mainstream political theory exploited and it contextualised the history of the European state's development in a global account of organisational change.

Kropotkin argued that the process of state-building could be protracted. It took the Russians hundreds of years to assert their control over the national groups in the Caucasus, for example.[90] But it followed a predicable path. Kropotkin did not use the term 'colonisation', but this was the idea he had: as the dominant group gradually appropriated the social, political and cultural functions of social life to itself in a particular territory, populations were homogenised. Local languages, religions, principles of allegiance, moral norms and rituals were all suppressed. As the Russian case demonstrated, it was possible to establish the limits of state sovereignty by resisting encroachments from competing powers rather than colonising within the state's territorial boundaries. In general terms colonisation described the extension of the principle of domination that mastership encapsulated but its ordering was coloured by the practices peculiar to the elites that prevailed in particular areas in particular periods.

As a process of cultural homogenisation, colonisation assumed the existence of diverse nationalities. Kropotkin borrowed from Renan to explain his conception of nationality, describing first what a nation is not, and then filling out a positive conception:[91]

> [A] nation is not an agglomeration of people speaking the same language – a language may disappear; not even an aggregation with distinct anthropological features, all nations being products of heterogeneous assimilations; still less a union of economic interests ... National unity, he said, is the common inheritance of traditions, of hopes and regrets, of common aspirations and common conceptions, which make of a nation a true organism instead of a loose aggregation. The naturalist would add to these essential features of a nation the necessary differentiation from other surrounding organisms, and the geographer, a kind of union between the people and the territory it occupies, from which territory it receives its national character and on which it impresses its own stamp, so as to make an indivisible whole both of men and territory.[92]

Kropotkin's habit of endorsing other writers' ideas often misleadingly implied a stronger correspondence than was actually the case. Following the example of his 'beloved Darwin' he always strove to 'bolster the school of thought' he intended to criticise rather than engage in polemics.[93] His adoption of Renan's definition was an excellent example of this approach insofar as his apparently consensual view provided a platform for Kropotkin to develop his own quite different view. Unlike Renan, who rejected conceptions that defined nations in terms of race, language and religion,[94] Kropotkin sometimes used nationality and race interchangeably. Despite his claims to the contrary, he treated language as an important factor in the construction of national identity. The 'community of language' made it 'impossible to refuse the name of a nation to the Merovingian France, or to the Russia of the eleventh and twelfth century'.[95] Importantly, language also provided access to literatures and folk traditions that disclosed particular ways of thinking. Finnish nationality, Kropotkin noted, had been kindled by the discovery of the Kalevala, 'the great Finnish epic poem', 'so grand in its cosmogonic conception and inspired with so pure an ideal'.[96] Languages were not fixed, but group perspectives were importantly shaped by the peculiarities of language use. The description in the volume of *Géographie Universelle* on Siberia and Asian Russia, which he prepared with Reclus, linked nationality to cultural practice and tradition, myths, religion and language.[97]

In distinction to Renan, Kropotkin also divorced the nation from the state. As John Breuilly notes, Renan's voluntarist account of the nation surrendered 'the idea that the nation was a cultural identity'.[98] All that was left to distinguish one group from another was the state. Indeed, Renan's contention that nationhood required groups captured within it to forget their separate histories and the violence that brought them into union accepted the very processes of colonisation that Kropotkin rejected.[99] The idea of the nation as a daily plebiscite, as Renan put it, was also alien to Kropotkin's worldview. While the ethnographic and geographical aspects of Renan's thesis appealed to him, as well as Renan's conception of the nation as a spiritual principle on which political solidarities were constructed, Kropotkin's central point was to distinguish the histories of nations from the development of official doctrines pursued by states in the modern era.

On Kropotkin's account, national differences were not fixed but neither were they artificial. Nations evolved. Kropotkin explained their specificity, as well as the character of international relations, both in terms of the influence of local habitats on the development of cultural practices – cultivation techniques, arts and so forth – and with reference to the physical obstacles to social interaction. With Russia in mind, he argued that the plateaux, high mountain ranges and large dry region caused social groups to live in relative isolation. Consequently, the differences between these groups were more pronounced than they tended to be in Europe, where climatic variations were less dramatic and movement by land and the waterways was much easier. The designation 'European' was as much an umbrella term as 'Turanien' or 'Finno-Tartare' and each embraced a large number of distinctive nationalities. Kropotkin's conclusion was that nationalities were flexible communities, as the development of common practices among the Europeans indicated.[100]

Capitalism was the dynamic for colonisation in the modern period, explaining both the historic rise of the state in Western Europe and the subsequent European colonisation of the rest of the world. Kropotkin gave an impressionistic account of the state's relationship to capitalism in the *Paroles d'un Révolté*, providing fuller account in *Mutual Aid, The State: Its Historic Role* and *Wars and Capitalism*, written in the early years of the twentieth century. In the later work he described how the locus of manufacturing and trading power shifted from the shores of the Mediterranean north, to Britain and the Netherlands, and how the extension of credit to the emergent political elites in these areas provided the momentum for state organisation in Europe. In his early writings, Kropotkin similarly linked capitalism to industrialisation and finance and indirectly to the state. The territorialisation of Western Europe had played a central role in the construction of an international market, but this was driven by the pursuit of commercial advantage, through industrialisation, and the investments of share dealers and financiers, whose returns helped bankroll political elites and support their military and administrative machines.[101] He also described states as vehicles for monopoly, a process of absorption that described the assumption of the functions of other bodies and establishment of unique and unmediated relationships with subjects. Monopoly was associated with the introduction of administrative machines and regulatory systems capable of ordering people's lives, from cradle to the grave as Kropotkin put it, enabling elites to tighten their grip on the behaviours of subjugated populations.[102]

The impact of capitalism was felt in the loss of village industry and the transformation of the rural environment: depopulation, urbanisation, mechanisation and the creation of transport systems that accelerated the export of mass-manufactured goods across the globe.[103] These changes were experienced in all European states, but progressively and in varying intensities, creating global power inequalities and intense competition. Relationships between West European powers and the rest of the world were defined primarily by economic domination – colonisation without territorialisation – although they could assume a political aspect. Capitalism's political and economic drivers combined to forge a supremacist civilising mission: the heaps of merchandise marketed by the bourgeoisie expressed cultural superiority. On the one hand, Europeans scoured the world to find outlets for mass-produced goods that domestic workers could not afford to buy, establishing markets in the Far East, America and Australasia. On the other, they searched for natural resources, particularly in mining, and the opportunity for lucrative investments in infrastructural development, notably railway construction.[104] In this sphere, colonisation often proceeded on the basis of an assessment of the overwhelming force that could be unleashed against non-European peoples to further European commercial interests. The violence of the process was not mitigated by political considerations, unless these were derived from a conflict of interest with a rival European power.[105]

Identifying England as the pioneer of capitalist development and Germany as the new dominant force on the continent, Kropotkin argued that inter-state relationships in Western Europe were characterised by aggressive competition, as Hobbes described sovereigns: with weapons pointing and eyes fixed. It was an order based on domination in which rival powers were set on a permanent war-footing and willing to engage in actual combat. Kropotkin acknowledged that European inter-state relations were complicated and constrained by historical rivalries, chauvinism and patriotism. States entered into defensive agreements, international pacts and alliances. The struggle for political domination in Europe was also an economic competition and this could either act as a spur to alliance or militate against cooperation. The Franco-Prussian war illustrated the dimensions of European rivalries. This was a conflict between powers battling for the control of seaports in the Baltic and the Adriatic; over the control of the investment markets in Asia, Africa and Turkey; and for the development of the African coasts, Polish plains, the Russian steppes, the Hungarian *pusztas* and the rose-covered valleys of Bulgaria.[106]

In Kropotkin's view, the geopolitics of the state system was wrongly described as anarchy. And defending Proudhon against those who reproached him for adopting a label associated with disorder, destruction and chaos, Kropotkin pointed to the reality of the international system to illustrate the prejudice for violence that 'order' concealed. The order of international states spelt deprivation, poverty, prostitution, continual war, servitude and massacres. Looking again to the example of the nihilists, Kropotkin noted that this soubriquet had first been applied pejoratively by 'fathers' to attack the disobedience of 'sons'.[107] Nihilists had made it their own. Likewise, Kropotkin argued:

> [W]e prefer 'disorder' to that sort of order .... which was 're-established' at Paris by the slaughter of 30,0000 workers ... We prefer a thousand times the disorder of the Anabaptists in the sixteenth century, of the revolutionists of 1793, of Garibaldi, of the Commune of 1871, and of so many others to whom the bourgeois dedicate the title – quite glorious in our eyes – of 'formenters of disorder'.[108]

Recognising the negative connotations of anarchy, Kropotkin reserved its use for the ethical disorder whose possibilities were revealed through the analysis of geographical science.

Global Communities

The intellectual context in which Kropotkin pitched his work is usefully summarised by Ellsworth Huntington, professor of geography at Yale University. Huntington was impressed by Kropotkin's theories on desiccation and used his findings to pioneer work on climate, linking changes in the physical environment to human actions.[109] The preface to his 1915 book *Civilization and Climate* notes a significant revision in the practice of the discipline. The 'science of geography' was no longer limited by the ambition to produce 'exact maps of the physical features of the earth's surface'. In the twentieth century 'it adds ... an almost innumerable series showing the distribution of plants, animals, and man, and of every phase of the life of these organisms'. Geography's purpose, Huntington continued, was to compare physical and organic maps in order to determine 'how far vital phenomena depend upon geographic environment'. Among the things to be mapped, he included 'human character as expressed in civilization'. There were a significant number of variables in this study: 'race, religion, institutions, and the influence of men of genius ... on the one hand, and geographical location, topography, soil, climate, and similar physical conditions on the other'.[110] Kropotkin's selection of criteria were not the same as Huntingdon's, and importantly included nationality, class, technology and the power of ideas, alongside the influence of spirited individuals. Yet Kropotkin's equally lofty ambition was to consider the dynamics that explained the movements of peoples and ideas: the distribution of 'races, beliefs, customs, and forms of property, and their close dependency on geographical conditions'; the 'aspirations and dreams of various races, in so far as they are influenced by the phenomena of nature'; and the 'distribution of human settlements in each country'. The 'great branch of geographical knowledge ... which deals with human families on the earth's surface', Kropotkin remarked, had not yet formulated laws to describe global changes or model the patterning of all of these variables. But geographers, ethnographers and anthropologists had begun to document the movements, migrations and modifications in human societies and it was possible, in principle, to think in terms of causality.[111]

Kropotkin developed this nascent theory of globalisation by uncovering the mainsprings of social evolution. Like Reclus, Kropotkin believed that it was possible to categorise the intellectual and ethical practices of national groups and assess their development.[112] Geographers were able to map the movement of ideas from ancient centres of learning in Libya, Athens and Rome, for example, or the spread of Abrahamic religions across the globe, and this exercise supported the classification of 'savage', 'barbarian' and 'civilised' behaviours.[113] These markers reappeared in *Mutual Aid* and *Ethics*, and Kropotkin clearly believed that it was possible to use this system of classification to identify higher forms of social practice and reveal the mechanisms that supported their expression. However, he did not impose a cultural history on the movement between these stages any more than he conflated nationality with colonisation. Civilisation was not benchmarked against modernity or modernisation: Kropotkin found that rural social systems in Spain, Russia, Italy and France were sociable, self-regulating and complex.[114] In *Mutual Aid* he observed that the ethical practices evident in peasant communities of " 'civilized" countries' were more or less the same in the 'Arab *djemmâa* and the Afghan *purra*, in the villages of Persia, India and Java, in the undivided family of the Chinese, in the encampments of semi-nomads of Central Asia and the Nomads of the far North', in short, in all sorts of places that were 'out of touch with modern civilization and ideas'.[115] Nor were 'civilised' standards reserved to nationalities that had been acculturated to European norms. 'We certainly must abandon the idea of representing human history as an uninterrupted chain of development from the pre-historical Stone Age to the present time.'[116] The development of human societies was not continuous, he noted in *Ethics*. Western Europe was one centre of social development in human history. India, Egypt, Mesopotamia, Greece, Rome, and Scandinavia were separate hubs and each had experienced periods of regression as well as progression. Equally, Kropotkin did not consider the behaviours of modern Europeans to be necessarily civilised. He often used the term with a good deal of irony. 'Until now', he argued, 'the Europeans have "civilised the savages" with whisky, tobacco, and kidnapping; they have inoculated them with their own vices; they have enslaved them.'[117] At other times, he spoke with revulsion. The 'mission of Europeans ... to civilise the lower races by ... bayonets', he noted, 'merely raises to the height of a theory the shameful deeds which Europeans are doing every day'.[118]

Anti-statecraft revealed that the organisational principles that groups adopted were a more important determinant of ethical development than technological sophistication and that 'higher' and 'lower' referred to the quality of the social relations that national groups cultivated with outsiders. The state system was a lower order because it fostered mutual aggression. Higher forms of social life would instead encourage the ethics that geographical science was designed to support. And in offering an alternative ethical system for non-state organisation, Kropotkin examined how popular aspirations dovetailed with global organisational trends.

Kropotkin's argument was that the world was now networked in ways that belied the territorial limits of states. Capitalism and commerce had established extra-territorial linkages through international trade and colonisation.[119] At the same time, previously isolated national groups were being connected through increasingly bold infrastructural projects. In Russia, the Trans-Siberian Railway was opening up even the most inhospitable areas of the interior, connecting European territories to the Pacific.[120]

The broad hypothesis that Kropotkin distilled from this approach was that modifications of social practice, whatever their cause, were linked to ideational transformations. These were typically countervailing and they may proceed from practice to theory or vice versa. For example, in

Ethics Kropotkin argued that the rise of the Roman Empire that eclipsed the flourishing Hellenic city-states stimulated the advance of Christian egalitarian ethical systems.[121] In the seventeenth century, the blossoming of philosophy and science unleashed a revolutionary force against the injustices of absolutist rule.[122] In the nineteenth century, capitalist decadence and state repression had similarly given vent to socialism. The story of nihilism was one local example of the way in which ideas and practices evolved. But, for Kropotkin, the Paris Commune was by far the most significant global event of the period.

Kropotkin's assessment of the Commune was remarkably similar to Bakunin's, which 'had been aimed as carefully at Marx as it was at capital and the state'.[123] Bakunin had characterised the Commune as a movement of the people, an intuitive expression of socialism. Likewise, Kropotkin argued that the Commune took its power from the popular movement that created it. Like Bakunin, Kropotkin judged the Commune to be a flawed expression of popular aspirations.[124] Bakunin had argued that the Communards 'did not have the time or the capacity to overcome and suppress in themselves a mass of bourgeois prejudices'.[125] Kropotkin concurred, putting the failures of the Communards down to their inability to break entirely with the habit of representative government and their reluctance to abolish individual ownership.[126] But this was not the most important lesson of 1871, even though it was an important one, especially from the perspective of Kropotkin's Russian propagandising.[127] More significant was the cultural shift that the Commune achieved in the process of its failure. Both Bakunin and Kropotkin imagined that future grass-roots insurrections would perfect the example of the Commune. 'The next international and solidarist revolution of the people will be the resurrection of Paris,' Bakunin declared. The Commune showed 'all the enslaved peoples … the unique way of emancipation and salvation', 'inaugurating the new era'.[128] On the tenth anniversary of the Commune, Kropotkin re-stated Bakunin's thesis. The Commune was the beginning of a 'new era' of revolutions in which the people were marching 'from slavery to freedom'. The Commune, he argued, remained 'the point of departure for future revolutions'.[129] Both, moreover, considered that the Commune expressed an internationalist ideal, alien to the state system. For Bakunin it aimed at the 'complete emancipation of the masses of the people and their solidarity … across and despite state borders'.[130] Likewise, Kropotkin described the Commune as a form of organisation that extended across 'artificial frontiers'.[131] Unlike the communes that were formed in the city-states during the medieval period, this new idea did not describe a bounded unit or discrete organisation. In 1871, the Commune had brought people together in networks that facilitated the direct management of production and the distribution of food, arms, clothing and other resources in crisis periods and beyond.[132] Future communes would realise the potential. Kropotkin imagined them as inherently limitless and without a sovereign: it was a generic term or synonym for the interactions of groups and individuals who recognised their equality but who saw no defined boundaries or barriers to their interconnection.[133]

Geographical science was hardly precise, but Kropotkin's point was that singular events, like the Commune, could have momentous, world-historic effects. The idea was a subversion of the great men of history thesis. Equally, collisions between ideas and practices resulted in changes that reverberated in social, political, economic and physical spheres. The outcomes were uncertain and there was no predicable sequencing of cause and effect. But this knowledge of global change was powerful because it suggested that the state's attempt to cement social relationships through hierarchy and domination were not only destructive, but also vulnerable to attack. Far from demonstrating the state's permanence, geographical science revealed that its deconstruction was imaginable. The world was in a process of constant flux. Capitalism had acted as a spur to the creation of a global infrastructure that surmounted the physical barriers to communal cooperation; the appalling social impact of capitalism and the state had encouraged resistance from within the global system in the shape of a mass movement for land reform; and tensions within the European state system had given rise to a new concept of grass-roots organising. In sum: geographical science suggested that the principles of fluidity that inspired anarchist organising were far better suited to global realities than the state was, even though it appeared permanent.

Global Transformation

The possibilities and uncertainties of Kropotkin's science of anti-statecraft come into view in his reflections on the study of geography and its potential to contribute to global revolutionary transformation. Kropotkin was passionately committed to the idea that science was 'an excellent thing' and that knowledge 'is an immense power'.[134] The task was to make sure that everybody benefited through education.

Kropotkin subdivided geography into four, eschewing the conventional division of the subject into physical and human branches. Physical geography examined the 'laws' governing Earth's surface. Oceanography involved the study of the seas, informed by meteorology, and the study of eco-systems, or what Kropotkin called 'the influence of local topographical causes on climate'.[135] The third branch, 'zoo and phyto-geography', examined global distributions of plants and animals and evolutionary processes of adaptation and modification, and the fourth, human geography, followed similar processes, also embracing anthropology, history and philology.

The power of geography, or any other discipline, to exercise a transformative effect depended on the manner of its teaching. Kropotkin made three recommendations to instructors. The first recommendation was to adopt an anti-disciplinary approach. Geography should be taught as Russian literature was in Russian universities: topics were elaborated by the pursuit of tangential ideas and intuitions, inspiring new insights into phenomena and the relationships between things. Teachers should aim to 'show the connection existing between all various categories of phenomena which are studied separately, to develop broader horizons before [student's] eyes, and to accustom [them] to scientific generalisations'.[136] The best pedagogues, Kropotkin remarked, 'understand what a precious auxiliary imagination is to scientific reasoning'.[137] The second recommendation was to develop knowledge from experience. Book learning had a place in knowledge acquisition, but 'humanitarian feelings cannot be developed .... if all the life outside school acts in an opposite direction'. Education 'must arise from the daily practice of the child' where, in fact, there was little teaching to be done, but a wealth of learning.[138] Kropotkin's third and last recommendation was to build knowledge through data and knowledge exchange.

This proposal had a practical as well as a principled dimension. Kropotkin railed against the duty for obedience and authoritative claims advanced as law, just as Bakunin had attacked the pretensions of scientific elites. Law had a theological root and a heritage of 'slavery, serfdom, feudalism and royalty'.[139] It was the opposite of science that, as the nihilists had argued, was always open to revision and modification. On a practical plain, Kropotkin also believed that geography required the development of global perspectives, beyond the reach of most individuals. Great ideas, he remarked, have their genesis in collective endeavour and come from the body the people, not from the heads of individual philosophers.[140] He distinguished between heimatskunde, the study of locality, and erdkunde, the understanding of the earth. Standing astride the Slavophiles' 'soil-bound' projects, which encouraged Russians to know their own country, and the outward-looking radicalism of the Westerners, Kropotkin defended both.[141] Heimatskunde was essential to erdkunde, but in the absence of erdkunde students would be held back from reflecting theoretically on the knowledge they had acquired of their locality and less likely to pursue 'spontaneous study'.[142] Travel and school-exchange were means of developing erdkunde. Another was to construct transnational scientific communities, at every level of learning. 'Each village school ought to have collections from everywhere: not only from all parts of its own country, but from Australia and Java, from Siberia and the Argentine Republic.'[143] Reciprocal exchanges in pursuit of erdkunde not only raised the level of technical knowledge they also provided a platform for the development of science from below. Perhaps above all, erdkunde evolved through the sharing of knowledge developed from multiple perspectives, including those outside Western Europe. The 'savants of Western Europe will object', but Kropotkin warned them that they:

> must recognise once [and] for all that every decade will bring within it … more and more important works, written in an ever increasing variety of languages. The true scientific man can no more ignore Scandinavian, Russian, Polish, Czechian, Hungarian, and Finnish scientific literature; and we must devise the means of systematically bringing all works of importance, written in any language, to the knowledge of the whole of the scientific world.[144]

The pedagogy that Kropotkin prescribed for geography was applicable to any subject, of course, but the special relevance of geography was its power to nurture global connections through the exchange of data and ideas and by collective reflection on the possibilities for adaptive change. In Kropotkin's mind, geography's special contribution to human knowledge was its capacity to help people mould their environments ethically.

Kropotkin's optimistic assessment of geography's value as a form of social practise did not mislead him into thinking that the kinds of change that he imagined possible were likely to result in uniform processes. In the 'struggle for freedom', he argued, 'each country must work out its own salvation'. Russia was 'bound to work out her liberty in her own way and with her own forces, however painful the way may be'.[145] His treatment of heimatskunde and erdkunde pointed to the same conclusion. The lesson that Kropotkin took from the development of geographical science was that the exchange of knowledge about the unpredictable laws of global development, patterns of geographical change and expected distributions would support an intellectual step-change in organisational theory, and one that dovetailed with the revolutionary pressure for social transformation.

Kropotkin's anti-statecraft indicated that there were a number of drivers for change. It was difficult to know whether the ravages of capitalism, revolt against slavery or rural deprivation would provide the spark for liberation struggles, or whether critical ideas in science, philosophy and ethics would help inspire ordinary people to despatch the parasites and criminals who were opposed to the development of new ways of thinking. Yet the reverberations of changes in one part of the globe, Kropotkin believed, would be felt across the world. By fighting for revolution in France, then, he also contributed to the struggles in Russia.

Conclusion to Part 2

Kropotkin described the work he completed for *Le Révolté* as the 'foundation of nearly all I have written later on'.[1] What did that mean? His early writings pointed up several themes: that anarchism was an ethical approach to politics; that the problems that socialists confronted were global; that science, construed poetically, offered a key to the resolution of those problems; that submissiveness and passivity were fatal barriers to social change and social solidarity was a catalyst for action; that change was a principle of life on Earth; and that fluid movements forged across diverse populations offered a model for cooperative living. Kropotkin presented these ideas in a distinctive way, using nihilism as his touchstone, but in developing his positions on nationality, slavery and the cementation of elite power, he aligned himself with Proudhonist and Bakuninist anti-authoritarianism. And his commentary on the Paris Commune formalised the ideological division that this alignment signalled. Yet there is scant evidence in Kropotkin's early writings that his identification with anti-authoritarian politics was a launch-pad for a theory resembling classical anarchism.

One of the foils for classical anarchism is Landauer's conception of the state as a social relationship, which we destroy by behaving differently. Kropotkin advanced a similar view. The relationships he sought to change were those that instilled obedience and slavishness, on the one hand, and command and supremacy on the other. In a recent discussion of Landauer's work, Dominique Miething notes the influence of the sixteenth-century French humanist Étienne de la Boétie on his work, specifically, la Boétie's observation that the capacity of a ruler to exercise his will over his subjects extended from a social and psychological capacity, not merely coercion.[2] Newman also draws on Boétie to explore post-anarchist principles, and the willingness of individuals to consent to their own subjection, comparing la Boétie to Landauer.[3] Kropotkin's analysis of nihilism touches on similar themes, but demonstrates how subjection is overcome through rebellious action: nihilism showed how. Kropotkin's description of the insurgence of nihilist women and his rebuttal of the literatures that ridiculed, objectified and demonised their rebellion richly illustrates the character of the dominating relationships he had in mind when he thought about the operation of power in the state. The activism he described in nihilism also exploded distinctions between public and private affairs. These women transformed socialist politics, injecting principles of mutuality and care into their relationships. Challenging their dependent status, they recast social relations on the basis of interdependence. He knew from his own personal experience how statism structured social relationships. And he knew how cultures of irresponsibility sustained monstrous regimes of domination, reproducing master–slave relationships in everyday behaviours:

> Having been brought up in a serf-owner's family, I entered active life, like all young men of my time, with a great deal of confidence in the necessity of commanding, ordering, scolding, punishing, and the like. But when, at an early stage, I had to manage serious enterprises and deal with men, and when each mistake would lead at once to heavy consequences, I began to appreciate the difference between acting on the principle of command and discipline, and acting on the principle of common understanding. The former works admirably in a military parade, but it is worth nothing where real life is concerned and the aim can be achieved only through the severe effort of many converging wills.[4]

It seems doubtful that Landauer intended his statement about changing behaviours and the state's destruction to be taken as an exhaustive account of anarchist struggle,[5] but assuming he did, Kropotkin clearly diverged. Unlike new anarchists Kropotkin believed the state to be more than just a set of social relationships. It was also a territorial unit that institutionalised slavery and a functional monopoly for the regulation and regimentation of political and social life. Because the state was also part of a geo-political system, geared to capitalism, it had a distinctively exploitative aspect. In whatever ways slavery operated across the world, the cleavage between those with property and those without cut across non-class oppressions. In all these guises the state had a real existence, made manifest in all manner of repressive activities, internationally, in social, political, economic and cultural domains.

The scientific approach that Kropotkin adopted to demonstrate the possibility of the state's destruction was inspired by nihilism. This approach was empiricist to the extent that nihilism was itself inspired by a deep scepticism about the claims to knowledge advanced by religious and philosophical elites. Kropotkin explained: 'the youth of Russia' stove to rid itself of prejudice, rejecting religious teachings, Kant, utilitarianism and tradition in equal measure. Kropotkin also pursued nihilist doubt against Hegelianism and Marxism, favourably comparing his naturalistic and materialist approach to 'the metaphysical conceptions of a Mind of the Universe, a Creative Force of Nature, a Loving Attraction of Matter, an Incarnation of the Idea, an Aim of Nature, a Reason for its Existence, the Unknowable, and so forth'.[6] Bazarov's view that there was no science 'in the abstract', only sciences, and that all principles were open to question, no matter how much they 'may be revered', struck a chord with Kropotkin.[7] In 1913 he repeated the point he made in *The Appeal to the Young*, describing anarchism as 'a principle which demands a complete reconstruction of all the sciences, whether physical, natural or social'.[8] But reading Turgenev through Chernyshevksy's eyes, he subverted the strict doctrine, rejecting the positivist separation of facts from values. Science described a particular claim to knowledge, but it was linked to power:

> The bourgeoisie is a force to be reckoned with, not just because it possesses wealth but *primarily because it has availed of the leisure afforded to it by wealth in order to train in the arts of government and devise a science that provides a justification for domination.* It knows what it wants, it knows that it is required if its ideal society is to survive, and until such time as the worker also wakes up to what is required and how to go about things, he is fated to remain enslaved to the possessor of that knowledge.[9]

Bazarov's remark that a 'decent chemist is twenty times more useful than any poet' did not resonate with Kropotkin.[10] Bazarov was a paragon of honesty and a dispeller of illusions. In 1897, Kropotkin told Maria Goldsmith that anarchists should examine the strength of their ideas in grass-roots movements with the 'candour of a Bazaorv'.[11] However, correcting Bazarov's rejection of poetry, Kropotkin approached the sciences as a thoughtful realist. The result was what Kropotkin called the 'inductive-deductive method', an approach to analysis that filtered empirical observations through values, recognising that what constituted knowledge in the world at any moment was itself constructed in this manner. The assertion that 'the inequality of fortunes is a "law of Nature," and that capitalistic exploitation represents the most advantageous form of social organisation' was an example.[12]

Malatesta's comment about the poetic quality of Kropotkin's science was perceptive. Yet, unlike Malatesta and Nettlau, who judged Kropotkin's anarchist science against a benchmark of genuine science, Kropotkin did not believe that there was anything that may be recognised as real science from which his approach departed. On the contrary, he considered that the sciences were conditioned by the ends to which they were put. The radical science that Kropotkin pursued as a geographer – and the sciences he implored the young to develop in tandem – were intended to support revolutionary ends. Scientists may adopt the same methods in their research, for example, gathering and collating statistical information, but as Vincent Barnett notes in his discussion of economics and statistics, competing theoretical approaches pointed to different scientific applications. The Russian school that Kropotkin followed emphasised observation as a process 'relating to a sequence of random events' rather than, as was the case in England and Germany, 'originating in the science of facts relating to the state'.[13] The detailed data collected by the Russian Geographical Society was intended to gauge the accuracy of competing economic theories. Kropotkin adopted the same approach in anarchism and used statistical data to support his proposed alternatives, scrutinise claims about the efficiency and effectiveness of government policy and highlight the problems that beset citizens exploited by capitalism. Scientists dealt with empirical data, but the questions they asked, the assumptions they adopted and the solutions they found were shaped always by their social, political and cultural perspectives. The difference between Kropotkin and Reclus, on the one hand, and Ratzl and Mackinder on the other, was not their ambition for geography or their understanding of geography's disciplinary range, but their contrary assumptions about the ontological status of the European state and the inevitability of colonisation.

Kropotkin's science did not reveal a pristine condition of uncorrupted sociability recoverable through revolution. There was no natural condition in the nature that geographers studied, although it may be more or less cultivated, exploited, barren, resource-rich, populated or inhabited. Since Kropotkin described evolutionary biology as a branch of geography, this conviction was significant. Kropotkin uncovered countervailing forces that were open to the interventions of human beings who lacked perfect knowledge of the world and who could not always foresee the consequences of their actions. It was clear, too, from Kropotkin's historical geography that the rise of the state in Europe was only the most recent manifestation of an organisational idea that had a much longer record. The statist and communalist principles of agglomeration Kropotkin identified in his anti-statecraft were defined in oppositional terms, but he set up the choice between these alternatives in much the same way that later social justice campaigners would argue about the possibility of realising alternatives to neo-liberal globalisation. The important difference between his view and the arguments put by alter-globalisers was that Kropotkin used adaptability to change as the criterion to assess alternatives. On Kropotkin's reasoning, questions about the justness of social arrangements could only be resolved by thinking about the ways in which struggles against territorialism and colonisation could be won. Knowledge of organisational resistance movements stimulated by these centralising forces was a useful guide in this respect. So, too, was history. His account of the failure of the city-states elicited important lessons about the robustness of social systems that divided urban from rural labour and about the risks of market accumulation. Kropotkin took these lessons to advocate anarchist communism, devise practical solutions for the disaggregation of industry from agriculture and to call on Western workers to support struggles for land reform. However, adaptability meant that organisational proposals were always open to revision. Recalling his time in Bern, Kropotkin remarked: 'We saw that a new form of society is germinating in the civilized nations, and must take the place of the old one ... The society will be composed of a multitude of associations ... This society will not be crystallized into certain unchangeable forms, but will continually modify its aspect, because it will be a living, evolving organism.'[14] Adaptability and revision also implied the possibility of dissent, hence Kropotkin's recommendation that 'conflicts which may still arise can be submitted to arbitration'.[15]

Kropotkin's rendering of the state as social relationship characterised by slavery and mastership did not lead him to establish an obviously gentler form of anarchism to Bakunin's, as new anarchists argued in the 1960s and 1970s, even though he spoke in a very different voice. As Martin Miller argues, Kropotkin keenly associated himself with Bakunin, writing a warm appreciation for *Freedom* in 1905. The ridicule that would later be heaped on Bakunin's head was already taking shape in Bernard Shaw's caricature Bakoonin-Siegfried[16] and the battle for Bakunin's reputation was already in swing.[17] Kropotkin was unable to scotch the legend of Bakunin's fondness for conspiracy, but he attested to his perceptive assessment of Nechaev's strengths and weaknesses as if in an effort to do so. He also drew on the personal traits that his detractors exploited to evidence his childlike, dictatorial and chaotic tendencies, as measures of high moral and intellectual virtue. On Kropotkin's testimony Bakunin might have found a home in the Chaikovskii Circle.[18] He had certainly earned a place in the history of socialist thought. When Bakunin sat down to write a letter the 'letter became a pamphlet, and the pamphlet a book'. But this was because Bakunin 'wrote for the needs of the movement' and, Kropotkin added approvingly, his work contained 'for the thinking reader, more political thought, and more philosophical comprehension of history, than heaps of university and state socialist treatises, in which the absence of deep thought is concealed under foggy dialectics'.[19]

The hardening of ideological divisions between anarchists and social democrats, particularly after the expulsion of anarchists from the congresses of the Second International in 1896, explains the ardour of Kropotkin's defence; his willingness to place himself on one side of this line and cement the differences through his identification with Bakunin reflects the militancy of his own positions.

Kropotkin's treatment of slavery was the first marker of his Bakuninism and it pointed to a distinctive idea of the state. As Robert Cutler notes, Bakunin developed his conception in the course of his dispute with Marx in the First International, arriving at his conclusions through his reading of Hegel. Kropotkin followed a different route, eschewing 'deep philosophy of history' for science, but his view that autocracy was an archetype for government in the state corresponded with Bakunin's view that 'all forms of government were merely various forms of Monarchy, that is, different forms of the despotism of some small number exercised against the vast majority'.[20] Kropotkin not only shared this view,[21] he also agreed with Bakunin's decoupling of state power from capitalist exploitation. These forces worked in partnership but were separate sources of domination. The economic inequalities that capitalism facilitated enabled elites to access the financial resources necessary to impose settlements on colonised peoples, as well as giving them an incentive to do so. Under 'even the most republican forms' of government, 'the slave to the soil and to the factory would always remain a slave unless private ownership of the soil and of the instruments of labour was abolished'.[22] But the political power that elites enjoyed and the grounds on which the oppressed were dominated were importantly derived from these settlements and the combination of force and fraud that maintained and legitimised them. The conditioning power of patriarchy was one example. Kropotkin's general view was that that economic emancipation was a key for 'religious and intellectual (clerical and academic) slavery'. Yet it would be 'utterly wrong to conclude that liberation from religious and intellectual servitude will come automatically once man is freed from poverty', he added.[23] The dynamic of political and economic power explained both why it was possible for a single global economy to support quite different regimes of domination and why it was possible for government systems to change, leaving mechanisms of economic exploitation intact. It also explained why Kropotkin argued that a change in economic power, namely the abolition of ownership that he believed underpinned capitalism, required a change in political institutions, which he imagined as the abandonment of representation by the recovery of individual sovereignty. On Kropotkin's account, the transfer of ownership from individuals to the state did not represent a change in economic power, even if it required a revolution to usher it in.[24] Extending the scope of rights or introducing new liberties within the state would alter the character of government but it would not challenge the principle of elite domination.[25] Following Bakunin, Kropotkin argued that elite rule was underwritten by a principle of right, and that this discourse justified basic inequalities that were corrosive of sociability. Both, then, were the target of anarchist critique.

The second indicator of Kropotkin's Bakuninism was his analysis of the Paris Commune. Following Bakunin, Kropotkin described the Commune as an expression of anti-authoritarian politics that had been opposed by the authoritarian German sections of the First International. This reading of the politics of the Commune grounded the divisions between anarchists and social democrats in a racialised language of Latin and Germanic socialisms. The language itself was ingrained in the European socialist movement and it mirrored the Slav/German polarity that Marx and Engels employed in the First International in the course of the dispute with Bakunin on the issue of Slav emancipation. Engels' view that the Slav peoples' failure to construct an independent state was a sign of their non-historic status has been described as a commonly held, impartial, nineteenth-century observation.[26] Having witnessed the fallout of this debate, Victor Dave, a member of the Belgian section, characterised it as naked racism. Bakunin had argued that the emancipation of the Slavs in Europe held the key to social revolution. Dave described Marx's response as 'chauvinist': the Slavs were the hereditary enemy to be annihilated and destroyed.[27]

In the aftermath of this argument Kropotkin adopted the uncompromising terms of the debate. In his essay 'The Paris Commune and the idea of the state', Bakunin had acknowledged that the Commune appeared in 'the country par excellence of political centralisation' but identified a cleavage between 'the scientific communism' developed by the 'German school' and the revolutionary socialism of 'the Latin countries'.[28] Reclus, who had participated in the Commune, similarly described the Franco-Prussian War as 'the crowning glory of Bismarckian politics, which came to fruition in a sentimental Germany'.[29] Kropotkin pushed this distinction a bit further. Indeed, whereas he was willing to acknowledge that the communes of the medieval period were neither Roman nor Germanic in origin, contrary to the claims of respective national historians,[30] he mapped the genius of the Paris Commune directly to the 'Latin' sections of the First International and its defeat to German statism. Kropotkin traced the observation back to Bakunin, and extended its application to the German socialist party. Bakunin, he argued, had rightly recognised that the triumph of 'Bismarck's military state' in 1871 was 'at the same time' the triumph of 'German State-socialism'. Kropotkin added: Bismarck was in fact 'the godfather'.

> At a time when the crushing defeat of France, the murder of 35,000 Paris workingmen after the fall of the Commune, and the triumph of the German Empire had opened a new period of reaction, which lasts till now, and when Marx and his friends endeavoured by means of all sorts of intrigues to transform the International Association created for the purposes of a *direct struggle against Capitalism,* into an arm of parliamentary politics in the hands of those workers who were going to pass over to the Philistine Camps – at such a time the Federalist Federations of the International, inspired by Bakunin, became the only strongholds against all-European reaction.
>
> To Bakunin and his friends we owe thus in a great degree that in Latin lands the revolutionary spirit, which formed a new force in the *labour* masses of these countries, was maintained.[31]

Kropotkin's conscious alignment with Bakunin produced some innovative lines of thought. By extending Bakunin's rejection of the state in the global analysis of territorialism, Kropotkin outlined an idea of colonialism that recognised the power advantages that Europeans enjoyed in the rest of the world without also framing liberation in terms of the superiority of Western ideas or the logic of modernisation. James Lehning argues that even into the mid-twentieth century Europeans represented themselves as 'civilized ... and colonial subjects uncivilized, inferior, and incapable of meeting the challenge of becoming like Europeans'.[32] Kropotkin observed the same tendency and showed how these attitudes inhibited the liberation of slaves in America and Russia.[33] He stood at some distance from liberals like J. S. Mill who imagined the possibility of improvement through the extension of European practices and values, for what constituted 'European' was in fact a tradition of domination. Kropotkin's analysis of the state challenged the validity of the distinction invoked between 'internal' and 'external' colonising processes, used by modern historians to describe the rise of the state. It also rejected the view, implicit to this distinction, that colonisation began after the rise of the European state.[34] For Kropotkin, colonisation was part of the process of state development. And by recognising the integrity of nationalities and distinguishing internationalist from nationalist struggles, Kropotkin anticipated what Maia Ramnath describes as the 'assertion of collective existence and demand for recognition' that serves 'as a stand against genocide, apartheid, systemic discrimination, or forced assimilation to a dominant norm'.[35]

Kropotkin's anarchism was not free from tensions, and one of these – linked to his analysis of the Paris Commune – also extended from his alliance with Bakunin. The aggressive pitch of Kropotkin's commentaries on the Commune is sometimes characterised as Germanophobic and to the extent that he believed that there were significant cultural differences between national groups, it is difficult to deny the charge. In *Modern Science and Anarchism*, Kropotkin pursued his theme by presenting a history of socialist thought that traced the tensions between 'centralists and federalists' in the First International to the enmity between the Jacobins and the Paris Commune of 1793–4. Robespierre and Babeuf were the progenitors of German Marxism and the Enragés were the bearers of Latin anarchism.[36] Yet the hostility that Kropotkin betrayed towards Germany was also linked to his anti-statecraft. He placed Germany at the heart of Europe. In the same way that historians have argued that its decentralised structure created instability in seventeenth-century Europe, Kropotkin suggested that Germany's unification was a destabilising force in the nineteenth-century state system. One way or another, 'European politics rested on the keystone of Germany'.[37] In socialist circles, the centrality of Germany fuelled an internecine debate about nations, states and revolutionary change that had rumbled on since the collapse of the First International. And in this context, Kropotkin's anti-Germanism was a not only a response to the view that Slav peoples were incapable of initiating socialist revolution, but a worry about the future of Russia. Kropotkin disputed the reasoning that informed Engels' observations and refused to accept his idea that '[s]ome small nationalities and languages had no independent future'.[38] For him, the Slavs supposed failure was their strength: neither a sign of their non-historic status nor a justification for their domination. Kropotkin's friend Bernard Kampffmeyer wryly observed the ease with which the 'almost fresh wounds that France received in 1870 and 1871' were forgotten when the German Kaiser sent his sympathies to the widow of President Carnot, assassinated in 1894 by the anarchist Casiero. Kropotkin was not blind to the international class alliances that political elites forged against resistance movements, but he did not share Kampffmeyer's confidence that a worker in one national group had 'no wish to enter the territory of his adversary in order to dominate and exploit' or that the capacity of workers to bring 'peace between the nations of the world' could be assumed.[39] There was as much cause for anxiety as for buoyancy in Kropotkin's understanding of progressive global change and the ways in which resistance politics may play out.

Kropotkin denied the charge, put to him by Georg Brandes, that he had a faith in the wisdom of ordinary people that bordered on the naive.[40] Read in the context of the geo-politics in which he situated it, his account of human sociability and his advocacy of self-government and free agreement are less easily misconstrued as indicators of blithe idealism. As Kropotkin explained to Brandes, his claims were less elevated. They were also more challenging, theoretically. Kropotkin believed that social groups were capable, and best placed, to make their own social and political arrangements. Carole Pateman makes the same point in her modern critique of contract theory: 'humans create their own social and political structures and institutions' but 'in theories of original contracts ... individuals give up their right of self-government to another or a few others'.[41] Principles of consent legitimised states but government was based on force. Arrangements imposed through a colonising process had no legitimacy, however persuasive the a-historical stories of political accord seemed to be. Kropotkin did not discuss the implications for political obligation, as modern scholars like Pateman have done, at least not in these terms. He did not ask whether or not individuals had a duty to obey. Instead, he reversed the terms of the question and asked why individuals were not prepared to rise up against oppression. Like Tolstoy, Brandes remarked, Kropotkin saw 'more cowardice than stupidity in the world'.[42] And he coupled his apparently dreamy view of anarchist organising with a demand for political responsibility.

Kropotkin's conception of responsibility had two interrelated aspects. He argued that the struggle for emancipation demanded the assertion of revolutionary will and he developed a conception of complicity to match it. His analysis of Tsarism convinced him that the fight against slavery required that the oppressed slough off their slavish obedience to masters and that those born into groups that were privileged in respect of burgeoning movements, join with them. For Kropotkin, this was not just a domestic campaign but an international struggle and it called on Europeans to enter into socialist struggle to agitate in support of the peasants' direct appropriation of the land. Kropotkin's analysis of European land movements convinced him that rural workers were already asserting their will. At the same time, he also recognised the ease with which oppressed groups were seduced by elite promises. Kropotkin's *Appeal to the Young* suggested that privileged, well-educated individuals had a role to play in the liberation struggles of underprivileged groups and in the amelioration of their poor living conditions. His discussion of the Russian revolutionary movement indicated that other nationalities were similarly well-placed to support the struggles of the landless. The implication was that those who chose to refuse this help or prioritise their own national interests aligned themselves with the dominating classes.

Kropotkin's polarisation of European traditions in his discussion of the Commune was a distillation of a cultural history that pitted written Roman law, private property and Byzantine rule against folk traditions, Indo-Germanic communism and Slavonic communalism and federation.[43] His view that the Paris Commune marked a new departure for the development of progressive revolutionary aspirations was contextualised by a geo-political analysis that located repressive power in Europe, and within Europe, in Germany. Struggling to replace representative government and abolish property ownership the Communards had inaugurated a new phase of international development. Its spatial location was explained by the tensions active within the European state system: the global domination of Germany, which exemplified the state principle, sparked resistance just as the extension of the Roman Empire had brought Christian ethics into being. On this account, Russia was the sick man of Europe, as liberals and socialists across the continent contended, but Germany provided the modern template for territorialisation and colonisation. It followed – in Kropotkin's view – that failure to make common cause with the forces struggling for free federation was counter-revolutionary, even if it appeared that the national groups captured within territorial blocs were themselves still subject to domination.

The implications of Kropotkin's position became increasingly apparent in the 1890s when the socialist movement divided on the question of political action. From Kropotkin's perspective, the call to organise in political parties and compete for electoral power was simply counter-revolutionary: it sought to perpetuate the systems of government that he associated with capitalism and it inhibited the development of free federation, which was the key to anarchy. That the policy of political action was pioneered by the German Social Democratic Party only confirmed Kropotkin's view that Germany had become the chief obstacle to socialist emancipation. Kropotkin's Germanophobia, however unpalatably it was expressed, was not an aberration of his thinking. Nor was it the result of a naive faith in French revolutionary traditions or a deep-seated Russian patriotism, at odds with anarchist internationalism. On the contrary, it was an assertion of internationalism, as Kropotkin understood it, and it was compatible with a commitment to socialist class struggle.

In his eagerness to follow Bakunin's example and write for the needs of the movement, Kropotkin invoked a separation between scientific work and activist writing, risking the loss of the comprehensiveness of his political vision. Kropotkin set out his understanding of class, exploitation and enslavement in his radical journalism, but other ideas about global change and the dimensions of nationality, also integral to his anarchism, were largely removed from his anti-statist and anti-capitalist critiques. The result was that Kropotkin unwittingly helped to conceal what was distinctive about his position in a generic radical discourse, while benchmarking anarchist politics against a set of cultural attitudes and policy differences that were stark, open to easy reduction and highly divisive. Coming out of Russia as a nihilist and a federalist, Kropotkin developed an innovative, creative anarchist politics, but one that was easily soaked up in the fluid, shifting but generalised argument of social-ist critique and subsequently swallowed up by stories of his scholarly erudition, self-sacrificing nobility and adjustment to British liberal cul-tural norms.

Part 3 Revolution and Evolution

Introduction to Part 3

The General Idea of Anarchy

As Kropotkin's exile advanced, he developed the ideas he had set out in the 1880s to challenge the cultural prejudices that dismissed anarchist organising as unviable. Publishing some of his best known work during this period, notably *Mutual Aid. A Factor of Evolution*, *The Conquest of Bread* and *Fields, Factories and Workshops: Or, Industry Combined with Agriculture and Brain Work with Manual Work*, Kropotkin set out an evolutionary, scientific conception of anarchism and explored a number of ideas about the economics of anarchy, cementing his reputation for scientism, utopianism and political reformism at the same time. In *The Conquest of Bread*, Alfredo Bonnano argues, Kropotkin rightly presented an idea of revolution as a process, but was unable to escape the philosophical conventions of his time and took 'scientific determinism' as 'his point of departure'.[1]

The strategy Kropotkin adopted to address issues of structural and cultural change in the 1890s and 1900s helps explain this dominant reading of his work. Kropotkin's ambition was to instil confidence in the revolutionary movement by explaining the possibilities for non-hierarchical organising and to challenge doctrines that seemed to suggest anarchism's redundancy. In pursuing this strategy, he continued to address a range of different audiences, appropriating dominant discourses and moulding them to his own purposes. Darwin was only one of the leading writers he recruited for the anarchist cause. As Matthew Adams has shown, Kropotkin also engaged with the anti-collectivist liberalism of Herbert Spencer.[2] Kropotkin's eagerness to show that significant cultural figures advocated ideas that tended towards anarchist conclusions was not entirely cynical: he made no secret of his admiration for Darwin. However, advertising these correspondences and borrowing the idioms of mainstream debate was a dangerous game and one that exposed Kropotkin to the criticism that he diluted his anarchism as a result. Yet the task Kropotkin set himself was to find a way of ensuring that the power to implement revolutionary change remained in the hands of oppressed groups.

Kropotkin's military experiences helped him formulate his ideas about the need to address the practical aspects of anarchist transformation. While his experience of leadership heightened his awareness of the stultifying consequences of authority relations, his tour of duty in

Siberia convinced him that the barrier to effective communal working was the artificial division between mental and manual labour. Ordinary people were perfectly capable of carrying out 'important schemes for reform' and would do so as long as those charged with their delivery understood that 'in serious work commanding and discipline are of little avail. Men of initiative are required everywhere.' Had 'all framers of plans of State discipline' passed 'through the school of real life' before they began 'to frame their State utopias', Kropotkin concluded, 'we should then hear far less than at present of schemes of military and pyramidal organization of society'.[3] What ordinary people lacked to fulfil their own needs, he concluded, was scientific knowledge and access to its 'joys' and 'immense power'.

> The masses want to know: they are willing to learn; they *can* learn. There, on the crest of that immense moraine which runs between the lakes ... there stands a Finnish peasant plunged in contemplation of the beautiful lakes, studded with islands, which lie before him ... there, on the shore of a lake, stands another peasant, and sings something so beautiful that the best musician would envy him his melody for its feeling and its meditative power. Both deeply feel, both meditate, both think; they are ready to widen their knowledge: only give it to them; only give them the means of getting leisure.[4]

Kropotkin drew similar lessons from his time working on *Le Révolté*. Confirming Brandes's assessment of Kropotkin's diagnosis of the problems confronting revolutionaries, he argued that workers and peasants did not need lessons in rebellion. The endurance of slavery was explained by 'widespread cowardice of mind and will'. The solution was the extension of scientific knowledge. Kropotkin's method was to:

> familiarize our readers – using plain comprehensible words, so as to accustom the most modest of them to judge for himself whereunto society is moving, and himself to correct the thinker if the latter comes to wrong conclusions. As to the criticism of what exists, I went into it only to disentangle the roots of the evils.[5]

By these methods Kropotkin hoped to instil confidence in the prospects of change. The paper listed the 'symptoms which everywhere announce the coming of a new era, the germination of new forms of social life, the growing revolt against antiquated institutions'. By watching, compiling and grouping these symptoms, Kropotkin intended to show 'their intimate connection' and persuade 'hesitating minds' that the ideas that shored up the status quo were giving way to 'advanced' conceptions that justified 'revolt against age-long injustice'.[6]

Kropotkin judged the urgency of his task by looking at the history of revolution, taking his lessons from the Great French Revolution. His study of the Revolution was published in 1909 but the commentary that featured in *The Spirit of Revolt* was an early example of Kropotkin's effort to contest accepted accounts.[7] The history of the French Revolution was a topic of considerable interest for anarchists, as it was for non-anarchist socialists. Alexander McKinley argues that it was a key plank for political reflection; in reviewing the events commentators were not so much concerned to document the history authoritatively but 'to use the Revolution and its actors in the modern-day struggle'.[8] Kropotkin saw no tension between these two aims and he developed an explicitly political framework for the analysis. While, as Matthew Adams shows, Kropotkin's theory of history illuminates the dynamism and spontaneity at the heart of his conception of evolution,[9] it also contained a valuable strategic message:

> History has a valuable lesson to teach us. She tells us that the revolution profits only those who have a clear conception of what they are out to achieve and who seek to make a reality of their own idea, without handing that task over to others.[10]

In his study of the Revolution, Kropotkin distinguished two forces for change: ideas and actions. The ideas were provided by intellectuals and they both prepared the ground for political change and underpinned the class tensions that later became apparent in the struggles between the Jacobins and the sans-culottes. The action came from the people and it supplied the dynamic force for change. However, in the course of the struggle against the King, the peoples' action gave the middle class an opportunity to wrest control of power in the state. By itself, Kropotkin argued, action was not sufficient to bring about revolutionary transformation.

In the run up to 1789, Kropotkin noted that 'the French middle classes ... had already developed a conception of the political edifice which should be erected on the ruins of feudal royalty'. The English and American revolutions made them realise that their dreams for power had the potential to assume an institutional form. Borrowing from a long philosophical tradition that stretched back to the writings of Hobbes, progressed through the Enlightenment of Montesquieu, Voltaire, Hume and Adam Smith and then to the seditious republicanism of Rousseau and Mably, the middle class found a rigorous justification for their power in the idea of representation and the right to property. No wonder, Kropotkin remarked, that 'the idea of a State, centralised and well-ordered, governed by the classes holding property in lands or in factories, or by members of the learned professions' triumphed: it was already in place, long before the fall of the Bastille. It 'was already forecast and described in a great number of books and pamphlets from which the men of action during the Revolution afterward drew their inspiration and their logical force'.[11]

Kropotkin acknowledged that the ideas that inspired the middle classes had also found their way into the Fourth Estate. 'By a thousand indirect channels the great principles of liberty and enfranchisement had filtered down to the villages and the suburbs of the large towns ... Ideas of equality were penetrating into the very lowest ranks.'[12] But these ideas failed to take a tangible form. The 'communistic aspirations' that Kropotkin attributed to the people 'were not formulated clearly and concretely'. They were expressed 'chiefly as simple negations: "Let us burn the registers in which the feudal dues are recorded! Down with the tithes! ... Hang the aristocrats!"' What the people lacked was a 'programme for political and economic organisation'.[13] By 1792 these 'vague aspirations' had prompted substantial experiments in communism, anticipating Proudhon's mutualism and the socialism of Charles Fourier and St Simon. These had been worked out 'from the needs of the moment' in the Gravilliers and Cordelier Clubs and in the Paris Commune.[14] But the Jacobins' terrorist machinery cut short the work of its advocates, Jacques Roux and the Enragés, and the programme of the middle class was secured.[15]

For Kropotkin, the political principles that the middle class turned to their own ends in the Revolution had lost none of their shine. He continued to celebrate the ideals of liberty, equality and fraternity advanced by eighteenth-century *philosophes*, and to that extent allied himself with Enlightenment ideals. Middle-class revolutionaries, he remarked, had 'drunk from that sublime font' and the 'eminently scientific spirit of this philosophy; its profoundly moral character; its trust in the intelligence, strength and greatness of the free man when he lives among his equals; its hatred of despotic institutions' were 'the source of all great ideas that have arisen since'.[16] Yet they remained 'abstractions' and were 'worth nothing if they cannot be brought to a practical issue'.[17] Rather than jettison the ideas as bourgeois, Kropotkin argued that anarchists should show how they may shape programmes for anarchy, empowering people to realise their full force and guard against their degeneration in the coming European conflagration. 'No struggle can be successful if it is unconscious, if it has no definite and concrete aim.'[18]

Kropotkin felt the need to flesh out the aims of anarchist change more keenly as the nineteenth century came to a close and events pointed to the popular revolution's defeat and perversion. He identified the main threat in the rise of electoral socialism. In 1910, he told readers of *Les*

Temps Nouveaux that the careerist politicians who warned against direct action resembled the bourgeois of 1789 who spoke out against the sans culottes.[19] Kropotkin had expressed his fears about the rise of parliamentarism in the socialist movement in the 1880s. Following the 1891 Brussels Congress of the Second International that voted down anarchist proposals for industrial struggle in favour of electoral campaigning, Kropotkin commented,

> the workers will not be troubling with the economic struggle any more. The economic struggle was all very well for dreamers such as Marx and Bakunin. But they, being practically minded, are going to concern themselves with votes. They will enter into alliances – some with the Conservatives, some with [Kaiser]Wilhem II – and they will get their men into Parliament. This is one item, the essential point of the Marxist gospel promulgated at the Brussels congress. This is to take priority over all the other resolutions.[20]

In 1893, following the Zurich meeting of the International, which introduced the policy of political action, binding socialist parties and unions to the struggle for 'political rights' and the 'conquest of political power',[21] *Freedom* wrote:

> [T]hat able and devoted revolutionist Karl Marx, left behind him a clique of personal adherents who … summed up his economic ideas into a sort of dogmatic creed, that which if any man ventures to dispute, he is an outcast from the orthodox church of Socialism. Morally incapable of reproducing what was great in their master, the Marxists have accentuated all that was least, and became notorious as unscrupulous wire-pullers and schemers for power. Having constituted themselves the priesthood of orthodox Socialism their aim is to place themselves at the head of the Labour Movement throughout Europe and to control its destinies.[22]

The decisive event, confirming Kropotkin's understanding of the fundamental division of the socialist movement, was the expulsion of the anarchists from the Congresses of the Second International at the London meeting of 1896. Wilhelm Liebknecht put the view of the German Social Democratic Party, which insisted on adherence to the policy of political action. 'There must be some kind of representation, some organisation, that embodied the centralised power and thought of the people', he argued in *Justice*. The anarchists' 'outcry against Parliamentarism is something very silly'.

> Our anarchistic and 'Revolutionary' enemies do not get tired with scoffing at our parliamentarism, which they pretend to consider as the most cowardly system, excluding revolutionary action and feeling. Well, these

'Revolutionists' apparently do not know that the two most really revolutionary bodies in history have been parliamentary bodies. The English Parliament which destroyed the Divine Right Monarchy of Charles the First, and the French Convention that sent the divine Right Monarchy of Louis the Sixteenth to the scaffold.[23]

Kropotkin's analysis of slavery treated both events as transformations of slavery, not fundamental revolutionary transformations. After the expulsion, he gathered at Holborn Town Hall with Malatesta, Reclus and others to discuss their response. Landauer summed up the German Social Democrats' position as follows:

> Their greed for domination and intolerance made us forswear the strife for political power and enter the struggle for the abolition of all authority. For this we live; and, however insulted and persecuted, we shall continue this work of propaganda for Anarchy.[24]

Following this division, Kropotkin redoubled his efforts to promote the practical implementation of anarchist alternatives. The need to propagate anarchist ideas was urgent, he told Alfred Marsh, the editor of *Freedom* in 1898. 'We must take advantage for spreading *our* ideas and show how they point us to see clear into matters – and to bring forward *our* ideas.'[25] The parliamentary policy that united reformist and anti-anarchist revolutionary socialists – 'Menshevists with Dictatorship Republicans' he said to Marsh[26] – threatened both to sap the energies of the popular mass movement and isolate the anarchists. As far as Kropotkin was concerned, the emptiness of the promises that these socialists made was obvious: in conniving in the systems of state that the eighteenth-century bourgeoisie had established on the backs of the people, they could only change the character of government, not its function. However, he recognised the appeal of the parliamentary strategy. The German social democrats were *'Radicals, sympathetic to the workers'* who 'do excellent work for the support of radical legislation … with some genuine interest in the working classes'.[27] Their danger was their attraction. The blend of 'statist and parliamentary infatuation' with 'the spirit of intrigue of Engels and Marx' aimed at 'making the workers' unions into a machine for wining Social Democrat seats in parliament'.[28] In the 1904 preface to the *Paroles d'un Révolté*, Kropotkin wrote:

> A whole school of socialists has even been established who claim to possess a science of their own, according to which it can be proved that revolution is a misconception. 'Discipline, submission to leaders – and everything than can be done for the workers will be done in parliament. Forget the gun, forget 1793, 1848 and 1871, help the bourgeoisie to

seize colonies in Africa and Asia, exploit the Negro and the Chinese with them, and everything will be done for you that can be done – without upsetting the bourgeoisie too much. Just one condition: forget this word, this illusion of revolution!'[29]

Kropotkin's attempts to meet the needs of revolutionaries took him in different directions. During his exile in Britain he sketched the ways in which an anarchist economy might operate, challenging orthodox Malthusian assumptions about scarcity in the process, and fleshed out a conception of evolutionary change that rivalled Marxist conceptions. In tackling these themes and promoting anarchist communist alternatives, Kropotkin importantly showed his indebtedness to Proudhon, as well as the areas in which he diverged from a variety of forms of anarchist individualism. The result was a robust, scientific, defence of anarchist ethics.

By simultaneously addressing middle-class intellectuals and working people, Kropotkin attempted to alter the political culture in favour of anarchism and implant ideas about organisation that would serve revolutionaries, at least during periods of crisis, while new ideas worked out in the course of physical struggles had a chance to germinate. Boldly setting his interpretations of leading intellectuals of the day against the orthodox readings used to justify inequality and oppression, Kropotkin attempted to convince his middle-class audience that their cherished-values properly supported anarchist conclusions. Pitting his socialism against the Marxism of social democracy, he worked equally hard to warn workers and peasants against the electoral strategies and radical promises of their would-be representatives and instil in them the responsibility for their own emancipation.

Anarchism: Utopian and Scientific

The premium that Kropotkin placed on the role of ideas and the value of imagining the implementation of anarchist practices conferred a utopian flavour on his anarchism. Because of the ways in which utopian socialism was commonly understood in nineteenth-century circles, Kropotkin was careful to qualify the nature of his utopianism, but he was also keen to show that anarchists had inherited the mantel of the innovative, experimental principles of the earlier generation of utopians, especially Robert Owen and Charles Fourier. The concept of utopia also helped Kropotkin to distinguish his own approach to design from contemporaries on the left and in the establishment.

Kropotkin presented several accounts of anarchist organisation, the most sustained being in the book *Fields, Factories and Workshops*. His willingness to outline his ideas and to use them as motivators for change attracted considerable criticism from within the anarchist movement, particularly from anti-communists. Kropotkin met these critiques and countered them by showing why his proposed solutions to the land question and slavery were superior to those advanced by individualists. These arguments highlight the grounds of Kropotkin's rejection of the individualist anarchism of Benjamin Tucker and the egoism of Stirner.

In the 1890s Kropotkin also openly confronted the professed anti-utopianism of the social democrats, and his development of the theory of mutual aid illuminated the gap that existed between the uncertainty of the evolutionary principles that ran alongside his utopian schemes and the confidence that anti-anarchist Marxist critics derived from their accounts of the logic of history. There was an ideal towards which evolution was pointing and this was the realisation of nihilist ethics. As a utopian, Kropotkin presented these ethics as the aspiration concealed in a tradition of political thought. Even though evolutionary processes were rooted in nature, anarchist ethics would never be fully realised unless their self-regulatory mechanisms were widely recognised. By attacking Social Darwininsm and supplementing biological evolutionary theory with an account of cultural evolution, Kropotkin challenged one of the theoretical mainsprings for statism and capitalism and demonstrated the advantages of anarchist institutions. In both practical and philosophical realms, utopia meant changing the environment in ways that enabled different behaviours to flourish.

Utopian Traditions

The warm reception of Kropotkin's *Appeal to the Young* by some of his social democrat political opponents attests to the willingness of even seasoned activists to recognise the interpenetration of socialist doctrines. In the 1890s fraternal relations began to break down in the face of the bitter dispute about the Second International's commitment to political action and the endorsement of exclusively constitutional methods. All parties to this debate began to look again at the theoretical differences that rationalised the factional division of anarchists from non-anarchists, an exercise often conducted through the critique of the opponent. It was during this period that the individualist tag was routinely applied to anarchism.[1] Stinerite became a blanket appellation in social democratic circles. And if anarchists were not Stirnerites, they were 'apostles' of Nietzsche, charged of treating morality as 'a fraudulent invasion of the rights of vigour, a rebellion of the weak multitude against the few who have overpowered them'.[2] Even anarchist-friendly William Morris adopted this tack.[3]

Following Marx's death in 1883, Engels became the guardian of Marxist orthodoxy and pre-eminent within the European social democratic movement. Yet not even Engels was able to steer the theoretical positions taken by European social democratic parties. The idiosyncrasies of British socialists organised in Hyndman's Social Democratic Federation (SDF) were a case in point. Engels' letters to Paul and Laura Lafargue are full of grumbles about the party's failings to grasp properly Marx's ideas, and complaints about its resulting policy miscalculations. The SDF were very good, he commented, at 'the dogmatic side of it', learning creed 'by heart' and reciting it 'like a conjurer's formula or a Catholic prayer'.[4] They were less good at applying Marx's insights to changing political situations.

Anarchists were not afraid of generalising Engels' description of the British movement to characterise social democracy as a disciplined, homogenous and unitary movement. A long history of expulsions from social democratic parties based on accusations of political heresy helped to encourage this view. Nevertheless, it was an overstatement. The variations of Marxist doctrine, combined with the sheer intellectual challenge of digesting Marx's ideas, resulted in considerable elasticity in the way in which scientific socialism was interpreted. One version of the orthodoxy, advanced in critique of syndicalism, intoned the key principles in a style reminiscent of Mr Memory in Hitchcock's *39 Steps*.[5]

> The Marxian analysis of the capitalist system is the only one that shows us the cause of the social evils that exist in capitalist society.
>
> Scientific Socialism is not 'up in the air' speculation.
>
> It is the result of generalisation drawn from economic facts.
>
> We reason from experience.
>
> The emancipation of the working class requires that they should lay hold of the science of the century.
>
> Mere sentiment and indignation against the wretched conditions does not meet the case. They must have recourse to intellect. It is, therefore, important that the working class should understand the two great laws discovered by Marx, and known as the Law of Surplus Value and The Materialist Conception of History.
>
> Surplus value is the difference between the wages received by the worker and the amount of value incorporated in the commodity he has produced ...
>
> The Materialist Conception of History is that the fundamental factor in the development of any society or nation is the economic factor.[6]

This dreary declamation of Marx and countless others like it provoked a critical response within social democratic ranks. William Morris's close associate Ernest Belfort Bax developed a markedly unorthodox interpretation that not only contradicted this kind of rigid orthodoxy, but also challenged the philosophy that Engels authorised. Re-injecting Marx with Hegel he imagined history as a spiral in which ideas acted on material conditions, leading to an increasingly happy condition defined, sociologically, as the dialectical overcoming of self-interest in community. Bax's 'religion of socialism' combined with Christian socialism and Comtean altruism to form the heady mix that seeped into the SDF's humanism. One fairly typical account in the journal *Justice* looked at the boundary between science and humanism and found that the two were just two sides of the same coin. Scientists followed Marx in economics and let their beliefs and actions be controlled by the calm, cold logic of reason. They were not devoid of emotion but did not let the moral crusade against capitalism take precedence over the realities of class war. Humanitarians acknowledged the operation of laws that Marx had revealed but fretted about repeated proclamations of their rigidity. Inspired by Rousseau and Ruskin, they took refuge in the idea that the spirit of man must also be altered in order to attain altruistic community.[7]

Kropotkin's discussion of utopianism touched on some of these themes, but the foil for his analysis was the critique of utopianism contained in the *Communist Manifesto* and Engels' *Socialism: Utopian and Scientific*, first published in French in 1880. The importance of these texts as the counterpoint for Kropotkin's discussion of utopianism is that they set out in a very clear way the divergence of socialist traditions from the early to the late nineteenth century. Engels had presented a sympathetic critique of the utopian socialists – Robert Owen, Charles Fourier and St Simon – but the contrast he drew between their work and Marx's became a litmus test to distinguish acolytes from dissenters.[8] George Pleckhanov's *Anarchism and Socialism* presented the crude thesis, fiercely criticised by anarchists, including Kropotkin. Kropotkin described Pleckhanov's influence in Russia as stultifying, a criticism that acknowledged the effectiveness of his propaganda.[9] A contributor to *The Torch* commented that in Pleckhanov's hands, utopianism was a convenient dumping-ground to rubbish all sorts of perceived deviations. The anarchists' refusal to accept the social-scientific laws that Engels credited Marx with discovering, were boxed as 'Metaphysical Dreamers, Idealists, Utopians and Bourgeois Socialists'.[10] As a way of sorting anarchists from non-anarchists the utopian epithet was even more reliable than the division over the question of political action that came to a head in the Second International 1896. The latter test was faulty as an indicator of doctrinal allegiance because it also captured anti-anarchist illegalists like Lenin and non-anarchist anti-parliamentarians like William Morris. In any event, Kropotkin told the veteran Bakuninist James Guillaume that utopianism was a distinction that he and his comrade Varlaam Cherkesov were keen to contest in order to counter the fatalism that social democratic doctrines encouraged.[11] Seizing on Engels' account of socialist history, Cherkesov agreed that there had been a historical shift in the development of socialism between the early century and the 1880s. However, departing from Engels, Cherkesov denied that it marked an intellectual progression and instead compared it to the co-optation of the radical Reformation by Luther and the theologians:

> Formulated and spread as a conception of the solidarity of human life, a life organised by society (hence the term Socialism) and not by the State, Socialism was, among the English and French really Socialist and not 'Social' Democratic. According to Robert Owen, St. Simon, Louis Blanc, Proudhon and the rest, he who said the word 'Socialism' thereby repudiated all idea of classes; for it was impossible to conceive of one Socialism as bourgeois or aristocratic and another as democratic ... toward 1840, Socialism began to spread in Germany. The faith of the universities

was entirely Hegelian and reactionary ... One section of German youth, imbued with reactionary philosophy ... declared themselves revolutionaries with the State and by the State. Marx, Engels and Lassalle were amongst them.[12]

Kropotkin also aligned anarchism with the utopian socialism of the early part of the century but, unlike Cherkesov, he excluded Proudhon from the category and treated him as the first anarchist. In *Freedom*, Kropotkin identified Robert Owen as the voice of working-class radicalism, placed Owen in direct relation to William Godwin and argued that anarchist communism was the heir to this tradition.[13] In *Modern Science and Anarchism*, he filled out this history of indigenous British socialism but this time established the connection to anarchism by revealing the resemblance between Proudhonian mutualism and the cooperative principles of William Thompson, John Gray and J. F. Bray – all Owenites. In America he tracked the history of Owen's utopianism to Josiah Warren's Time Store.[14]

Matthew Adams argues that Charles Fourier was Kropotkin's favourite utopian socialist.[15] The attraction was perhaps explained by the influence of Proudhon, who was similarly fascinated by Fourier and had printed most of his works as an apprentice. Either way, Adams's contention is borne out by the remarks he makes in his *Memoirs*. Following the footprints of the three bearers of the utopian tradition appointed by Marx and Engels, Kropotkin tracked St Simon to social democracy and, perhaps anticipating Bookchin, Owenism to English and American 'trades-unionism, co-operation, and the so-called municipal socialism ... hostile to social democratic State socialism'.[16] Fourier's path led to anarchism. Together with Owen, Kropotkin argued, Fourier had bequeathed an idea of 'free organically developing society, in opposition to the pyramidal ideals which had been copied from the Roman Empire or from the Roman Church'.[17] Of all the utopians, Fourier embraced an idea of organisation that Kropotkin characterised as anarchistic: ' "Take pebbles," ', said Fourier, ' "put them into a box and shake them, and they will arrange themselves in a mosaic that you could never get by entrusting to anyone the work of arranging them harmoniously." '[18]

Kropotkin's fondness for Fourier's ideas was matched by queasiness about his practical proposals.[19] Fourier had proposed the organisation of communities, the phalansteries, as havens for socialism within existing society. Kropotkin disliked this idea of escape – and although he exercised considerable sway on the growth of the British of communal movement,[20] giving sympathetic advice to would-be community-builders, he put his weight behind more ambitious transformative proposals.[21] Kropotkin also rejected what he described as the monastic, barrack-room regimentation of utopian schemas, including Fourier's libertarian 'phalanx'. He was also suspicious of models fashioned on ideals of brotherhood or fellowship. It was a mistake, he argued, 'to manage the community after the model of a family'.[22] Kropotkin was attracted to Fourier's idea of harmony, but purely as a dynamic principle. Taking his lead from modern science – chemistry, physics and astronomy – he treated the idea as a process of adjustment,[23] which succeeded on the condition 'of being continually modified'.[24] In the entry for anarchism published in the *Encyclopaedia Britannica* in 1905, Kropotkin accordingly distinguished between the state, as a body in which harmony was achieved by the forcible restraint of complex, vibrant social movements, and society, as a condition where harmony reigned as 'an ever-changing adjustment and readjustment of equilibrium between the multitudes of forces and influences'.[25]

Kropotkin's critical stance towards Fourier and the utopians captured his general ambivalence about the concept of utopia. Like Marx and Engels, Kropotkin was keen to distinguish science from utopia and assert anarchism's scientific credentials. In a curious echo of Marx's refusal to write 'recipes for the ... cookshops of the future',[26] Kropotkin argued that Bakunin's anarchism contained no 'ready-made recipes for political-cooking'.[27] But because of the way in which he understood science, Kropotkin was able openly to invest anarchism with a utopian dimension, in a way that Marx and Engels were unable to do. Strictly speaking, he argued, 'the word "Utopia"' should be applied to 'the idea of something that *cannot* be realised'.[28] Yet ideas that were deemed impossible were too often those that challenged the status quo. For example, it was the 'Utopists' who argued for the abolition of serfdom in Russia and slavery in the American South; and when they won the battle, albeit partially, they 'proved that *they* were the really practical people'.[29] Contrary to his seeming disparagement of utopianism, Kropotkin's view was that it was not only possible to imagine alternatives to social reality, but that it was necessary to do so. He endorsed Edward Bellamy's utopian novel, *Looking Backward*, for doing just that. Kropotkin disputed Bellamy's 'authoritarian organisation of production' and argued that his earlier book *Equality*, which he described as Proudhonian, 'was superior to his Utopia'. Nevertheless, Bellamy had exploded dominant convictions about the permanence of existing social relations. His imaginative work showed that socialism 'is not impossible and that the obstacles are neither technical difficulties nor the individual tendencies of man, simply inertia, stupidity, indolence and the slavishness of thought'.[30]

Probing the relationship between anarchism and utopia, Kropotkin found the real difference between the two in the method each used to question reality. Utopians worked through abstraction. Looking at the development of utopian thinking in France, he noted that the utopias of the seventeenth and early eighteenth centuries 'were based on a faith in the power of Reason, and on the faith that morality is the inherent property of human nature'.[31] Here, Kropotkin argued, the term ' "Utopia" ought to be limited to those conceptions only which are based on merely theoretical reasonings as to what is *desirable* from the writer's point of view'.[32] The Jacobins were utopians in this sense: as the representatives of the middle classes who dreamed of appropriating the powers of kings, they republicanised an abstract idea of right. Like some modern sociologists, Kropotkin remarked, utopians of this stripe start 'from a few principles' and develop them 'to their necessary consequences, like a geometrical conclusion from a few axioms'.[33] In fact, anyone who believed that it was possible to order society according to a favoured principle was a utopian in this pejorative sense. 'All the science of government, imagined by those who govern' was utopian. The outcomes of these fancies were not pretty. Kropotkin listed 'the Catholic Empire of the Popes, the Napoleonic Empire, [and]the Messianism of Mackiewicz'.[34] As utopias they fell into the category of a 'lovely Christmas dream'.[35] In contrast, anarchy was beautiful, but it was constructed through resistance and not based on an abstraction.

Anarchy and Utopia

In 1873, Kropotkin answered affirmatively the question he put to the Russian movement: 'must we occupy ourselves with an examination of the ideal of a future system?' The exercise encouraged activists to express their hopes, reflect on their persistent prejudices and challenge their 'mental timidity'.[36] Forty years later, reflecting on the process by which destructive passions may be transformed into constructive possibilities, Kropotkin posed the following question: '*Which social forms best guarantee in such and such society, and in humanity at large, the greatest sum of happiness, and therefore the greatest sum of vitality?*'[37] His idea, which extrapolated from the Paris Commune, was one where 'the consumption of commodities, their exchange and their production' was 'communalised' according to the idea of free federation, resulting in the abandonment of central and municipal government.[38]

As Ya'acov Oved argues, the guiding principle of Kropotkin's future planning was 'well-being for all'.[39] In showing how this may be secured, his aims were ambitious but not extravagant: to 'leave nobody without food, shelter and clothing, is the first and imperative duty of each popular movement inspired by Socialist ideas'.[40] This goal led him to make a number of practical proposals about work, education and production. In *Fields, Factories and Workshops*, he called for the abolition of the division of labour, referring both to the 'monotonous and wearisome'[41] piece work it implied and the numerous pernicious sub-divisions that production for profit entailed: production from consumption; 'brain work' from manual labour; and agricultural from industrial labour.[42] In order to enable individuals to re-master artisan crafts that could be practised in small workshops and to design, manufacture and operate machinery, Kropotkin also called for the introduction of scientific education. Kropotkin had included universal access to 'theoretical education' as a plank of his 1873 programme. He remained a keen advocate of education reform thereafter, putting his weight behind Francisco Ferrer's Modern School Movement[43] and lending his support to Louise Michel's London International School. Every human being, he argued, 'without distinction of birth, ought to receive such an education as would enable him, or her, to combine a thorough knowledge of science with a thorough knowledge of handicraft'. Individuals may choose to specialise, but 'general education must be given' in both areas.[44] Kropotkin referred to 'éducation intégrale', an idea pioneered by Fourier and taken up by Bakunin and Paul Robin, with whom Kropotkin had corresponded in the 1870s.[45] In Kropotkin's formulation, integral education meant 'a new exposition of all sciences', the 'teaching of all sciences, from the most abstract to those of sociology, the economic, the physiological psychology of the individual and crowds' and 'teaching which, by the practice of the hand, on wood, stone, metal, will speak to the brain and help to develop it'. Everyone would learn *the basis of every trade as well as of every machine*, by labouring ... at the work-bench, with the vice, in shaping raw material, in oneself making the fundamental parts of everything, as well of simple machines'. Each would also become familiar with the 'apparatus for the transmission of power, to which all machines are reduced'.[46] Dubbing the European school model as a 'small prison for the little ones',[47] Kropotkin not only called for a system of education that mixed practical and theoretical training, but also education through play, independent research and problem-based learning.

Kropotkin's proposals were designed to transform education by reversing the polarity that capitalism forced between work and school. Rightly understood, education was a springboard that enabled individuals to find out about the world and their own propensities, not a vehicle to support the state's demands to compete in the global economy. However, Kropotkin did not imagine the dissolution of the boundaries between education and work through pleasure, as Fourier had done in his schemes for attractive labour. He also stopped short of suggesting the transformation of labour through art, as Morris advocated. Kropotkin's general rule was that any work 'necessitated by the conditions of life can, and in time will, be accompanied by pleasure'.[48] This meant that work that served no social purpose and was imposed only for work's sake would be abandoned. Picking oakum was the best example of labour that 'nobody needs', but there were plenty of other tasks – usually those tailored to the satisfaction of the demands of the idle rich – that were also unnecessary.[49] Kropotkin's concern to reduce the time that women devoted 'uselessly' to childcare and housework raises a host of issues that feminists have since debated: for Kropotkin it pointed to the communalisation of labour and the transformation of social life that was not only labour-saving, but also convivial. Kropotkin fully expected that the nature of work would change as a result of the re-balancing of economies towards local production.

Anticipating the use of technology to support 'agreeable work' he imagined a 'revival of art' along the lines proposed by 'Ruskin and his school': changing work practices changed environments.[50] In *The State: Its Historical Role* he linked ancient Greek art, the brilliance of the Renaissance and the beautiful crafting of everyday objects directly to unhurried, leisured labour.[51] Following this model, Kropotkin assumed that integrated labour would similarly enable workers to do what they desired and that the work they chose to do would suit their particular inclinations: women would no longer be 'the slaves of the community'. Everyone would find work interesting because it would be varied. And it would not be 'wearisome' because it would be off-set by copious leisure time and because older workers – those more than forty years of age – would probably cease performing any manual tasks. Betraying his own love of learning, Kropotkin elevated education as a necessary and progressive stage in childhood development and blurred the boundaries between education and labour by treating work as a field for continuing education. When he thought about leisure, he estimated that 'one half of the working day would remain to everyone for the pursuit of art, science, or any hobby that he or she might prefer'.[52]

Kropotkin considered changes in production as a critic of the laws of political economy. His aim was to direct discussion away from the labour theory of value, the Ricardian 'article of faith' that 'says to us: "In an absolutely open market the value of goods is measured by the quantity of work socially necessary to produce those goods."'[53] Kropotkin had Marx in his sights when he made this remark and subsequently criticised Marx's development of the law on the grounds that it legitimised the introduction of labour hierarchies in socialism.[54] Yet his attack was more far-reaching and extended to Proudhon and indeed all those who had adopted it, as well as his foremost political adversary.[55]

In different ways both Proudhon and Marx had appropriated a set of ideas about market exchange and a concept of value that took its meaning from a cultural context that had been shaped by the exploitative practices their analyses were designed to reveal. Seeking to uncover the contradictions in the laws formulated by classical economists was a waste of time because these were not laws at all.

Given that Proudhon only assumed the orthodoxy in order to show how its premises undercut the justification of individual property ownership that were said to derive from them, Kropotkin's charge was harsh.[56] Indeed, his bracketing of Proudhon with Marx made even less sense in the light of his adoption of Proudhon's arguments about the exploitation of collective property and his claim that the 'evils of the present economic system' extended from slavery or the '*forced* necessity of the worker to sell his labour power', not from 'its faculty to absorb surplus-value'.[57] Yet Kropotkin's main concern was to argue that the science of political economy had to be re-cast, just as he had recommended in the *Appeal to the Young*. His proposal that it should be framed as a 'physiology of society' directed towards the 'study of the ever-growing sum of *needs* of society and the means ... for satisfying them' was made in this spirit. While Proudhon's arguments supported Kropotkin's advocacy for communism, the mutualist schemes with which Proudhonism had become associated since his death detached issues of labour and exchange from the problems of capitalism and the state and so undermined this ambition, encouraging Kropotkin to disassociate himself from Proudhon's economics.[58]

Kropotkin devolved the determination of social needs to communal and regional units. His idea of an intentional community was 'whole city of, at least, 20,000 inhabitants',[59] although this may be broken down, as he believed it had been in the medieval city-states, into 'districts, streets, parishes and guilds'.[60] The size of regions was less easy to estimate. Some of Kropotkin's calculations were made using existing territorial boundaries. However, following the geographical contours of nationality, Kropotkin referred to the 'aggregation of individuals, large enough to dispose of a certain variety of natural resources' and resisted imposing regions on nations.[61] Importing this conception into *Fields, Factories and Workshops* he explained that

[e]ach nation is a compound aggregate of tastes and inclinations, of wants and resources, of capacities and inventive powers. The territory occupied by each nation is in its turn a most varied texture of soils

and climates, of hills and valleys, of slopes leading to a still greater variety of territories and races. Variety is the distinctive feature, both of the territory and its inhabitants; and that variety implies a variety of occupations.[62]

Whatever size the regional unit may be, Kropotkin also imagined that 'a large development of free groupings for the satisfaction of the higher artistic, scientific, and literary needs and hobbies' would be active within them and link them to multiple groups across the globe, supporting knowledge exchange and understanding of the world, just as he outlined in his pedagogy.[63] In *Mutual Aid*, Kropotkin drew attention to the growing number of international sports clubs, nature societies, scientific bodies, literary and artistic associations, educational alliances and religious and charitable unions to show how these might operate.[64]

As Rob Knowles argues, integration was Kropotkin's central principle of production.[65] His bold idea was to abandon the existing system of international division, which designated 'the whole of humanity into national workshops having each of them its own speciality'[66] and replace it with a scheme in which each region 'produces and consumes most of its own agricultural and manufactured produce'.[67] He did not imagine that trade would cease but, as Peter Ryley observes, argued for its limitation 'to the exchange of what really must be exchanged'.[68] Kropotkin understood the change as a step towards the abolition of capitalism, explaining trade specialisation as a utopian fantasy of English 'economists and political men' eager to exploit the 'marvellous inventions' of the late eighteenth century to their advantage.[69]

Fields, Factories and Workshops demonstrated the possibilities of integrated production in considerable detail. Kropotkin calculated how much land could be put to productive use and demonstrated how soils could be improved in order to increase yields. He highlighted the virtues and efficiency of the domestic or 'petty' trades and the opportunities that existed to develop small industry by mechanisation and electrification. After visiting the Channel Islands in 1890, 1896 and 1903,[70] Kropotkin became a keen advocate of market gardening, also practised with enormous success in France,[71] and the new techniques of glass-cultivation 'perfected' in Guernsey.[72] All this made possible the full integration of agricultural and industry, 'so as to bring the factory amidst the fields' and facilitate production '*for the producers themselves*'.[73]

Kropotkin's excitement about the possibility of integrated production was further fuelled by his analysis of existing economic trends. Contrary to the predictions made by social democrats that the concentration of capital would lead, through competition, to a decline in the number of capitalists, Kropotkin argued that the *'consecutive development of nations'*[74] towards industrial division had not reduced the number of 'petty trades'. These often operated precariously but their 'transformation … into great industries goes on with a slowness which cannot fail to astonish even those who are convinced of its necessity'.[75] Cherkesov took up a similar position, pushing the economic analysis. In place of Marx's theory of concentration, Cherkesov provided a thesis of capital's democratisation: it was this process that had enabled financiers to amass vast wealth while creating a thriving small business class, neither reducing the number of capitalists nor the rate of profit. Workers were kept in poverty and finance capital was indeed concentrated in the hands of an elite, but the success of the capitalist system was built on the elite's ability to spread some of the benefits of exploitation through shareholding and investment. 'If a financial company is not a Panama' Cherkesov argued with a nod to corrupt speculative deals, 'the participants, instead of being expropriated, are enriched'.[76]

Kropotkin's sketch of integrated production was well received, finding an audience with anti-industrialist agrarians and those worried about food security, as well as with revolutionary socialists of Kropotkin's stripe.[77] Even while casting aspersions on Kropotkin's claims to have shown that needs could be met, Charles Vickery Drysdale, a founder member of the Men's League for Women's Suffrage, admitted that his 'idea of "integration" as opposed to the extreme division of labour, is sound in that it tends to develop complete, self-reliant human beings instead of uninterested automaton'.[78] For Kropotkin the special significance of the integration of production was that it provided a single solution to the two most pressing problems to emerge from his critique of the state: the land question and the 'most fatal error' of the ancient and medieval city-states, namely, the social exclusivity that extended from the 'neglect of agriculture'.[79]

Yet shifting the ground of political economy forced Kropotkin to confront a key theoretical challenge: the problem of scarcity that Thomas Malthus had defined and that Drysdale, speaking as president of the Malthusian League, pressed. The argument that unchecked population increase would always outstrip the growth of resources ran like a persistent sore through Kropotkin's writings, as it had earlier been a bugbear for Godwin and Proudhon.[80] Kropotkin's rejection of Malthus became a central tenet of the theory of mutual aid and the focus of his critique of T. H. Huxley. In Huxley's socio-biological rendering of Darwin's work, the overpopulation thesis explained the idea of individual competition and inter-species struggle which Kropotkin contested. Eventually, in order to reduce the dependence of Darwin's biological theory of natural selection on the idea of chance variation, also predicated on individual competition arising from scarcity, Kropotkin re-cast Darwin as a professed but closet Lamarckian.[81] In his economics, he treated Malthus's supposed law of political economy as a cloak for the perpetuation of injustice. And in response to Malthusian critiques such as Drysdale's, which suggested that the provision of needs was always conditional on the reduction of population growth-rates, Kropotkin explained scarcity just as he had explained Russian famines: both were avoidable results of slavery.

By Kropotkin's estimations, Malthusians wrongly posited their law on an already faulty set of economic propositions. Their conclusions were skewed by their failure to take account of the manufactured shortages of foodstuffs designed to keep demand and prices high, the waste of natural resources and the under-utilisation of labour. In his Russian manifesto Kropotkin calculated that each worker 'now supports on the average (in Germany and France) three people besides himself (in France almost four people) of whom only one is a member of the worker's family, whereas the other two (almost three in France) are parasites'.[82] Where production was geared to profit, moreover, technological innovations were not turned to good use. Fortunes were made by flooding markets across the world with cheaply produced manufactured goods, churned out by domestic labourers who were paid at subsistence and consequently unable to afford them. Because nations refused to remain tributaries of Britain and instead replicated the model of divided labour and production that it had initiated, the world was actually awash with unnecessary goods but still unable to meet basic needs. Capitalist markets were responsive to profit, not the demands of the poor. Kropotkin sometimes pointed to the wasteful luxuries produced for the rich to make the point,[83] but as the twentieth century progressed, he looked increasingly to the operation of the arms markets and the structural constraints on production imposed by the lending powers of the international banks.[84] In 1919 he realised that capitalism had not in fact provided for a transition to socialism, such that needs could be met, leaving aside the possibility of leisure. The post-revolutionary famine was stark evidence of chronic under-production in Russia.[85] Nevertheless, Kropotkin not only rejected Malthus, he disputed neo-Malthusian proposals for birth control, so great was his loathing for the market and his conviction about its distorting effects. The solution to scarcity, he insisted, was not the restriction of population growth but intensive cultivation, the expansion of manufacturing and decentralised, integrated production. In turn, this necessitated communism.

Anarchism with Adjectives

In the 1880s, Spanish anarchists worried about the sectional fragmentation of anarchism. Concerned to avoid the imposition of pre-determined plans in revolutionary situations they coined the phrase 'anarchism without adjectives' to describe a tolerant, open-ended approach to revolutionary practice.[86] Kropotkin was sympathetic to this approach, insofar as it referred specifically to the collectivism of Spanish anarchists and the possibility of taking local decisions about the practices of production and land distribution, which may be individual or collective.[87] This was the view that he associated with Bakunin, too, and he commended Bakunin for refusing to determine 'in advance what form of distribution the producers should adopt in their different groups'.[88] Kropotkin's conviction that rural distress would spark a mass movement of direct expropriation also encouraged him to think that these questions would be resolved as matters of fact or as 'practical' questions, not according to preordained ideals.[89] At the same time, Kropotkin was also steadfastly communist and keen to demonstrate the flaws of rival schemes of ownership.

Kropotkin argued for communism at the 1880 Congress of the Jura Federation, alongside Reclus and Carlo Cafiero. He differentiated his ideal from earlier monastic, mystical and authoritarian forms that took their lead from Jacobinism and that subordinated individual to community interests. Kropotkin's concern was to distance communists from collectivists who, he argued, accepted the principle of individual ownership and justified more or less restrictive systems of property alongside nationalisation. In order to avoid confusion between this collectivist idea and the collectivism that anarchists had once embraced to signal their rejection of authoritarian communist traditions, Kropotkin recommended the re-adoption of the communist label.[90] In *Modern Science and Anarchism*, Kropotkin added some historical detail to this baffling picture and distinguished anarchist communism from authoritarian communism, mutualism, collectivism and Marxism. Authoritarian communism was the egalitarian tradition that advocated dictatorship and terrorism. Mutualism was a system that combined the rejection of the state with a principle of exchange that enabled individuals to claim ownership in the things they produced.[91] Collectivism or 'state capitalism', as Kropotkin preferred,[92] combined the mutualist idea of individual remuneration for work with a collective principle of ownership, vesting the control of large industry and public services in the state. Marxism or 'scientific socialism' combined collectivism with authoritarianism.[93] Anarchist communism was anti-statist, as Proudhon's mutualism had been, and, therefore, anti-authoritarian and anti-collectivist. But it also rejected the idea of labour remuneration, which Proudhon did not.

This rendition of socialist history enabled Kropotkin to detach Proudhon's arguments for common ownership and against private accumulation, which he had espoused in the Chaikovskist manifesto of 1873,[94] from the individualism of Benjamin Tucker with which Proudhonist mutualism was associated, and that Kropotkin rejected.[95] Moreover, it had the virtue of divorcing Bakunin, who had called himself a collectivist, from Marx.

In his defence of anarchist communism Kropotkin pitted the principle of distribution according to need against the alternative: distribution according to work. This move sorted the four currents within socialism into two bundles: authoritarianism, mutualism and collectivism fell into the collectivist category leaving anarchist communism to define communism. However, Kropotkin's chief concern was to link collectivism with the politics of social democracy and individualism, turning the social democratic accusation that anarchism was individualist on its head. This strategy created enormous resentment in social democratic circles. *Justice* flatly denied the accusation of collectivism and suggested that Kropotkin knew 'as much about economics ... as a monkey knows about driving a motor car'. He was as 'wayward as a boy and as illogical as a woman'.[96] Undeterred, Kropotkin pressed the point against them and argued that neither collectivists nor individualists were able to accept the distinctive feature of communism, namely, the abolition of the wages system because both proposed schemes which rewarded individuals for their time or effort. In whatever ways these operated, they were wage systems and Kropotkin argued that they negated socialism by inscribing it with a structure of social relations that negated the communist principle of need.[97]

Kropotkin identified a series of flaws in wage systems. A serious practical problem was the 'difficulty of estimating the *market* value, or the *selling* values, of a product' and of determining whether average times or actual times would be used to calculate the effort of production.[98] But this pointed to a more serious theoretical issue. Proudhon had argued that the value of individual labour was in fact impossible to measure, not only because a large proportion of work was organised collaboratively but also because labour had a social dimension. Each worker depended on the labour of others: for the development of their skills, the production of their tools and availability of their materials and the construction of their workplaces. Proudhon concluded that individual property was unjust because it enabled those who claimed the right of ownership to appropriate the social product of labour.[99] Kropotkin similarly argued that labour was typically collaborative[100] and that it was an inherently social activity, though he expressed the idea differently to Proudhon:

the duration of time given to any work does not give the measure of social utility of the work accomplished, and the theories of value that economists have endeavoured to base, from Adam Smith to Marx, only on the cost of production, valued in labor time, have not solved the question of value. As soon as there is exchange, the value of an article becomes a complex quantity, and depends also on the degree of satisfaction which it brings to the needs – not of the individual, as certain economist stated formerly, but of the whole of society, taken in its entirety. Value is a *social* fact.[101]

Kropotkin acknowledged that the tensions in the wages system gave rise to different problems in collectivism and individualism. With an eye to securing the common good through the state, collectivist schemes had a special degenerative tendency. Cafiero had made the point in 1880 when he argued that the possibility of securing individual advantage set socialism on a slippery slope. 'It would require just one more step to be taken for counter-revolutionaries to introduce rights of inheritance' and to countenance property transfers.[102] Kropotkin argued even more strongly that collectivists typically approved the introduction of wage scales, discriminating between '*qualified* or professional work and *simple* work'.[103] Individualists confronted a different problem because they rejected the state and left the determination of work and the principles of exchange to individuals. While this position seemed to promise effective self-regulation, Kropotkin accused Tucker of short-sighted naivety. Tucker argued that the rights of each individual would be limited by the equal rights of others. Yet in conferring the right, he also admitted the necessity of its enforcement and thus remained inured in statist practices.[104] 'He who intends to retain for himself the monopoly of any piece of land or property; or any other portion of social wealth, *will be bound to look for some authority* which could guarantee to him possession.'[105] Landauer agreed: 'the individualist Tucker is insofar a state socialist as he is totally dependent on the state'.[106]

In different ways, both collectivist and individualist schemes reinstated the coercive social relations that prevailed in capitalist states. As Cafiero argued: individual remuneration was 'the root of more or less sizable accumulation of wealth, according to the greater or lesser merits, or rather, greater or lesser shrewdness of the individual'.[107] Kropotkin similarly described the coercion integral to wage work as the mainspring of capitalist oppression. Capital's 'faculty of absorbing surplus-value' was a result of the accumulation that was explained by 'the forced position the worker is placed to sell his labor-power'. Capitalism impoverished workers, but it secured their enslavement through dependency: ' "Speak not of liberty – poverty is slavery," ' Kropotkin declared.[108] For as long as the worker 'continues to be paid in wages he necessarily will remain the slave or the subordinate of the one to whom he is forced to sell his labour-force – be the buyer a private individual or the State'.[109] In return for wages

> the worker sells himself to the one who undertakes to give him work; he renounces the benefits his labour might bring him ... he renounces his right to make his opinion heard on the utility of what he is about to produce and on the way of producing it.[110]

In contrast, communism ensured that individual needs would be met and that workers were able to determine the nature and extent of their work without compulsion. Not only was the system attractive, but because work was undertaken freely, it was also free. This last claim was fiercely contested in anarchist circles, and while social democrats were content to wrangle about the applicability of Kropotkin's critique to their politics, individualists disputed the libertarian credentials of anarchist communism.

Communism, Individualism and Freedom

The individualist critique of anarchist communism had a number of dimensions. The basic complaint fastened on the issue of communism and revolutionary violence. Henry Seymour, Kropotkin's one-time collaborator in *Freedom*, condemned anarchist communism on these grounds.[111] Yet individualists were no more uniform in their attitudes to violence than communists. Not all individualists championed 'Christian non-resistance', Victor Yarros protested, and some, including him, interpreted the principle of self-defence to mean 'against tyrants all means are justifiable'.[112]

Benjamin Tucker's considered critique of anarchist communism extended from a defence of the principle of individual sovereignty and a version of the labour theory of value, influenced both by Stirner and Proudhon. As Wendy McElroy explains, Tucker elided sovereignty with self-ownership, treating liberty as the idea that 'every human being, simply by being human, has an inalienable moral jurisdiction over his or her own body and over what he or she produces'. He interpreted the labour theory to mean that 'all wealth belongs unquestionably to the laborer'.[113] Communism was illiberal, on this view, because it sought to realise an abstract 'religious' ideal of social relations and force individuals to comply with it, denying them of their just deserts, too. Tucker's friend, the Stirnerite John Henry Mackay, argued that communism was a form of fanaticism. In his fictionalised account of the Victorian London anarchist scene he contrasted the sober, reasoned anarchism of Conrad

Auban to the wild, impassioned Bakuninism of Otto Trupp. As a communist, Mackay remarks, Trupp espoused a doctrine that Auban recognised as a utopian fantasy:

> [H]is dreams reared the structure of the future of humanity: they built it high, broad, and beautiful … Everybody would be contented; all hopes fulfilled, all desires satisfied. Labor and exchange would be voluntary; nothing henceforth to determine their limits, not even their value. The earth belongs to all equally. Each has a right to it as he has a right to be a human being. And he reared the proud structure of his thoughts – reared it to the heavens! …
>
> This creed of Communism, which is as old as the religions that have made the earth not a heaven, but a hell, he called Anarchism.[114]

Kropotkin's answer to this accusation was to distinguish self-ownership from the principle of sovereignty and to defend the latter as an anarchist principle of freedom, realisable only in communism.

Kropotkin acknowledged that sovereignty was commonly understood as a core concept of state, linked to the power to legislate. However, in his account of the rise of the European state, he highlighted the duality of the concept and the ways in which it had become de-contested in the period since the European city-state's decline. In *Modern Science and Anarchism* he re-phrased the dialogue that he had invented in the *Paroles d'un Révolté* to illustrate the process of the theoretical transformation: ' "Love your neighbour," said Christianity … but it hastened to add by the mouth of the Apostle Paul: "Slaves obey your masters," and "No authority but from God's will" – thus legitimising and deifying the divisions between masters and slaves.'[115]

Detaching sovereignty from the state, Kropotkin re-cast it as a principle of freedom that encapsulated the idea of independent judgement. Extending the anarchist tradition beyond its European 'invention' in the 1870s, Kropotkin selected the stoic, Zeno of Crete, as an 'exponent of anarchist philosophy' because he rejected the state in favour of free communes and 'proclaimed the sovereignty of the moral law of the individual'.[116] In *The State: Its Historic Role* he similarly described the members of the city-states as people of 'free initiative, free agreement', who 'saw in the individual the starting point of all society'. The dissenting movements that drove the radical reformation took as their motto: 'the conscience of each individual being thus his only law'. These religious men did not accept the authority of the Bible but maintained 'the only obligatory rule of conduct is the one that each individual finds for *himself*'.[117]

Kropotkin's idea of harmony led him to find the analogy for freedom in free movement. Citing the work of the chemist D. I. Mendeleev, whose student Kropotkin had been, he noted that 'all bodies, simple or compound, borrow their individualities from the characters of the movements which the atoms perform within the molecules'.[118] In political theory, modern science supported Fourier's insight: freedom was a condition that 'results from the disorderly and incoherent movements of numberless hosts of matter, each of which goes its own way and all of which hold each other in equilibrium'.[119] Analysing freedom as movement, Kropotkin identified the paradigm for unfreedom in imprisonment. This view appeared to chime with Hobbes' contention that 'whatsoever is so tied or environed as it cannot move ... hath not liberty to go further ... living creatures whilst they are imprisoned or restrained with walls or chains ... are not at liberty to move'.[120] However, perhaps drawing on his prison experiences, Kropotkin amended Hobbes's idea.

Kropotkin understood the special privations of being kept in 'very small, very dark, and very damp' cells.[121] But he did not conclude that imprisonment collapsed into physical restraint; not all prisoners were restricted in this way. Exiles in Siberia and many forced labourers received similarly harsh treatment as those locked in cells. Their movements were tightly regulated and they were disallowed from returning to their home environments, but they frequently lived in colonies with their families and they were able to move about.[122] Whether or not Kropotkin's conception of freedom was influenced by his experiences, he identified the unfreedom of imprisonment with regimes of punishment not the prisons and the physical shackles on action that were their grotesque symptom. Imprisonment negatively affected the free 'disorderly movements' of individuals and ideas by ordering them in particular ways, not necessarily by immobilisation. Kropotkin measured the effects by looking at the psychological toll that prison took both on inmates and warders, and the social divisions it created between them.[123] He described the tangible impact by the narrowing of individuals' capacity to act and the sphere for action. 'In prisons as in monasteries, everything is done to kill a man's will. He generally has no choice between one of two acts.'[124] Each was turned into 'a docile tool in the hand of those who control him', incapable of acting on independent judgement. This, Kropotkin argued, was *the most terrible condemnation of the whole penal system based on the deprivation of individual liberty*.[125]

From apparently Hobbesian premises, Kropotkin came to contrary conclusions. Hobbes had argued that free movement resulted in chaos, instilling fear that prompted reason and enabled individuals to escape the violence of the state of nature by accepting terms for their restricted free movement and judgment. As Hobbes was inspired by geometry, Kropotkin theorised using geography: fear enslaved individuals by fixing the boundaries of legitimate free movement, undermining independent judgement and institutionalising violence as a means to contain and repress change. Freedom demanded the removal of the institutional constraints that perpetuated domination and inequality; but communism was only anarchist for as long as the codes that communities adopted remained open to challenge:

> [T]he individual would be *free*, in the sense that his freedom would not be limited any more by *fear*: by the fear of a social or a mystical punishment, or by obedience, either to other men reputed to be his superiors, or to mystical and metaphysical entities – which leads in both cases to intellectual servility (one of the greatest curses of mankind) and to the lowering of the moral level of man.[126]

Returning to his critics, Kropotkin understood the individualist anarchist idea of freedom as a spin on the Hobbesian conception. Tucker's notion was summed up in the phrase: 'mind every one your own business'.[127] Stirner's principle, described as 'the right to ... full development', was less obviously Hobbesian.[128] Kropotkin acknowledged that these conceptions were rooted in diverse philosophical traditions: unlike Tucker, Stirner was a Hegelian. Nevertheless, Kropotkin argued that both reduced liberty to a defence of rights and were similarly negative insofar as they required the 'full liberation of the individual from all social and moral bonds'.[129] For Kropotkin, this was nonsensical and contradictory since this right to non-interference either required a special body to enact protective laws, establish 'standards of punishment' and deal with transgressors, or it left individuals free to secure their rights by their own powers. Fastening on the negativity, Kropotkin described individualism as punitive, arguing that 'the policy of non-interference now so greatly favoured is a bad habit acquired since the State found it convenient to assume the duty of keeping order'.[130] Anarchists were people 'who demand absolute freedom, nothing but freedom, the whole of freedom'[131] but they championed liberty as a primary value knowing that it was, in fact, unachievable except as a measure of what was desirable. In real society 'man is *never free*'.[132] Kropotkin's conception of sovereignty assumed that the abstraction of the individual from the social order was a theoretical fiction that legitimised oppression. In contrast, Kropotkin proceeded on the basis that individuals were participant in a continuous collective process of ordering. Communism did not expect individuals to conform to a lofty religious ideal, as the Stirnerites feared. It was merely a principle of distribution that provided the best conditions for liberty by protecting social groups from the forces that militated towards the re-emergence of slavery. Kropotkin once remarked that 'liberty is as dear as bread'.[133] By the same token, the conquest of bread – providing well-being for all on the basis of need – enabled individuals to live freely in interdependence. Kropotkin's idea of freedom would never satisfy those who understood liberty as independence. And he acknowledged the difference between the two perspectives, as if to indicate that he understood their incommensurability. Believing that his conception of anarchy was more a-tuned to the aspirations of the subjugated than individualist doctrines, he anticipated that critics would object that the anarchy he imagined was fit only for angels. Kropotkin denied this and responded by outlining his evolutionary ethics.

The Nature of Evolution

Kropotkin's critique of T. H. Huxley's conception of the natural world in *Mutual Aid*, his extended analysis of natural selection and environmental adaptation in the years after its publication in 1902, and his last efforts show the naturalistic root of anarchist ethics all attest to the central place Darwin occupied in Kropotkin's thought. Like Proudhon, he was also interested in August Comte's sociology and he gave significant attention to Herbert Spencer liberalism, as Matthew Adams points out.[134] These interests in evolution coalesced around Darwin because of the way in which Kropotkin consciously merged the biological and cultural planes of the general theory of evolution.[135] In 1907 he argued, the 'old distinction between scientist and philosopher bids fair to become extinct ... each invades the other's realm; the scientist theorizes on origin and cause; the philosopher adopts scientific methods'. Kropotkin located his own work 'somewhere in the borderlands'[136] and argued that Darwin occupied a similar space. Realising that his work 'was not limited to biology only', Darwin recorded in his diary: 'My theory will lead to a new philosophy.'[137]

Darwin, it seemed, had thrown down a gauntlet, leaving others to flesh out the political implications of this philosophy. The prevailing cultural theories bridled natural selection to a theory of individual competition, painting an amoral picture of the world. Spencer's work was a leading example. Spencer accepted natural selection as the primary mechanism for biological evolution and leaned towards Lamarckianism to explain the transmission of character traits. This analysis legitimised the tailoring of social systems to competition such that individuals (people and nations) were able to benefit from the exploitation of their skills and talents, free either to ignore or behave charitably to lesser beings. Over time, the weak would be weeded out and the character traits evident in the fit would be transmitted to future generations.[138]

Kropotkin's Lamarckian reading of Darwin's biological thesis prioritised species cooperation over individual competition as the principal factor of evolution, setting the dichotomy between anarchic and statist systems that he had sketched in his social geography on a new scientific foundation. Much of the work that Kropotkin produced after the publication of *Mutual Aid* focused sharply on the science of biological transmission and appeared unrelated to this sociological project. Yet his attempt to downplay or even discredit natural selection and show that Darwin also leaned towards Lamarck was part of his argument that evolution should be re-set on an anarchist path. Kropotkin worked tirelessly to show that species fitness was linked to the inheritance of environmental adaptations in part to defend the scientific integrity of mutual aid as a factor of evolution but above all to contest neo-Darwinian theories of transmission that appeared to indicate that species development followed a mechanistic, predetermined course. August Weismann's widely celebrated germ-plasm theory was Kropotkin's principal target.[139] Kropotkin described it as Hegelian: Weismann wanted to do for biology what Marx had done for economics, he told Georges Herzig, his friend from the days of *Le Révolté*.[140] Lamarckianism was Kropotkin's preferred idea that species fitness should be assessed by the quality of the environments individuals helped to create. His discussion operated in two ways. On the one hand, he contested Spencer's conception of nature as red in tooth and claw, which Huxley also absorbed, to undermine the idea that nature was an anti-social condition, necessitating some kind of discipline, either worldly or divine, to secure cooperation. On the other, he presented an evolutionary account of ethics to reveal the movement of philosophy towards anarchist ethics.

Kropotkin identified the Social Darwinian thesis – encapsulated in Spencer's catchphrase 'the survival of the fittest' – with Hobbesian political theory and the idea that in nature 'man is a wolf to man'.[141] His rejection of this thesis weighed the claims of abstract political theory against anthropology. Instead of adjusting the characteristics that philosophers attributed to individuals in order to re-model their behaviours in the hypothetical state of nature, as Locke amended Hobbes, Kropotkin instead produced a mass of material to show how societies were in fact constructed. The evidence showed that humans exhibited the social and moral instincts that most non-human animals displayed. Kropotkin did not consider the social construction of these groups, but accepting the boundaries between them he treated the difference between humans and non-humans as one of degree, not essence.[142] Like non-humans, humans developed languages, enabling them to express social sentiments and articulate moral rules. Unlike non-humans, humans were also able to learn from non-humans, and those living in close proximity to non-humans mimicked their cooperative behaviours.[143]

Kropotkin's rejection of the Social Darwinian view did not suggest that nature was good. Kropotkin criticised Rousseau's 'idealization' of the noble savage just as he rejected Hobbes' picture of the war of all against all.[144] Moreover, while he treated sociability as a fact of nature, he highlighted the variety and complexity of social practices: there was no single condition that could be called natural. Invoking Darwin, Kropotkin described how humans developed divergent traditions, becoming increasingly divided from non-human societies and from other spatially and temporally located human groups. Individuals in all groups – human and non-human – adopted the same test to assess moral action, and this was a principle of social utility: what was good contributed to species preservation, what was bad militated against it.[145] However, there was no agreement on the substance of this rule within communities, let alone between them. Indeed, Kropotkin subscribed to the anthropology of Élisée's brother Elie Reclus, who argued that outsiders could not legitimately pass judgements on social behaviours they were not party to and could not fully comprehend. In *Primitive Folk*, which Kropotkin read, Reclus noted how the 'civilised are always repelled at first by the uncivilised', explaining this 'repugnance' as 'the outcome of ... ignorance' and prejudice 'unfavourable to savages'.[146] In *Mutual Aid*, Kropotkin sometimes let his own prejudices slip, sought explanations for behaviours he took to be unsavoury and assumed that readers would share his responses. Nevertheless, he avoided absolute judgements. Observing the mutual revulsion that Europeans and non-Europeans felt on encountering each other's traditions Kropotkin noted a pervasive and 'pronounced lack of mutual understanding ... between human societies in different stages of development'. It made as much sense to moralise about, say, infanticide among so-called savage peoples as it did to 'judge the "morality" of worker-bees when they kill drones in their hive'.[147]

Pulling the rug from under Spencer's Social Darwinian reading of nature explained the origins of moral instincts, but left the mechanisms for ethical change and the 'criterion for judging' alternative options unspecified.[148] This judgement required 'a higher moral ideal, capable of giving to civilised nations the inspiration required for the great task that lies before them'. Evolutionary ethics filled the space. Kropotkin explained: this 'new, realistic moral science' was 'a science free of superstition, religious dogmatism, and metaphysical mythology ... permeated at the same time with those higher feelings and brighter hopes which a thorough knowledge of man and his history can breathe into men's breasts.'[149]

Ethics was Kropotkin's fullest, if still incomplete, statement of this moral science. It traced a history of ideas from the rise of the Greek city-states to the twentieth century. The discussion ranged over philosophical and cultural movements – stoicism, Christianity, utilitarianism, the encyclopaedists, utopianism, German idealism and Anglo-Scottish enlightenment – and hovered over individuals: Plato, Epicurus, Hobbes, Kant, Hegel, Comte and Spencer were among the key writers examined. Kropotkin ordered ideas and movements in a number of series that explored the ways in which explanations of the origin of moral sentiments, their character and the drivers of ethical behaviour were outlined, reconfigured and refined. Kant stood in a chain defined by science and reason that extended back from Bacon and forward to Darwin. Bentham and Mill were part of a string examining the motivations for morality that stretched from Aristotle and Epicurus to Darwin and Spencer. Nietzsche was linked to the amoralism of the sophists, Mandeville and Stirner as well as to the ethical individualism of Godwin and Spencer. Kropotkin highlighted their insights and flaws to draw out some of the persistent themes: Epicureans and utilitarians jettisoned metaphysics to show that all action is directed towards happiness and inspired by egoism, but they failed to explain the forces that led individuals to renounce 'that which would undoubtedly give … pleasure'.[150] Christians introduced principles of equality and forgiveness, but relied on subordination to an invented deity to ensure compliance.[151] Kant 'asserted that we must lead a moral life because such is the demand of our reason' but was unable to 'find in man the source of respect for the moral law'.[152] Nietzsche voiced 'a passionate desire of *personal independence*' but was led wrongly 'to conclude that all morality must be thrown overboard'.[153]

The story of philosophy's evolution illustrated both the soaring ambition of human aspirations and its continual thwarting. Kropotkin explained the disappointment as a result of excessive abstraction and the failure of philosophers to properly ground their ideals in social practice. Finding the remedy for philosophy's failure in Darwinian evolution, he reaffirmed philosophy's ambition by arguing that the intersections and overlaps of various series outlined a 'universal law of organic evolution'. This had three 'consecutive steps': mutual aid, justice and morality.[154] Kropotkin credited Proudhon with cementing the second stage and establishing justice as 'the fundamental principle of all morality'.[155] Whereas previous philosophers had elevated the principle and remained blind to the incidence of slavery and social division, Proudhon had set the idea of justice against the reality of social injustice. By revealing the contradictions between the standard and the practice, Proudhon thereby established justice as a dynamic goal. Developing Proudhon's insights,

Kropotkin argued that the third step, morality, which he described as 'unstable' and 'the least imperative of the three', was a spontaneous reaction to injustice.[156]

Kropotkin described the prompts for justice and ethical development as principles of obligation, inverting conceptions in political theory to show why some individuals disobeyed, responding to contradictions even at the cost of their own interests. He was particularly inspired by the work of Jean-Marie Guyau. Guyau, Keith Ansell-Parson explains, treated obligation as 'a primitive, impersonal impulse ... prior to philosophical reasoning' and explicable in naturalistic terms.[157] He argued, Dario Padovan notes, that 'individual and social action were the result of a *moral fecundity* that existed in each individual, of a *surplus* of life-force that should be directed towards the Other'.[158] Adapting Guyau's idea, Kropotkin identified obligation with altruism. Altruism was sometimes wrongly conflated with egoism, although this described mere self-interest or the instinct for self-preservation, concepts Kropotkin used interchangeably. Because egoism necessarily operated in social settings, it bore 'the character of reciprocity'. Yet it was distinct from altruism that, properly understood, described self-sacrificing acts that were performed without expectation of 'compensation in return'.[159] Similarly, egoism was rooted in reason, whereas altruism sprang from passion. Moreover, as the 'unconsciously Anarchist thinker',[160] Guyau also argued, altruism was unconscious and wilful, rather than conscious and habitual. Altruism was other-regarding insofar as it impelled actions that compromised egoism, but self-regarding in that it enabled individuals to live in good faith. It appeared elevated and rare, yet Kropotkin found plenty of illustrative examples in everyday life: mothers who suffered for the sake of their children, men who preferred suicide to risking injury to loved ones by the transmission of illness or disease, strangers who jumped into rivers to save others from drowning. Kropotkin's friend, the artist G. F. Watts, sponsored a monument in London's Postman's Park to commemorate these ordinary acts of altruistic mutual aid.[161] However, Kropotkin returned to nihilism to reveal its revolutionary character.

Refusing to be bound by inherited moral codes, nihilists first applied utilitarian tests to re-construct morality: what caused pleasure was good, and what caused pain was bad. The language was Bentham and Mill's. However, in nihilism it was filtered through a Chernyshevskian lens.[162] Aware that Dostoevsky had satirised the image of the rational, utopian self-interested socialist that he found in Chernyshevsky's writing,[163] Kropotkin offered an interpretation that made room for passion. When they threw existing morality overboard, nihilists unleashed a critical energy that was felt in sympathy and compassion. Sofia Perovskaya exemplified nihilist vigour. Kropotkin argued that her plotting to kill the Tsar was inspired by a loathing for the distress she saw around her. Unable to tolerate the injustices perpetrated by regime, she was impelled by her sympathy for the suffering to make her passions count.[164] She was an individualist who defined her well-being in relation the pleasures and pains of others. Kropotkin dubbed this kind form of individualism 'perfect egoism' or, returning to Pisarev, 'thoughtful realism'.[165]

Kropotkin's Proudhonian conception of justice implied that there was no end to ethical development. In 1873 he argued that to 'define a system in which there is absolutely no room for any injustice' was impossible and 'fruitless'. With the 'abolishment of some injustices that exist now even the conception of justice, of good and evil, of the good and the bad, of the useful and harmful, will be modified'.[166] His notion of morality reinforced this conclusion. Even the justice that anarchist communism established was open to wilful disobedience. Admittedly, Kropotkin did not consider himself 'a great negator' in the vein of modern insurrectionary anarchists.[167] Like Proudhon and Bakunin he coupled destruction with construction. Nevertheless, Kropotkin's maxim 'in building we shall demolish'[168] captured a similar spirit. He acknowledged that, as cooperation in communism fostered new traditions and customary practices, it was also likely to breed 'fear of change, and inertia of thought'.[169] In any social context, habitual practice was a break on change but no social system was capable of eradicating the tensions at the heart of social life. Human beings simply were not angels. Returning to the history of the city-states and their historical degeneration, Kropotkin distinguished between battles 'that kill' and those that 'launch humanity forward'.[170] War fell into the first category. It had never been a 'normal condition of life' and it had emerged with militarisation and priestly rule.[171] Yet its antonym was not peace. The *variety, conflict, even* that characterised all social development was the mainstay of social change. It was manifest in the assortment of mutual-aid societies that blossomed under the radar of the state, poised to form the backbone of the international networks of anarchy, and evident in each one of us. Kropotkin identified associations for 'exploitation, resistance to exploitation, amusement, serious work, gratification and self-denial' – and saw these as reflections of all that 'makes up the life of an active and thinking being'.[172] Kropotkin's promotion of arbitration as a process of conflict-resolution consistent with individual sovereignty and free agreement was another explicit acknowledgement of the tensions inherent in social living and the difficulty of forging relationships unmediated by self-appointed authorities.

In theory, altruism functioned as a form of eternal vigilance against social degeneration. And if, in practice, individualists still worried that Kropotkin's plans would result in the subordination of egos to the religious creed of communism, as John Henry McKay put it, his response was that communism was itself dependent on the empirical confirmation of his thesis. Without wilful altruistic disobedience, there could be no communism. Kropotkin observed that Proudhon had ascribed 'great importance to idealization' in social struggles. The 'development of *culture*' – material conditions – and 'of *civilization*' – intellectual conditions – depended on 'ideals' assuming 'the ascendancy over petty daily cares, when the discrepancy between the law ... and actual life ... acquires the proportions of a glaring, unbearable contradiction'.[173] Evolutionary ethics promoted this view and was itself a contribution to social transformation. If Kropotkin was wrong about altruism and his own idealisation proved unpersuasive, he was also mistaken about the prospects for communist revolution. In this case, the tendency of evolution, conditioned by the state, was towards death.[174]

The Revolution Will Not Be Historicised

'Liberty or death!' entered the lexicon of revolutionary action during the American War of Independence. Usually invoked as an exulting, rallying cry, it also captured the horrendous prospect of revolutionary collapse that socialists began to contemplate in the early twentieth century. Kropotkin's assessment of the counter-veiling pressures on evolutionary development posed the choice between anarchy and the state in these stark terms and he was indeed circumspect about the prospects for liberty. His formulation, mutual aid or death, more closely resembled Rosa Luxemburg's socialism or barbarism than the romantic maxim of the American rebels. Admittedly, Kropotkin did not share her good estimation of the policies that European social democratic parties had pursued in the period following the defeat of the Commune. Yet, just as she re-evaluated the vigour of European socialism towards the outbreak of the 1914–18 war, Kropotkin harboured similar doubts about the popularity of anarchist doctrines and the likely kindling of a pan-European Commune movement.[1]

Unlike the eighteenth-century patriots, Kropotkin understood revolution as a process, not a marshalling of militias, as their call presupposed. At the start of his exile in France, when he believed that Europe stood on the brink of revolution, Kropotkin argued that the crisis sparked by the land question presented an opportunity for transformation. The ensuing struggle was likely to be protracted and shaped equally by the potential of popular movements to resist new forms of revolutionary domination as by their power to liberate themselves from the forms of enslavement that had arisen in the aftermath of the English, America and French revolutions in the seventeenth and eighteenth centuries.

Kropotkin's writings on revolution can be read as contributions to this struggle. His commentaries on social transformation set out insurrectionary and organisational principles for anarchists. He demonstrated how small groups of activists could harness the strength of mass movements and showed how those movements might be sustained in times of crisis, and insulated against elite usurpation of their power.

Kropotkin continually reviewed the prospects for revolution in the latter decades of the nineteenth century and in the early years of the twentieth. His judgement broadly balanced the rise of militant labour activism in the 1890s, on the one hand, against the influence of social democracy, the fracturing of the Second International and the pull of jingoistic dogmas on the other. While Kropotkin remained committed to revolutionary transformation, he became increasingly concerned that constitutionally bound struggles for reform through the achievement of electoral power would divert the urban proletariat from transformative action, locking it into the institutional logic of inter-state competition and cutting it adrift from the rural struggle. The apparent dovetailing of German social democratic doctrines about the civilising power of capitalism with the imperialist agendas of European states exacerbated Kropotkin's fears that the parliamentary politics of the Second International was not just theoretically muddled and strategically wrongheaded but fundamentally counter-revolutionary.

As the nineteenth century progressed, Kropotkin talked more openly about the possibility of a European war. His commentaries on war indicated a pronounced bias against Germany, consistent with his view that the demise of the Commune in 1871 had marked a victory for German reaction. Nevertheless, his decision in 1914 to support the Entente's campaign appeared to fly in the face of his principled rejection of capitalism and the state and it isolated himself from most of his comrades, notably Malatesta. Their bitter dispute illuminated a tension between Kropotkin's conception of solidarity, which was based on the defence of nationality, and Malatesta's idea that called for the transcendence of national differences through class-based resistance to capitalism and the state. Moreover, unlike Malatesta, who argued that there was nothing to choose between a German or French victory, Kropotkin thought that the results were likely to be significant: the victory of Germany meant the extension of the militarised Prussian model of government. This outcome would rebound on the political culture of republican France and liberal England, even though both were imperialist and capitalist. But Kropotkin's principal concern was the impact of a German victory on Russia. His conviction that the federal re-organisation of the Tsarist Empire, supporting anarchy against statism, was conditional on the diminution of German influence, tipped him towards the Entente in 1914. For Kropotkin, the defeat of Germany was the option that offered the best hope of restraining state-centralising tendencies and maximising the space for future anarchistic evolutions.

The Spirit of Revolt

George Woodcock explains Kropotkin's conception of revolution by measuring his personal enthusiasm for insurrection and plotting its gradual downward trajectory. The wisdom and frailty of age, political pessimism and domestic comfort are all relevant factors in this assessment of Kropotkin's understanding. As early as 1887, Woodcock argues, 'agitation had ceased to be the main purpose of his activity'. Enjoying the security of his suburban refuge, Kropotkin did not want to become embroiled 'with the authorities'.[2] The following year he began to apply himself 'more than ever before to writing' and started the 'sociological work on which his reputation … was to rest'.[3] Although Woodcock fails to set out his notion of revolution explicitly, his analysis relies on a dichotomy between revolution and evolution and a rejection of punctuated change hypotheses that imagine moments of accelerated, cataclysmic change within processes of gradual, nearly imperceptible modification. Employing this distinction, Woodcock further uses a Blanquist idea of insurrection as a political model for revolution. Not un-coincidentally, then, he finds that at the same moment that Kropotkin turned his attention to mutual aid – evolutionary theory – his commitment to revolution began to wane and his assessment of its likelihood matured. When he wrote for *Le Révolté*, Kropotkin 'saw in every strike or bread riot a hopeful omen of the disintegration of the great national states'. And because he 'expected a Europe-wide revolution', Woodcock suggests, Kropotkin adopted a correspondingly revolutionary stance.[4] When, in the 1890s, 'the note of extreme optimism' started to fade, Kropotkin's work was 'less preoccupied with ideas of revolutionary action', '[l]ess tinged with violence'. And instead of dreaming about the post-revolutionary future, Kropotkin instead exhorted anarchists 'to apply their principles in the organisation of social life here and now'. Sensibly adjusting his ideological ambitions to fit the political realities Kropotkin concluded that the 'role of the anarchist must for a long time be one of permeation'.[5]

Assessing the development of Kropotkin's revolutionary career by his enthusiasm for the barricades, Woodcock spends little time discussing one of his key early texts on revolutionary action, *The Spirit of Revolt*, although he notes its popularity and influence.[6] Written as an urgent call for action while Kropotkin was indeed bullish about the vulnerability of European states to the mounting pressures of insurrectionary land reform movements, this essay examines the strategic problem of revolutionary change and looks at the relationship between the revolutionary avant garde and mass grass-roots movements.

Looking back on the essay in 1909 Kropotkin told Herzig that the popularity of Paul Brousse's principle of propaganda by the deed motivated him to set out his ideas. His misgivings about Brousse's doctrine were heighted by the fervent promotion of illegalism by Serraux, one of the delegates to the 1881 London Anarchist Congress.[7] The Congress, which Malatesta had helped organise in an attempt to rekindle the International and unite anti-authoritarian revolutionary socialists, singularly failed in this aim but notoriously resolved to advance the study of '[t]echnical and chemical science' to further the anarchist cause.[8] Kropotkin guessed correctly that Serraux, whose real name was Égide Spilleux,[9] was a spy and he feared that the Congress's endorsement of propagandistic acts would be taken by activists as a go-ahead for the kind of sensualist, egoistic amoralism that was popularly linked to nihilism and that he associated with Nietzscheanism. As Cahm points out, Kropotkin misremembered that *The Spirit of Revolt* had been published prior to the 1881 Congress, not in response to it, as he told Herzig.[10] Moreover, the context in which he wrote his essay was shaped as much by his concerns about Paul Brousse's drift towards possibilism as it was by the endorsement of propagandistic acts.[11] Indeed, he gave vent to these concerns in his broader rejection of bourgeois socialist democracy – a topic he addressed in *Paroles d'un Révolté*. Kropotkin discussed the latter as an electoral phenomenon and as a Jacobin principle of dictatorship and flatly rejected both as oxymoronic.[12] Nevertheless, in examining the interrelationship between popular struggles and political activism Kropotkin also outlined some of the central tenets of his punctuated evolutionary theory of change. And his retrospective defence of *The Spirit of Revolt* highlights the consistency of Kropotkin's conception of revolution and the tenuousness of Woodcock's account of his doctrines.

The Spirit of Revolt can be read as the counterpart to the *Appeal to the Young* in the sense that it seeks to prompt individuals to enter into resistance struggles to build bonds of solidarity with disadvantaged groups. Whereas the *Appeal* emphasises the power of educated youth to alleviate the suffering of the poor, *The Spirit of Revolt* calls attention to their capacity to shape political cultures through action. While the *Appeal* seeks to open the eyes of apolitical youths to social injustice, *The Spirit of Revolt* assumes that these radicals are already aware of their complicity in oppression and prepared to give up their advantage and rebel against it. In the language of *Ethics*, they already feel the contradictions between ideal justice and the reality of injustice and have the wherewithal to make the leap to morality. In the essay, Kropotkin uses nihilist tropes, just as he does in the *Appeal*, to make this point. The opening argument refers to the cultural schism between fathers and sons and mothers and daughters, to periods of social disequilibria and the emergence of ideational conflicts that illuminate the unfairness of existing political and economic arrangements. As if extrapolating from his history of nihilism, *The Spirit of Revolt* argues that the conflict between new ideas and old traditions casts established moral principles and social practices into question.

Action is the major theme of the essay. Theoretical analysis, Kropotkin argued, importantly helps activists flesh out their principles and formulate their ideals, but dramatic deeds reach a far wider audience and penetrate more deeply into public consciousness than philosophy.[13] Political movements establish their profile and reputation through their deeds: action is the most effective channel for communicating political ideals. In actions, activists learn about the concerns of ordinary people, even those on the fringes of popular struggles, otherwise detached from mass movements. They can build trust through their exploits and in moments of crisis their reputations will guarantee the value of their words, increasing the standing of anarchist doctrines against non-anarchist alternatives.[14] Kropotkin's message is that rebels should embrace their discomfort with established mores and act on their passions: just as the application of scientific knowledge in the service of the oppressed closes the gap between egoistic desires and altruistic impulses, courageous action frees the daring from their own degeneration and their complicity in systems of oppression.[15]

A significant segment of the essay is devoted to a candid discussion of tactics and the escalation of revolutionary violence. Kropotkin outlined a strategy based on provocation and constant disruption. To help activists think about the possibilities he sketched what he believed to be the most successful methods employed in the period leading up to the French Revolution, wrongly sidelined in historical accounts of its famous set pieces. Anarchist actions, he argued, may take an individual or collective form and they may have a 'tragic' or 'humorous' tone.[16] There were a number of ways that activists could interject in popular movements: circulating pamphlets that exposed and ridiculed the scandalous, seedy behaviours of elites; producing fliers and placards that captured popular demands in simple slogans; and organising satirical carnival performances. These were all good ways of altering the temper of public opinion. Organising illegal demonstrations and popular general assemblies supported the articulation of popular aspirations. By burning effigies of despised public figures, instigating property destruction and targeted assassinations, radicals audaciously demonstrated their commitment and solidarity with the discontented. Similarly, the adoption of revolutionary aliases and calling cards to claim responsibility for multiple acts of property damage and personal assaults enabled disparate activists to enhance the romantic, mythologising image of the revolutionary while creating alarm and spreading confusion in the enemy's ranks. Multiple and sustained actions unsettled elites and disturbed the social peace, eventually creating discord between hawks and doves within governing circles. Goading the hawks to institute tyrannous measures to quell unrest tended to embarrass the doves, exposing divisions and creating instability, and also forcing typically half-hearted and mistimed political concessions. The panicked compromises that revolutionaries secured laid bare the meagre limits of reform and the incapacity of government to deal with protest, encouraging even the most passive victims of oppression to be guided by their passions and enter into struggle.[17]

The role of minorities, Kropotkin argued, was to assist the subjugated to secure its own liberation. This starting point assumed the existence of a cultural and political gap between the radical minorities who were alert to the sources of their own oppression and the causes of social injustice and mass movements that, because of their disadvantage, were ill-equipped to articulate their aspirations or formulate their goals. History taught that the dynamic for revolutionary change extended from the incessant struggle against domination and slavery, but Kropotkin conceded that 'whilst the people might not be found wanting in terms of powers of attack, it has all too often been short of mental audacity and commitment to reconstruction'.[18] Kropotkin did not use the term 'avant garde' to describe the minority and was intolerant with those who believed in the redemptive power of the revolutionary vanguard. As Reszler notes, nothing was 'more alien to the philosophy of Kropotkin than the gratuitousness of Art for Art's sake and the anti-social aristocracies of the Bohemians and the artistic groups' associated with this tag.[19] However, his analysis chimed with the ideas of the Paris veterans of 1848 who claimed a role for art as an instrument of revolutionary propaganda and agitation.[20] Minorities precipitated change, but were not in command of it. Indeed, Kropotkin supposed that minorities were dependent on mass movements for their liberation. Alert to the nature of domination, these minorities were powerfully creative rebels.[21] Yet unless they garnered popular support, their radical ideals existed only in the ether, at best realised on the margins. 'No handful of people, however energetic and talented, can evoke a popular insurrection.'[22] Mass action was required in order to sweep away the institutions and practices that constrained radical aspirations and develop new social forms. Anarchist revolution was thus a matter of closing the gaps between social actors, an accomplishment that depended on the ways in which both radicals and mass movements responded to historical processes and situations.

The interconnection of revolutionary forces imposed considerable constraints on the actions of minorities or, at least, on the character and timing of actions, although these were not always obvious. Indeed, some of the tactics Kropotkin extolled in the *Spirit of Revolt* were not immediately distinguishable from the wrongheaded exploits he linked to propaganda by the deed. In his letter to Herzig, Kropotkin commended the spirited actions of Santo Casiero, guillotined for slaying the French President, Carnot, in 1894 and Michael Angiollo, garrotted three years later for his killing of the Spanish Prime Minister, Antonio Cánovas, even though both were widely condemned in the mainstream press as terrorists. The difference, Kropotkin told Herzig, was that the spirit of revolt described an act undertaken by individuals in conflict with the regimes they attacked and whose hatred for its abuses meant that they could not act otherwise. Spirited revolutionaries, Kropotkin argued in *Anarchist Morality*, were ethical actors. They responded impulsively to the injustices they saw others endure and struck out against tyrants, just as anyone who was neither a coward nor a brute would intervene to restrain a man beating a child.[23] Unlike propagandists of the deed, revolutionaries empathised with others, and their compassion distinguished their actions from those undertaken by political actors who used violence in order to dominate.

Kropotkin was relaxed about the possibility that spirited revolutionaries may be driven by the force of their passions to act rashly and sometimes disproportionately and he took a common-sense approach to determination of motivations. On the first point, he admitted that the 'mud' of bourgeois rule was likely to splash 'far and wide' and that the 'revolt against such a society will sometimes assume forms that will make us shudder'. In the event of mass revolution, socialists were likely to find that the 'ferocity of the rulers of to-day will have left its furrow in the people's minds'.[24] In the 1790s Jean-Paul Marat, scourge of the Court, tribune of the people and flawed hero of the Revolution, had 'understood the sudden accesses of fury in the people and even considered them necessary, at times'.[25] Kropotkin was clearly speaking through Marat, endorsing this position. And in doing so, he perhaps forgot that the violence meted out on the oppressors might possibly extend to despised minorities, such as the Jews. In both cases, however, he argued that wilfulness acted as a brake on revolutionary excess, gainsaying a host of modern criminologists who argued that anarchists lacked the intellect to properly exercise will.

Psychologists seeking to explain anarchist terrorism linked violence to utopianism or 'predominance of the visionary imagination'. One writer, evidently not given to basic arithmetic, explained how this propensity overwhelmed the 'critical judgement' of 'generally half-mad, half-imbecile, half-criminal individuals'.[26] The celebrated criminologist Cesare Lombroso offered a precise diagnosis of anarchist deviance.

His pioneering science of physiognomy was applied to detect 'noble' behaviours in those displaying 'a very large forehead, a very bushy beard, and very large and soft eyes'. The ignoble, those guided by reason but lacking moral sensibility, presented with facial asymmetry and protruding ears: hereditary anomalies linked to species degeneration.[27] Perovskaya was one of Lombroso's models of nobility, although images of her rarely showed significant facial hair. Marat and the anarchists were resolutely labelled degenerate. Michael Schwab, one of Lombroso's anarchist subjects and a victim of the injustice of the Haymarket Affair, complained about his lack of attention to detail. Writing from his prison cell, Schwab protested that Lombroso had ignored the photographic evidence in his possession that clearly contradicted his damning analysis.[28] Kropotkin took a different tack and instead appropriated Lombroso's theory of degeneration in order to contest his dubious science. It was prisons and prison environments that accounted for species decline, always breeding vengeance and confounding justice.[29] Prisons were '*the* nurseries for the most revolting category of breaches of moral law'.[30] The prisoner, 'regulated and ordered', dehumanised and 'treated as a numbered thing' was fashioned into an unfeeling, manipulative, 'rancorous' being.[31] Prisons stoked resentment through mistreatment while simultaneously de-moralising individuals by enforcing compliance through discipline. Kropotkin's conclusion was that 'transgressions against the established principles of morality' resulted from 'a want of firm Will'.[32]

Revolt was an act of wilfulness that extended from the love and practice of freedom and it tended towards moralised behaviours. In *Anarchist Morality* this is precisely the point that Kropotkin made: 'the more you are accustomed by circumstances, by those surrounding you, or by the intensity of your own thought and your own imagination, to *act* as your thought and imagination urge, the more will the moral sentiment grow in you'.[33] The formula was a re-statement of Proudhon's dictum that 'liberty the mother, not the daughter of order'. As Victor Yarros put it, 'the command of a man to himself is essentially different from the command of governor to the governed'. The former implied responsibility; the latter depended on accountability.[34] Thus, the submissive and those broken by enslavement, unused to taking responsibility for their own actions, were more prone than the self-willed to follow established routines unquestioningly and less able, therefore, to reflect on their impulses and practices. Revolutionaries critical of inherited traditions and willing to throw existing morality overboard, were by the same token less inclined to behaviours likely to distress the groups they identified with than those who continued to follow inherited practices or obey dictates from above. The size of their ear lobes, still less the bushiness of their beards, was not the relevant consideration and Kropotkin recommended that Lombroso take a careful look at the social conditions that allowed 'criminals of authority' to thrive, in order to grasp the capacity for moral action.[35]

Kropotkin's discussion of the public reception of revolutionary acts reinforced this point. Deciding of the rightness of actions, he argued, was a matter for common debate and not, especially, philosophy. Gauging the intentions of others was tricky, but the evaluation was something that ordinary people were able to do. Tellingly, in *Anarchist Morality* Kropotkin presented the public verdict on Sofia Perovskaya and the Executive Committee as a dialogue. ' "These men and women" ', it was said, ' "had conquered the right to kill." ' Louise Michel, who embodied the spirit of the Commune, had been similarly exonerated: ' "*She had the right to rob.*" '[36] Sympathetic sketches of activists, such as Kropotkin's accounts of Soloviev and Perovskaya, were clearly designed to sway the public's deliberation. Kropotkin also felt that the balance of harms was also relevant to the process. In his correspondence with Herzig, he included Mariya Spiridonova in his list of spirited revolutionaries. Because of the beating and sexual violence she had suffered at the hands of police, hell-bent on wreaking revenge for her assassination of General Luzhenovsky in 1905,[37] her case provided a particularly shocking illustration of the privations that revolutionaries were prepared to suffer for the sake of their actions, and one less easily sentimentalised in martyrdom than execution. Whatever Kropotkin's feelings were about this case, in the aftermath of the 1905 Russian revolution he noted that acts conventionally dubbed terrorist by ruling authorities 'become a general phenomenon' during revolutionary periods. This being so, it was important to 'keep in mind that the purpose of every terrorist act has to be measured against its results and the impression produced by it'.[38] The public were likely to take a wide range of factors into account in forming their judgements. If, therefore, 'an act is to produce a deep impression', the right to undertake extraordinary actions '*must be conquered*'.[39] Activists could take whatever actions they deemed appropriate, but were also required to consider the public intelligibility of those acts and the extent to which they expressed the concerns and aspirations of the intended audience.

As well as establishing the role of minorities in revolutionary struggles, the action Kropotkin sketched in *The Spirit of Revolt* underlined the protracted nature of revolutionary change. Anarchist revolution, Kropotkin commented, was an immense task. Not only did anarchists confront a pervasive cult of statism, reinforced through schools, the press and in a vast body of literature, they also faced significant practical problems: the rule-bound and divided workforce that capitalism had created was hardly equipped to run an economy capable of withstanding sustained counter-revolutionary onslaughts and meeting the tasks of anarchist reconstruction. Revolution was 'the sudden overthrow of institutions ... the outgrowths of centuries past' and 'the sudden uprising of new ideas and new conceptions'. It was also rightly described as a festival, Kropotkin argued, if it strove for 'the liberation of all'.[40] But '[n]o revolution falls upon us from the skies',[41] Kropotkin warned. These rapid, abrupt revolutionary events depended on the convergence of a number of different factors: 'a widely spread economic revolt, tending to change the economical conditions of the masses, and a political revolt, tending to modify the very essence of the political organisation'.[42] Movements 'of ideas' and the transcendence of despair by hope were also crucial ingredients.[43] The storming of the Bastille had been preceded by hundreds of 'partial' revolts. Similarly, 'scores of ... machine wars took place' in Britain and Germany 'before '48'.[44] It was a mistake, therefore, to confuse revolution with a jacquerie, street warfare, a 'military parade'[45] or 'the bloody conflict between two parties'.[46] It was equally erroneous to think that it was only a party or to suppose that 'everything will sort itself out for the best' without effort, energy and 'a commitment ... that people have rarely displayed in previous revolutions'.[47] Bringing the forces of revolution into alignment and ensuring that there was sufficient strength behind mass revolts to sustain revolutionary change was an enormous undertaking, involving years of preparation and activist commitment.

Prefiguring Prefiguration

Applied across the spectrum of his thought rather than to a narrow period of his career, Woodcock's description of Kropotkin's conception of revolution as the application of principles 'in the organisation of social life in the here and now', usefully highlights the prefigurative aspect of his thinking. Like the *Appeal to the Young*, *The Spirit of Revolt* addressed directly what groups and individuals were able to do in the present in order to shape the future. And it did so by attending to the social relationships forged through revolutionary action as well as by laying bare the nature of oppression in direct action. In common with contemporary conceptions of prefigurative practice, this persistent theme in Kropotkin's writings on revolution derived from a rejection of instrumentalist doctrines that justified the means of action by the efficacy of the goal's attainment, and it provided a significant ground for his rejection of Marxist social democracy.

Kropotkin set out the tenets of his theory in *Anarchist Morality*. Like Stirner, he traced the origins of the means–ends doctrine to religious thought, although he did not see it as particularly Jesuitical, as Stirner did. An instrumentalist thread, he argued, ran through Christianity, Buddhism, utilitarianism and even some forms of nihilism and anarchism. Nor did Kropotkin argue, as Stirner did, that the error of the doctrine lay in the sanctification of the end – the 'hallowing' of the means following its prior consecration.[48] In Kropotkin's view, it was the reluctance to specify the ends properly that lay at the heart of prefiguration. Looking at the question of workers' associations, he argued that that first task of any organisation was to decide on its 'final *objective*'. It was only possible to set out 'a proposed course of action *in conformity with the ends*' once these objectives had been agreed.[49] Instrumentalists also adopted this approach, Kropotkin noted, giving some comfort to Stirnerites keen to show the religiosity of anarchist-communism. However, their specification of ends was ethically bankrupt. The Christian doctrine took this form: 'An action will be good if it represent [*sic*] a victory of the soul over the flesh; it will be evil if the flesh has overcome the soul; if neither then it will be indifferent.'[50] Non-Christian doctrines had a different colouring. Whereas Christians approved all acts that led to recompense in the afterlife, utilitarians endorsed behaviours that increased happiness in the material world. Yet 'however atheistic, however materialistic, however anarchistic they believe themselves',[51] they followed the same precepts, justifying ends by encouraging the conscious calculation of reward. In other words, they were uniformly egoistic. Consequently, whereas Stirner battled against the 'spooks' imposed on individuals to define their essence and predetermine their goals, Kropotkin focused on delimiting the range of possible means by specifying the ethical value of anarchist ends. Sharing Stirner's concern for the 'complete liberty of the individual' and rejecting the right that 'moralists have always taken upon themselves to claim, that of mutilating the individual in the name of some ideal',[52] he nevertheless refused to relinquish the idea of an ideal. Indeed, he mocked the possibility of doing so. 'Every philistine has his ideal,' he commented.[53] Bismarck's vision of blood and iron was one, powerful example. That most were repellent, as Bismarck's was, did not detract from the need for anarchists to outline the goals they wanted to achieve, before turning to consider the best ways of tailoring the means for their attainment.

Kropotkin referred to the golden rule to describe the ends of anarchism – '*Treat others as you would like them to treat you under similar circumstances*'[54] – but more helpfully specified his understanding of the precept by linking it to a set of virtues and passions. Many of the virtues

Kropotkin commended had a distinctly muscular tinge. Chief among those he championed in *The Spirit of Revolt* – courage, daring and audacity – were identical to the qualities that Machiavelli required of princes to meet the necessities of statecraft. Cowardice, submission and panic were anarchist vices. Following Guyau, Kropotkin called on anarchists to 'be *great* in your every action' and to 'venture into danger … throw your strength without taking count of it'.[55] However, the princely virtues that Machiavelli linked to military prowess were attached more broadly in Kropotkin's work to social struggle. Moreover, Kropotkin resisted the Machiavellian gendering of virtue and the exclusive attribution of virtue to men. Women displayed virtues, too, usually in ways that were 'unknown and almost always misprized'.[56] Kropotkin seemed unsurprised by this neglect, perhaps because he believed that women in bourgeois society constituted a special sub-class within the exploited (rural workers, skilled and unskilled labourers were the other key groups) and their devaluation reflected the pervasive social inequality on which women's oppression was based.[57] In another departure from Machiavelli, Kropotkin added self-sacrifice to his catalogue and he scoffed both at caution and prudence in ways that Machiavelli would likely have disapproved. Kropotkin rejected brutality as Machiavelli warned against cruelty, but further distancing himself from princely realpolitik, he championed compassion, empathy and devotion and rejected 'lying', an important weapon in the Machiavellian armoury, as 'repulsive'.[58] Equating lies with dishonesty and mystification Kropotkin reportedly told Lenin in 1919, 'We don't need covers; we must ruthlessly expose each lie, everywhere.'[59] Perhaps decisively, Kropotkin rejected fearfulness, which princes were counselled to inspire. Kropotkin staked anarchy on love, a virtue that Machiavelli described as fickle, and hate, for the very reason that Machiavelli rejected it: because it made rulers vulnerable. Just as Machiavelli hung the order and greatness of the prince on fear, he rooted anarchy in the greatness of trusting, truthful and fearless individuals.

By the cultivation of these virtues and in giving free reign to passion, the golden rule became an instrument of anarchist freedom. So re-cast, reciprocity meant:

> We do not wish to be ruled. And by this very fact, do we not declare that we ourselves wish to rule nobody? We do not wish to be deceived, we wish always to be told nothing but the truth. And by this very fact, do we not declare that we ourselves do not wish to deceive anybody, that we promise to always tell the truth, nothing but the truth, the whole truth? We do not wish to have the fruits of our labor stolen from us. And by that very fact, do we not declare that we respect the fruits of others' labor?[60]

This reading of the golden rule underpinned Kropotkin's anarchist ends: the ability of individuals to live unmediated lives. His analysis of the monopolising tendencies of the state convinced him that 'all direct union' between individuals was being eroded in favour of 'the principle of submission and discipline'.[61] Three hundred years of state development had resulted in the destruction of society. 'To-day we live side by side without knowing one another ... everything ends to alienate you from one another.'[62] Not even the Church was able to provide autonomous spaces for communal interaction. Having been once party to the state's rise it was rapidly being subsumed by it and in modern societies individuals were increasingly united solely through the law. Relieved of the burden of negotiating disagreements and differences directly, they were required only to cultivate 'the virtue of being equally its slaves'.[63] Prefigurative politics involved reclaiming the power of negotiation by the practice of reciprocity and, importantly, the assertion of individual force. Kropotkin referred to Guyau's idea of *overflowing life* where the *'power* to act' is realised through an unconscious *'duty* to act'[64] to describe the principle he had in mind.

This determination of the anarchist end demarcated Kropotkin's anarchism from Stirner's. As an egoist, Stirner divorced power from duty. Duty spelt commitment and promising, concepts that Stirner rejected: 'Because I was a fool yesterday I must remain such my life long. So in the State-life I am ... a bondman of myself. Because I was a willer yesterday, I am to-day without a will: yesterday voluntary, to-day involuntary.' The solution was to recognise 'no *duty*, not *binding* myself nor letting myself be bound'.[65] Kropotkin's rejection of conscious calculation in favour of unconscious living opened up a theoretical channel for commitment based on 'loyalty (keeping our word)',[66] making solidarity possible. From his perspective, Stirner's rejection of ends looked like a defence of self-interest that hallowed all means employed for the realisation of the individual will, held sacred.

Tailoring means to anarchist ends meant endorsing only those strategies that supported the direct action of individuals. The 'task of reconstructing society on new principles', Kropotkin noted, fell exclusively to the 'collective spirit of the masses'.[67] This was inevitably the case because the ends of anarchy demanded the abolition of slavery in its psychological as well as its structural dimensions. Anarchists were compelled to act for themselves and should also know that they were strong enough to live by themselves.[68] Kropotkin disagreed with Tolstoy's judgement of Napoleon, criticising *War and Peace* for overlooking 'entirely ... the immense influence that the young Bonaparte had acquired over the minds of men, when he was imbued with the ideas of the advanced

Jacobins, when he inspired with enthusiasm the *sans-culottes* armies'. However, he wholeheartedly endorsed Tolstoy's view that 'historical events develop independently of the will of those individuals to whom historians attribute importance, and that it is the state of mind and the actions of the masses which decide the battles and shape the events of universal history'.[69]

Overcoming slavish habits was a difficult task, Kropotkin realised. In Western Europe the grip of monopoly bred a *'narrow egoistic spirit which stands in direct contradiction to the spirit which Co-operation is intended to develop'*.[70] Economic competition and authoritarian schooling similarly encouraged slavish behaviours: rivalry, back-stabbing and the desire to secure power-advantage.[71] But Kropotkin pointed to the example of the legal emancipations of the 1860s to illustrate the feasibility of anarchist means. Those calling for complete emancipation at the time had been mocked as utopians. In Russia, 'the peasants, who revolted with sticks against guns, and refused to submit, notwithstanding the massacres' demonstrated their practicality. The slaves were reputed to be 'improvident, selfish brutes'; in rising against their oppressors and rebuilding their villages they were in fact 'becoming Men'.[72]

Kropotkin argued that anarchist ends were necessarily incompatible with the means of political conquest proposed by authoritarian socialists. Government, 'whether it be constituted by force or by election; be it "the dictatorship of the proletariat", as they used to say in France ... and as they still say in Germany, or else an elected "Provisional Government or a Convention"' were all ruled out.[73] These means reduced revolution to an event in which the existing levers of political power in the state were seized in order to bring about economic change. However, it did not follow that authoritarian socialism was not prefigurative or that anarchists and Marxists shared the same ends and diverged only on the means. Kropotkin took the contrary view and argued that authoritarian socialism was prefigurative, perfectly matching authoritarian means to equally authoritarian ends. The state socialists' Babouvist fantasy of political conquest was entirely appropriate to the realisation of a system of production based on compulsory labour and the 'organisation of industrial armies, especially as regards agriculture' – abhorrent to Kropotkin's defence of small economy.[74] Similarly, movement regulation and respect for revolutionary elites[75] were part and parcel of a vision of 'social organisation' in which 'an "army" of workers severely "disciplined"' obeyed 'the word of a "dictatorial chief", or group of chiefs'.[76]

Kropotkin linked these different conceptions of change to competing conceptions of history. His view of revolution as a process of change in which actors became increasingly self-determining through direct action was reliant on ordinary political judgement but did not treat individuals as agents of historical processes. The social democratic conception linked revolutionary transformations to changes in the material conditions of production and it was underwritten by a 'philosophy of history' that assumed that state centralisation and the rejection of local autonomy were 'foregone conclusions'.[77] Naturally, as Belfort Bax argued, social democrats interpreted this philosophical doctrine in different ways. While the 'extreme materialist view' reduced all change to economic causes, Bax's modified interpretation imagined that other factors – psychological and ideological – operated independently of economic changes and that each followed 'its own distinct line of causation'.[78] Yet however it was understood, the materialist doctrine described an idea of history that had a discernible logic. In Bax's version, economic changes had propelled history forward to a point where intellectual, ethical and aesthetic drives were now poised to predominate as the main drivers of change. This view implied that vulgar materialists were right to treat bare economics as the force of historical change hitherto, but wrong to ignore the ways in which materialism had altered evolutionary dynamics. Both perspectives were equally open to the view that it was possible to grasp 'the meaning of historic development in the past',[79] even if there was considerable disagreement about what that meaning may be.

Referring to the ejection of the anarchists from the congresses of the Second International, Kropotkin observed that socialists were 'compelled … under penalty of ostracism' to accept this model of change.[80] Choosing banishment, he cast all of this talk of the logic of history aside and contrasted his conception of social tendencies to misnamed laws of scientific evolution. Kropotkin rejected both the philosophy and the political doctrines that attached to this determination: the scientific socialists' thesis of immiseration and the " 'Law of self-annihilation" discovered by their great thinkers' that preached that 'no substantial change is possible … until the number of capitalists has been reduced by their mutual competition',[81] delineating both the course of class struggle and the emergence of class consciousness.[82] Some men 'speak of stages to be travelled through … [T]hey … work to reach what they consider to be the nearest station and only *then* to take the high road leading to what they recognise to be a still higher ideal'.[83] 'Humanity was not a rolling ball, nor even a marching column,' Kropotkin commented. Societies developed, but each phase was 'a resultant of all the activities of the intellects which compose that society; it bears the imprint of all those millions of wills'.[84] Revolutionaries did not have history on their side. They had to make it themselves. There was nothing greater than the beings that inhabited the world. If this sounded bleak, Kropotkin thought it was a consoling thought, for being without gods or masters meant that rebels were free to impress their desires upon it. There was no better time than now to exploit detectable social trends to meet anarchist ends.

Kropotkin's contention that communism was the best system to guard against the return of exploitation highlighted the need for the rebellious to construct the bare bones of the future integrated economy in the process of their struggles. This approach to prefigurative change was shaped by his analysis of the Commune. Kropotkin's overriding concern was with the security of the revolution during periods of conflict and, in the longer term, by the smooth organisation of complex economic systems. The Communards had realised far too late in the day 'that a supply of food to the population, which was deprived of the means of earning it for itself, ought to have been the Commune's first duty'.[85] Kropotkin suggested a remedy in *The Conquest of Bread*: the title encapsulates his contention that finding 'bread for the people of the Revolution' must 'take precedence over all other questions'.[86] Beyond the Commune, the wider question Kropotkin posed was how an economy geared towards production for profit could be reconstructed to meet needs? The only answer, he ventured in 1919, having witnessed the dislocations of the Russian economy, was by the self-organising activities of the producers. State socialist plans, 'which lead inevitably to the dictatorship of a party' were a non-starter: even assuming the willing cooperation of the workforce, it was impossible for any government to manage the economic system or to anticipate the management problems that were likely to arise. However, it was possible for producers to imagine how they may direct existing economic processes to meet revolutionary contingencies in advance of crisis periods. And in doing this, Kropotkin argued, they would not be plotting programmes for some fantasy of ideal existence. They would be starting to change '*life*'.[87]

Agents of Change

Kropotkin's appeals to urban industrial workers to support the struggles of rural land movements assumed a new importance in the light of his proposals for integrated economics and his analysis of the logistics of revolution. In the 1890s the emergence of the syndicalist movement seemed to offer a solution. Coinciding with the so-called second industrial revolution, radical unionism became a powerful force during this period, seeding powerful movements across Europe, in North, Central and Latin America, Sweden, Japan, Egypt and South Africa.[88]

Kropotkin's interest was stirred by the Spanish movement,[89] although he paid close attention to global radical union struggles during the years leading up to war. Indeed, his saturation coverage of the topic, he admitted, probably irritated his readers.[90]

Syndicalism divided anarchist opinion, although as Schmidt and van der Walt show, the lines of division were very fluid: rival parties to the debates argued about the relationship between anarchist communism and anarcho-syndicalism often without pinning down what was meant by these labels.[91] Rather than identifying himself as a partisan or antagonist of radical labour organising, Kropotkin approached the relationship between anarchism and syndicalism strategically, using the strength of radical unionism both to gauge the prospects for anarchist change and to evaluate the revolutionary commitment of competing socialist factions. In the first decade of the twentieth century, this analysis supported Kropotkin's increasingly polemical critique of German socialism and his assessment of the essentially statist and imperialist character of German politics.

Kropotkin traced the modern history of the movement to Owenism, but argued that the idea of labour association was an older one, re-emerging in the wake of the destruction of the medieval guild system and in defiance of state prohibitions on labour organising introduced across Europe in the eighteenth century.[92] Forced to struggle against legal and extra-legal repression in order to establish their labour organisations, workers importantly pioneered strike action to secure their demands.[93] For Kropotkin, this experience shaped the defining characteristics of radical unionism: unions were mutual aid associations that emerged to fight against labour injustice and exploitation by the '[d]irect struggle of labour against [c]apital'. In the early nineteenth century the principle of radical union organising was championed by Proudhon and Owen and it was their followers who provided the impetus for the formation of the First International and who pushed for the incorporation of the commitment to workers' self-emancipation in its statutes.[94] Rudolf Rocker narrated a similar story of union development, but stressed both the evolutionary passage of anarchism through the revolutionary union movements and their symbiotic relationship in his conjunction of anarcho-syndicalism.[95] According to Kropotkin's genealogy, syndicalism was only the most recent manifestation of radical labour activism. It was 'a new name for tactics long since resorted to with profit by British workers ... on the economic field'.[96] It had developed in parallel to anarchism, but the two currents were quite distinct. Anarchists did not confuse syndicalism with anarchism, any more than they pretended to have invented it.[97]

Kropotkin was enthusiastic about the mass base for anarchist organising that syndicalism offered. In part, this was because he was deeply sceptical about the insurrectionary alternatives, describing the idea that 1,000 armed men could make a revolution as a Blanquist illusion.[98] In the other part, his enthusiasm reflected his appreciation of the power that radical unions had in their grasp. Because global capitalism was reliant on industrial production and international trade, urban labourers – most especially miners and dockers – occupied a pivotal place in the struggle against exploitation. 'No one' he told European and American workers should 'underrate the importance of this labour movement for the coming revolution': it was charged with reorganising production 'on new social bases'.[99] Writing to Grave in 1903, Kropotkin dismissed Nettlau's claim that syndicalism had stalled the spread of anarchism, putting his negativity down to an individualistic tendency to treat anarchism as a radical philosophy for the educated.[100] The engagement of a revolutionary core in the worker's movement was essential, Kropotkin told Grave.[101] Labour movement organisations were 'the real force capable of accomplishing the social revolution'.[102] Writing in the early years of the new century, he made the same point to Alexander Berkman. The labour unions were the 'mass the great mass – *those who made the revolution – those who are the only ones to make them*'.[103]

Kropotkin's embrace of syndicalism was comparable to Malatesta's.[104] Neither adopted an uncritical view: both argued that unionism lacked anarchism's breadth of vision and both worried about the bureaucratic tendencies of union organisation. In his address to the 1907 Amsterdam Anarchist Congress, Malatesta highlighted the risks that attached to paid positions and to creeping officialdom.[105] Kropotkin agreed. Moreover, because their primary concern was to wrest control of industry from the owners, union leaders risked losing sight of the need to transform production. 'We go further' and 'say that the workers will never attain their emancipation if they do not abandon the fallacy of the state'.[106] Even explicitly non-hierarchical anti-statist syndicalists were often quite rigid. While he agreed to write a preface for Emile Pataud and Emile Pouget's syndicalist utopia, *How We Shall Bring about the Revolution*, Kropotkin felt that their ideas were still overly governmental.[107] They were 'bureaucratic syndicalists', he told Grave, who leaned too much on the syndicates and too little on the community.[108] Yet like Malatesta, Kropotkin also saw the syndicates as excellent vehicles for anarchist propaganda. Writing about individual and mass action in *La Révolte* he argued that the power of individual initiatives was their power to '*awaken the spirit of revolt in the mass*'.[109] Addressing a London audience in 1892, Kropotkin called on anarchists to 'permeate the great labour movement'.[110] In his correspondence with Grave he made the same point: syndicates should be seen as auxiliary organisations, open to hosting anarchist revolutionary cells.[111]

While it perhaps appeared opportunistic, the strategic role that Kropotkin ascribed to syndicalism in the struggle for anarchist revolution dovetailed with his understanding of prefigurative change and his conception of mutual aid. As Rocker observed, the two main purposes of the syndicates were to defend 'the interests of the producers within existing society' and 'prepare for the practical carrying out of the reconstruction of social life after the pattern of Socialism'.[112] Unlike Malatesta, Kropotkin believed that these aims were consistent with anarchists objectives: by entering into these new unions, he thought anarchists could steer syndicalists towards meeting the contingencies of revolution and resist state aggression. For Malatesta syndicalism was inherently contradictory, for the first objective tended to reinforce divisions between workers, particularly the unionised and un-unionised, whereas the second pointed to what he called the 'moral solidarity between proletarians' realisable only by 'sharing a common ideal' that will 'transform society' and 'make new men of them'.[113] In contrast, Kropotkin was unperturbed by the producers' self-interest, not only because it bore the character of reciprocity but also because struggle itself supported structural change. Strike actions in France, Spain, the US and Ireland in the late 1870s persuaded Kropotkin that strike action was a motor for anarchistic organisation. In order to overcome isolation and abandonment, strikers needed to establish effective communications networks and systems of mutual support, to construct 'resistance associations for each trade in each town', amass 'resistance funds' and forge federal unions with trade associations in other towns, leading to the formation of national and trans-national networks.[114] Despite the strictures of Pataud and Pouget's syndicalist vision, the process of self-emancipation pointed to the transformation of the global economic infrastructure. Solidarity was also forged through this process, more easily than Malatesta imagined because Kropotkin did not share the same conception. Malatesta defined solidarity in terms of the formation of a general interest and the transcendence of particular interests achieved through classlessness.[115] Using the idioms of mutual aid, he defined solidarity as the 'harmony of interests and sentiments'.[116] Kropotkin argued otherwise. Wary of the harmony of the phalanstère, he also warned against appeals to sentiment 'to brotherly feelings' and 'to moral principles'. This was the form that communism took before 1848 and that Proudhon had rejected.[117] Kropotkin had no greater ambition to remodel workers or to sink their differences. The struggle against capital was not about the formation of an identity, but liberation from its domination. How individuals understood socialism or anarchism was not Kropotkin's concern, unless or until it diverted unionists from their activism.[118] In 1901, when he called for the formation of an International Federation of Trade Unions, Kropotkin imagined 'Conservative, or Liberal, Nationalist or Internationalist, Social Democrat or Anarchist' workers ranged against 'Conservative, Liberal, Jingo or anti-Jingo' capitalists.[119] The tensions between workers may well result in conflicts, but direct action bred resistance and that was enough to advance change. At the end of the 1911 British rail workers strike, Kropotkin told Grave that the compromises of the union leadership did not detract from the real power of the action: 'the *spirit* of the masses was superb'. With some irony, he referred to *The Times* leader that described syndicalism as the 'fruits of Socialistic teaching … absolutely reckless in its methods'. *The Times* was 'intelligent', Kropotkin told Grave.[120] Direct action indeed threatened to unleash 'all the forces of disorder and anarchy' on the world, just as the paper warned.[121]

Kropotkin's conclusion that the implementation of direct action was the test of syndicalist power was amply demonstrated in his commentaries on strike actions. The truth of his general rule, that strikes 'awaken revolutionary spirit'[122] was borne out by workers in the Netherlands, France and Italy.[123] Strikes, 'once "a war of folded arms"' were 'turning to revolt', he argued in 1907.[124] The Milan general strike of 1904 was an inspirational model. Here, the workers' refusal to work was revolutionised by their accompanying declaration of intent. They were no longer prepared to starve 'with their arms crossed'. They would take what they needed and reorganise production, *'for ourselves, who work, for those who come to work with us by our side'*.[125] Kropotkin similarly represented the Russian general strike that started in Moscow in October 1905, as a key moment for the revolution: it unified the urban population with the peasantry, lending support to the rural insurrections that had taken place across Poland, the Baltic States and the Ukraine. The two-month period of the strike was Russia's moment of freedom, Kropotkin contended. Workers, peasants and artisans, even the most timid, took their liberties, according to anarchist principles. The action triggered risings along the entire length of the Trans-Siberian Railway, he argued. Encouraged by Blanquists, Moscow workers ill-advisedly called a second strike in December – a 'fiasco' that failed to secure bread and weakened the people's resolve and capacity to fight.[126] Nevertheless, Kropotkin maintained that in the course of the October struggle 'A NEW NATION WAS BORN'.[127] As he told the audience in London's East End, the revolution ultimately only secured a set of promises, still to be honoured. But 'the main point is that these promises were *wrested by the people* and still more so that they were wrested by means of a *general strike.*' Other workers should continue on the same path:

> Don't expect anything from would-be guardians. But in every factory, every building yard, every workshop, and every mine, establish *yourselves the order of things which by common accord, you will find proper to establish*. But remember this: Don't allow others to interfere! It is *your* affair and *you* have to settle it.[128]

Kropotkin painted the failures of direct action in equally dramatic terms. Perhaps the most striking example was his condemnation of British workers' failure to strike in protest against the Boer War. In a speech delivered in London in 1901 Kropotkin described the instigators of war as 'shameless money-grabbers', but he blamed the workers for its pursuit. 'They alone can put an end to the abominations committed against women and children in their name.' But instead of putting 'their foot' on it, the 'Labour Unions of London' did nothing and were complicit by their passivity. Referring to a mass meeting held to protest against the concentration camps the British initiated, *Freedom* published an indictment: 'you have not realised your responsibilities over this war ... the corpses of these murdered ones are in evidence against you'.[129] British workers were not only answerable for this war, but also in the 'abominations that are committed in England's name in ... North Africa and in famine- and plague-stricken India'.[130]

Kropotkin's analysis of the revolutionary power of workers' direct action significantly raised the temper of his critique of social democracy and the Second International's electoral strategy. In the 1880s Kropotkin's concern was to highlight the efficacy of direct action. Spanish building workers won the eight-and-a-half-hour day *'by the strike'*, whereas in France 'workers toiling for fifty *sous* per eleven hour shift are told: "Put us in Parliament, and, once we have a majority ... we will vote through the nine hour day."'[131] Rehearsing precisely the same argument ten years later in the London eight-hour-day campaigns, Kropotkin prescribed British labourers the Spanish tonic.[132] The policy of the 'German social-democrats', he argued was 'to turn the International in to a political party', leaving the workers' organisations 'hamstrung'.[133] Time and again he stressed that workers had to choose between direct action and the International's constitutional policy, greeting each transgression of the official line as a victory. In 1904 he observed that the Milanese strike went ahead *'against'* the advice of socialist leaders and *'in spite* of their opposition'.[134] In consequence, the strike was not merely a struggle against the bourgeoisie, it was also a test of the workers' resistance to social democracy. The two were as one. Referring to the fraught relationship between the German Social Democratic Party and Free Association of German Trade Unions, Kropotkin noted in 1906 that the German Social Democrats had dropped their long-standing opposition to the 'independent organisation of trades'. But he was not impressed. Two years before socialist leaders ruled union and Party membership incompatible, he argued that the agreement reflected the Party's ambition to absorb the workers' associations. Their goal, '*government socialism*' or '*government capitalism*',[135] was diametrically opposed to the First International's commitment to worker's self-organisation.

Kropotkin not only read the rejection of direct action as a vote for capitalism and the state, but also for imperialism. Parliamentary socialists who opposed the general strike had an interest in maintaining the 'present capitalistic State' that exploits the labour of 'millions of men in Eastern Europe, Asia, and Africa'.[136] Kropotkin's accusation struck a chord with Bax's critique of Eduard Bernstein. In an intemperate debate conducted during 1896 and 1897 Bax accused Bernstein of advancing a theory of socialist development that sanctioned German imperialist expansion as a regrettable but necessary stage of capitalist development, thus leading to socialism. Rejecting this vulgar reading of Marx, Bax also repudiated Bernstein's juxtaposition of economic underdevelopment and barbarism.[137] Kropotkin similarly attacked Bernstein's suggestion that colonialism somehow advanced socialism, denouncing him as a Fabian '*à outrance*'.[138] Moreover, acknowledging that Hyndman, like Bax, had been staunchly opposed to 'the policy of spoliation in India and Egypt', in contrast to the Fabians and 'that disgusting acrobat B. Shaw', Kropotkin took Bernstein's position to describe the rule. Reviewing social democratic policy from 1885 to 1901 he told Marsh: 'I deeply feel that the attitude of the Social Democrats ... especially at the last elections has done more to give a free hand to the Imperialist than anything else.'[139] Kropotkin held the German Social Democrats responsible for this imperialistic turn. And because he did not believe, as Bax did, that it was possible to conduct a revolutionary electoral strategy against capitalism, he treated the argument between advocates of political and direct action as an expression of the struggle between capital and labour. In 1912 Kropotkin asked himself how the image of 'Germans ... jubilating with red flags and torchlights at their steadily increasing electoral successes', would lead workers to answer the question: 'What would be the outcome of the now inevitable world-conflict between Labour and Capital?'[140] The answer he gave to this question at the war's end was that the push against direct action had allowed imperialism to seep into the workers' movements to secure capital's victory.

> As the workers are beginning to take part in political power, the contagion of colonial imperialism is infecting them too. In the last war the German workers, as much as their masters, aspired to conquer cheaper man-power for themselves – even in Europe, that is in Russia and the Balkan peninsula, as well as in Asia Minor and Egypt ... and on their side, the French and English workers showed themselves to be full of indulgence for similar conquests on the part of their governments in Africa and Asia.[141]

Syndicalism's Achilles' heel had been dramatically exposed. Direct action failed to take sufficient root in Europe to prevent the degeneration into war. Unable to forge international solidarity, European workers struggled for the control and possession of capital, not their liberation from its yoke.

War and Revolution

Kropotkin's assessment of the instrumental role that German social democracy had played in diverting the energies of workers towards political action was the key factor explaining his decision to support a defensive war against Germany in 1914. He had anticipated the outbreak of war in Europe long before the fighting started, not just because the competition for markets brought states into conflict with one another, but also because he treated the defeat of the Commune as the first round of a struggle of the oppressed for emancipation, on the one hand, and state domination in Europe, on the other. The reverberations of the Commune's defeat had been felt across the Continent, both in the organisation of pan-European and indeed global radical and socialist movements, and in the constant manoeuvrings of European states. Just as Kropotkin thought that the manner in which revolutionaries organised themselves was crucial to socialism's success, he also believed that the outcome of these power struggles would profoundly influence the fortunes of the revolutionary movement. In this context, the German-led initiative in the Second International to undertake political action amounted to collusion in the aggressive, expansionist policies of the Prussified German state. And in 1914 the failure of German labourers to resist the nationalist pressures active on them appeared to him as an endorsement of the Kaiser's plans for European domination, in the same way that British workers' placidity in the South African war had seemed to indicate their collusion in imperialist oppression. Believing that it was just a matter of time before Germany mounted another invasion of France, Kropotkin made no secret of his antipathy for Bismarck's Germany and the Kaiserreich. He also laid out his views about what the French response to this new invasion should be nearly ten years before the war started. Nevertheless, when Kropotkin's letter to Gustav Steffen was published in *Freedom* in 1914,[142] his belligerent critique of German aggression and, perhaps above all, his defence of Russian integrity shocked his comrades, effectively splitting the anarchist movement. Equally astonishing was the language of Kropotkin's Farewell Letter of June 1917, where he referred to the civilisational contest between 'Western democracies' and 'the Central Empires' – the 'striving to achieve Progress through a steady growth of ... inner forces' on the one hand, and the 'obsolete ideals of outward expansion' on the other.[143] Malatesta's accusation, which was supported by most leading anarchist intellectuals, was that Kropotkin had betrayed his principles. He had lent his name to a war that had nothing to do with human emancipation, and everything to do with securing the advantage of militarised capitalist states.[144] Whether or not Malatesta was right to condemn Kropotkin's stance, his charge of treachery is difficult to maintain: Kropotkin's position was consistent with his conception of anarchism and he defended it in these terms. He supported the campaign against Germany even though he accepted that the war was a result of capitalism and statism. However, he separated the analysis of the war's causes from its effects and evaluated these by distinguishing between war, as an act of colonisation by conquest, and revolution, as an act of national rebellion.

Kropotkin's pamphlet *Wars and Capitalism*, published in 1914 from articles written two years earlier, is a pithy restatement of the critique he first advanced in *Paroles d'un Révolté*. In it, he describes war as the result of economic competition and colonisation. European powers battled for supremacy on the Continent in order to maximise their control of global markets. This struggle not only involved constant jostling for control of land – to exploit raw materials, gain access to cheap labour and command seaways and ports – but also technological advantage. European politics was characterised by permanent instability for, unable to contain the industrialising, urbanising forces that competition stimulated, European states modernised in turn, creating new pressures to expand, extend and conquer. When the 'industrial wave, in rolling from West to East' reached Russia the result was 'brigandage in Persia'.[145] Banks were integral to this process, extending credit to colonising states in order to benefit from the investments that global exploitation facilitated and receiving, in return, the protection of those states ever keen to secure favourable lending rates.[146] The London stock exchange was the single most important player in the 1904–5 Russo-Japanese war, Kropotkin told Brandes, just as it had been instrumental in the South African and the Sino-Japanese wars.[147] Equally, the Rothshilds' refusal to buy up Alexander III's debts, on account of his anti-Semitic policies, explained why the Tsar buried his objections to republicanism and sought alliance with France in 1892.[148]

Kropotkin maintained this position at the end of the war. What the war proved, he argued in 1920, was the madness of hoping for peace in a world given to capitalist exploitation.[149] However, he never thought that capitalism functioned independently of states: it was reliant on them. In 'Europe and America' Kropotkin argued, 'States are constituting monopolies in favour of capitalists at home, and still more in conquered lands, such as Egypt, Tonkin, the Transvaal, and so on'. The Marxists' concept of 'primitive accumulation' thus mis-described the relationship of state to capitalism. The reality was that 'new monopolies have been granted every year till now by the Parliaments to all nations to railway, tramway, gas, water, and maritime transport companies, schools, institutions and so on'. The Trans-Siberian Railway was another example of a state-led colonising project.[150] The state, he argued, was 'the first foundation of all great capitalist fortunes' and 'has ever been'.[151] Moreover, capitalism assumed its character from the political cultures in which it operated. Reviewing the experience of the 1905 revolution, Kropotkin argued that it would be irrational 'to restrict our fight to an exclusively economic program and not take part in the ongoing political struggle against autocracy'. The fight against autocracy was precisely where Kropotkin's revolutionary career had begun and he regarded it as 'one of the most harmful forms of statehood because it gives the State such enormous powers'.[152]

The relationship between the state and capitalism complicated Kropotkin's response to war because it established a ranking for international domination that bolstered his Germanophobia. Germany came out at the top of his table because Prussified Germany was as autocratic as Russia and also economically dominant. When Kropotkin examined the complex treaty system pioneered by Bismarck, he considered the different ways in which the machinations of European states had played out: from Russia's alignment with Germany against France and Britain, forged through a mutual desire to preserve autocracy against socialism and its useful idiot, liberalism, to the plotting of Russia's virtual dismemberment by Britain, Germany and Austria.[153] But he continually returned to Franco–German rivalry because of his conviction that the defeat of the Commune had set-back revolutionary hopes in Europe. In 1896, he remarked on the ascendancy of the 'military utopias of German Socialism'.[154] Three years later he outlined the dangers of German Caesarism:

> The triumph of Germany was the triumph of militarism in Europe, of military and political despotism; and at the same time the worship of the State, of authority and of State Socialism, which is reality nothing but State Capitalism, triumphed in the ideas of a whole generation. If these ideas crib and confine the European mind at present, and even the minds of revolutionists, we owe it in great measure to the triumph of the military Germany Empire.[155]

The combination of industrial might and political reaction made Germany the greatest threat to European political cultures. Kropotkin continued: 'if France is inclined to slide down the slope of Caesarism instead of being the vanguard of the Communist Communalist movement towards which her evolution tended, it is also in consequence of the disaster of 1870.'[156] By 1905, he had no doubts about France's contamination and he pointed to the anti-Semitic anti-Dreyfusards and the success of the populist, dictatorial Boulangist movement as evidence.[157] In the letter to Steffen, he reiterated the argument: 'Since 1871 German had become a standing menace to European progress.'[158] In his broadside against Kropotkin, Malatesta argued that there was nothing to choose between the triumph of German 'militarism and of reaction' and 'Russo-English (*i.e.*, a knouto-capitalist) domination in Europe and in Asia, conscription and the development of the militarist spirit in England, and a Clerical and perhaps Monarchist reaction in France'.[159] Kropotkin disagreed. It was absurd to think that the iron rule of Germany would be the same as the iron rule of France he told Herzig, a year before the war's outbreak.[160]

Kropotkin continued to defend the principle of national liberation alongside this analysis of relative state oppression. In 1897, he reaffirmed his view that national struggles had a social dimension. The "purely nationalist character' of nationalist movements was a fiction'.[161] Anarchists should play their part in these campaigns, just as they engaged with workers' organisations. This meant defending cultural expression – language, song and so forth – while reserving 'the first bullet' for the aspiring national dictator and the 'first noose' for the 'lord and estate-owner'.[162] Kropotkin's position, which was derived from his analysis of state colonisation and a key element of his critique of Tsarism, was a principle of self-emancipation. Writing to Herzig, he argued that real internationalism would only be attained by the independence of each nationality, small or large, compact or diffuse, just as anarchism resulted from the independence of each individual.[163] Internationalism thus imposed obligations on other national groups, namely, to support the most oppressed victims of state and capitalism. Even where 'people have not risen up against ... exploitation' Kropotkin told Maria Goldsmith in 1897, 'we must stand by them'. His list of most oppressed peoples included 'the blacks in America, the Armenians in Turkey, the Finns and the Poles in Russia'.[164] Internationalism also prohibited conniving in the oppression of others. In *Anarchist Morality*, he argued, 'we ourselves, would asked to be killed, like venomous beasts, if we went to invade Burmese or Zulus, who have done us no harm'.[165]

Every war was a disaster, Kropotkin wrote in *Les Temps Nouveaux*, in a discussion of the Russo-Japanese war.[166] Indeed, the technological developments in arms production indicated that the coming European conflagration would be particularly horrendous. Unlike the donkeys who still anticipated a colonial-style campaign in 1914, Kropotkin had adjusted to the realities of modern warfare. Wars, he noted, 'no longer consist of a mere massacre of hundreds of thousands of men in a few great battles': they are 'fought on a front ... of thirty-five to forty miles'. Soldiers could expect to be fired on by 'several hundred pieces of ord-nance' that would obliterate the landscape and drive them 'to madness' – to hurl 'hand-grenades' and guncotton at one another and then face successive waves of 'attacking columns', forcing them to engage in hand-to-hand combat, rolling in the trenches 'like wild beasts, striking each other with the butt-end of their rifles and with their knives, and tearing each other's flesh with their teeth'.[167]

Kropotkin also denied that wars were ever liberating. In his study of the French Revolution, Kropotkin recorded Marat's indictment of the Girondin's warmongering: 'It is because you do not wish to appeal to the people that you wish for war.'[168] Engaging the German army in 1792 was a strategy designed to defeat the King while also limiting the reach of the revolution. Since then, wars had had the same effect. It was an illusion to believe that the emancipation was the positive result of the Crimean war, or that the Civil War in America secured the abolition of slavery.[169] Just as the decrees of 1793 settled the land question in favour of the bourgeoisie, these wars facilitated the transformation of chattel to bond slavery.[170]

The response to war, which had also accounted for progressive change in the past, was revolutionary resistance. In 1905 Kropotkin set out his position in a critique of the proposal for a conscripts' gen-eral strike, put forward as an anti-militarist revolutionary action in the event of German invasion. Rejecting the policy Kropotkin argued that anti-militarism was wrongly defined as a refusal to fight and that it really described a willingness to resist militaristic forces of reaction. This was the idea embraced by sans culottes in August 1792 when the people took up arms against the Swiss Guard and the King and fought for the expropriation of the commons. It was also Bakunin's principle, Kropotkin argued, and the one implemented by the Commune.

That Kropotkin's conception of anti-militarism was at odds with prevailing liberal conceptions is not surprising. Guglielmo Ferrero's influential study, which analysed militarism as a form of barbarism that undermined civilisation and progress towards justice, was based on premises about the 'pacific equilibrium' of the international world that Kropotkin wholly rejected.[171] But his conception was also out of step with a number of radical conceptions, notably feminist analyses that borrowed Kropotkin's principle of mutual aid to develop gendered theories of violence,[172] and those that extended the analysis of slavery to explain patriarchy, linking militarism to sex slavery and coerced reproduction.[173] Kropotkin's conception differed, too, from other anarchist understandings. Guy Aldred placed capitalism at militarism's heart. Indeed, capitalism was 'a system of militarism' that encompassed 'servitude of subservience to laws and customs which subsist ... to perpetuate the horrors of class-rule', the 'immoral authoritarianism of marriage laws, priestly pretence, political paternalism, and scientific and scholastic professionalism'.[174] Kropotkin, in contrast, treated militarism as an aspect of statecraft, linked specifically to war and the monopoly of violence, not generally to conflict. Returning to the idea of the conscripts' strike, Kropotkin argued that general strike was the right tool for workers to use in order to frustrate wars in which they were not involved. He therefore decried the anti-Russian pro-Japanese chauvinism of the English press, establishment and radical alike, during the 1904–5 war. However, in instances of conquest general strike was entirely mistaken: armed resistance was a reasonable response.[175]

Sharing Kropotkin's view that revolution was the best remedy for war, Malatesta may well have argued that Kropotkin's anti-militarist neutrality in the Russo-Japanese war illuminated the faultiness and inconsistency of his anti-German position in 1914.[176] Indeed, Kropotkin's internationalism resulted in other troubling judgements. In contrast to the paternalist and anarchist-friendly Josephine Butler, he was silent about the prospect of Boer oppression of the indigenous population when he called on workers to resist anti-British imperialism in South Africa.[177] Later, balancing Western intervention against Bolshevik domination, Kropotkin argued that while there was plenty to oppose 'in the methods of the Bolshevist Government', the Allied invasion was still worse: 'every armed intervention of a foreign Power necessarily results in a reinforcement of the dictatorial tendencies of the rulers.'[178] The messiness of these decisions reflected the realities that anarchists confronted. 'We do not fight abstract concepts of the state but the existing governments that oppress nations.'[179]

Facing up to the French failure to implement the revolutionary plan hatched in 1792, in 1914 Kropotkin held fast to the principle of national defence against oppression. As the Manifesto of the Sixteen put it, 'we would have preferred to see that population take ... its defence in its own hands'.[180] But the threat of German colonisation outweighed the feebleness of the French revolutionary spirit. To desert the French cause, Kropotkin told the Dutch anti-militarist Domela Nieuwenhuis, was to legitimise the colonial domination of the French by the Germans, compounding the exploitation that ordinary people suffered under capitalism.[181] Above all, perhaps, it was to frustrate the revolutionary aspirations of national groups in the East. Kropotkin's letter to Steffen described Germany's 'warlike spirit' to be 'absolutely incompatible' with the formation of the federations that national groups in the Tsarist empire were on the verge of building.[182] Instead of attaining their independence, Finland and Poland would become German provinces and the hope of emancipation glimpsed in 1905 would be snuffed out. For a fleeting moment in March 1917, between the fall of the Tsar and Lenin's arrival at St Petersburg's Finland station, Kropotkin thought his dream was being realised:

> Is it not grand? All the old-regime authorities *in the villages* and provincial towns swept away, free democratic self-government, the soldier becoming a citizen – almost nobody – to take the defence of the rotten regime, capital punishment abolished, the prisons opened, *the Finnish Constitution restored* the Red Flag floating on the Peter-and-Paul fortress ... and all that realized with comparatively very little bloodshed.[183]

Conclusion to Part 3

In his critical, melancholy reminiscence of Kropotkin, Malatesta made a number of significant claims about his anarchism. First, it traced a progressive evolution, leading to emancipation understood as a singular condition. Like Malatesta, Kropotkin was an optimist, who saw 'things rose-coloured'. They both hoped for 'an early revolution which would realize our ideals'. But in Kropotkin's work, this optimism fuelled a rigid theorisation of anarchy, for he was also a scientist and a 'social reformer', 'pressed' by 'the desire to know and the desire to bring about the well-being of humanity'. Second, Kropotkin was fully immersed in the conventions of his time. He 'professed the materialist philosophy which dominated the scientists of the second half of the nineteenth century' and 'wanted to reduce all to a unity'. Third, his 'conception of the universe was rigorously mechanical' and consequently deterministic. According to Kropotkin's system, individual will 'does not exist and is a mere illusion'. Malatesta continues:

> All that was, is, and shall be, from the orbits of the stars to the birth and decay of a civilization, from an earthquake to the thought of Newton, from the perfume of a rose to the smile of a mother ... all did, does and will happen by the fatal consecutive series of causes and effects of a mechanical character, leaving no room for the possibility by variation.[1]

Because he gave 'no power' to the idea of will, Kropotkin was also unable to defend key anarchist principles. Malatesta argued that 'ideas of freedom, justice and responsibility' had 'no meaning and do not correspond to anything real' in his anarchism. In fact, while Kropotkin was 'very severe on the historical fatalism of the Marxists', he fell into a form of 'mechanical fatalism' which was 'much more paralysing'.[2]

Malatesta's critique has seeped into a number of contemporary critiques of Kropotkin's classical stance. Just as David Miller invokes Malatesta to support his judgement of Kropotkin's 'fatalism',[3] Alfredo Bonnano repeats Malatesta's accusation that Kropotkin 'put the international anarchist movement to sleep' by 'proposing an ideology of waiting'.[4] Saul Newman, too, refers in passing to Malatesta's critique: his attack on the Kropotkinian scientific project was driven by a radical anti-theory of anarchism based on a commitment to insurrectionary practice, leaving a philosophical void for post-anarchism to fill.[5]

Unilike Landauer or Stirner, Malatesta has not yet been described as a precursor of post-anarchism. And he did not probe classical anarchism's observed faulty ontological and epistemological foundations. However, his intuitive sense of the shakiness of Kropotkin's anarchism serves as a useful testing ground to consider some of the central arguments of contemporary critique of the classical tradition. Indeed, because Malatesta advanced his arguments in terms that Kropotkin would have recognised and understood, his criticisms present none of the problems of translation that sometimes emerge when political idioms are imported into philosophy.

The strongest of the three criticisms Malatesta levels against Kropotkin is the first: Kropotkin's optimism led him to believe in the inevitability of revolution. Contrary to Woodcock's suggestion, Kropotkin neither gave up on the idea of revolutionary transformation nor changed his mind about the possibilities for anarchy. His commitment to revolutionary change underpinned his sustained attack on social democracy and reformism and propelled his engagement with syndicalism. Optimism perhaps overstates the brightness of Kropotkin's political thought: his analysis of environmental change and social evolution always left open the possibility of degeneration and regression as much as it promised rejuvenation and growth; his enthusiastic descriptions of anarchy's possibility were paralleled by warnings of the state's morbid growth. Yet Kropotkin's anarchism was resilient and Malatesta was right to explain this feature of his politics by his science. Kropotkin's conception of the world in constant flux encouraged him to think in relational terms. Not even the most dramatic setbacks could eclipse totally the possibility of recovery, not even global war. Kropotkin cut the cloth of his political aspirations to fit what he took to be the readiness of labour movements to instigate change. And in doing so, he let go of his lofty hopes of seeing the rise of revolutionary communal movement across Europe. Even so, he continued to talk about the potential for social reconstruction. Writing to an unnamed correspondent in 1915, Kropotkin wrote the 'burden of the war is *terrible*'. In Russia, however, 'all the classes take part in helping the country to live it through. They conquer the rights of taking part in the life of the country by *practising* these rights'. Russia was not in revolution, but with the French example still uppermost in his mind, Kropotkin hinted that this remained a distinct possibility:

Have you come across my book on the *French Revolution*. One sees there what an importance the *sections* of Paris acquired for imposing their will in political and economical matters, simply by taking into their own hands, first the sale of the estates of the clergy, and when war broke out in 1792 – the choice of the volunteers, their equipment, their sending to the front, the correspondence with them, the supply of labour to the unemployed and so on. It was a striking chapter in the Great Revolution.

Now something – of course on a much smaller scale (we are not in the midst of a Revolution) – takes place in the Society at large – peasants and intellectuals alike – taking part in the efforts to live through this calamity. Never before anything similar happened. It *will* bear fruit. I very much regret to see that the factory hands do not realize this fact. Only in taking part in the efforts of the country to live through this calamity will they affirm their rights of reconstructing society and discovering the ways of doing it.[6]

Malatesta's description of the rigid theorisation of anarchy that fuelled Kropotkin's optimism raises a question about the way in which he applied his ideas to politics, particularly in respect of the war. Kropotkin's antipathy for German social democracy and this conflation of all things German with statism exposed the tensions in his conception of the state and the difficultly of reconciling his analysis of European geo-politics, which emphasised the economic and cultural dimensions of global change, with his critical political theory and historical sociology of the state, which examined the principles of statecraft and the colonising dynamics of state formation. When he drew these strands of analysis together Kropotkin weighed the destructive tendencies of statecraft more heavily than the monopolising processes active within states. Kropotkin may have sympathised with British anti-statists who protested the centralising tendencies of war and bemoaned the introduction of the Defence of the Realm Act, the Board of Education, the Ministry of Information and the 'secret and subtle channels of inspiration' devised to govern 'communal conscience and public opinion'.[7] But he explained the shift towards 'autocracy' within liberal states as an adjustment to global forces operating on all domestic governments, not as an extraordinary corruption of eternal liberal values. This analysis explained why, after spending a lifetime attacking Tsarism, Kropotkin judged the significant harms of Russian autocracy to be less pernicious than the global effects of German Ceasarism. Kropotkin did not let up on his attacks against the autocracy. In the aftermath of the killing of miners in the Lena goldfields Kropotkin told Scottish workers in 1912 that '[t]errorising the workmen by periodical massacres is part of the present methods of the Government of Russia'.[8] But his judgement was that Russia simply lacked Germany's dominating power. Russia was expansionist but was also on the brink of internal collapse.

Woodcock describes Kropotkin's decision to support constitutionalism in Russia in 1917 as a straightforward denial of his anarchist rejection of revolutionary government.[9] Yet Kropotkin's position was consistent with his analysis of the pressures active on the Tsarist regime. Kropotkin had long argued that the overthrow of Tsarism would bolster the independence campaigns of the ethnic groups contained with the Empire. Kropotkin's anarchism similarly led him to argue for a resolution of the land question that supported international federation and communism. Even allowing that Kropotkin was moved by patriotic fervour, 'the onesideness' of his position, Camille Berneri argued, was also an expression 'of his federalist faith'.[10] In 1920 Kropotkin reaffirmed his commitment to the ideal of a decentralised federation of nations based on the independent self-government of 'the constituent parts of the Russian Empire – Finland, the Baltic Provinces, Lithuania, Ukraine, Georgia, Armenia, Siberia, and so on'.[11] Yet acutely aware that he was out of step with the bulk of the Russian revolutionary opinion, he had assumed that the popular movements would opt for constitutional change. Contemplating the possibility in 1902 he argued, '[I]f I speak of the coming Constitution it is not because I see in it a panacea. My personal ideals go far beyond that. But, whether we like it or not, it is coming.'[12] In the event, Lenin's 'strongly-centralised Dictatorship of one party', modelled on the 'Centralist and Jacobinist conspiracy of Babeuf'[13] eclipsed this possibility. Kropotkin's resilient belief in the future formation of 'a federation of free rural communes and free cities' survived, but he probably felt that constitutionalism offered a more secure ground than Bolshevism for future anarchistic change.[14] After all, it was Lenin's forerunner Robespierre who had called time on Roux's anarchistic Paris Commune.

Kropotkin's view that communism and economic integration offered the most robust structural defence against the reappearance of slavery and exploitation helps sustain Malatesta's view of his tendency to rigid theorisation and that his anarchism was reductive. However, the charge is overstated, insofar as the comment was intended to highlight his adoption of a model for anarchy. Malatesta was right that Kropotkin was militant about the economics of anarchy. Moreover, Kropotkin's vision tended towards scientific innovation. While he shared Reclus's profound concerns about the degradation of external nature and the ways that human life disrupted the delicate ecology of the planet,[15] his vision of agrarian socialism, Brian Morris rightly notes, called for the application of smart technologies.[16] Focused on finding ways to resist centralisation and monopoly, Kropotkin linked the abuse of technology to capitalism. It was production for profit that encouraged capitalists to 'rush like a flock of sheep into every new branch of production ... regardless of the usefulness or noxiousness of the goods'.[17] Similarly, Kropotkin attributed the loss of light industry and local artisan craft – the petty trades – to the international division of labour that swamped markets with goods for the middle class while maintaining the producers in poverty. Keen to overcome the problems of divided labour and reduce total labour time, Kropotkin was receptive to the mechanisation of production. Writing lyrically about 'the pleasure than man can derive from the consciousness of the might of his machine, the intelligent character of its work, the gracefulness of its movements, and the correctness for what it is doing', Kropotkin invoked John Ruskin and William Morris to support his contention that industry was compatible with art,[18] but simultaneously rebuked Morris for his 'hatred of machines'.[19] The reprimand opened up a breach in the tradition that Woodcock traces to Lewis Mumford. Instead of doing away with the rug, as Mumford recommended, Kropotkin embraced the vacuum cleaner.[20] Machines were ornaments, in Mumford's terms, and technology was a neutral 'amalgam of tools and applications that can be used for good or bad ends, but have no inherent moral or political content'.[21] From the perspective of contemporary eco-anarchists like Uri Gordon Kropotkin fell squarely within a modernist anarchist frame. At the same time, however, he was happy to entrust the conservation of the natural environment to its inhabitants, who loved and appreciated it. And in distinction to Reclus, he saw no need to involve an aesthetically inclined citizenry to beautify the environment, in the same way that painters created landscapes.[22]

Malatesta's second charge, that the effect of Kropotkin's theory was to reduce all 'to unity' was true, but not in the sense that the critique implies. Kropotkin's anarchism was directed towards harmony, a unity of sorts, but one rooted in movement and diversity. Kropotkin's argument was that the cooperative practices he identified in nature exploded the myths of anarchy-as-chaos that Social Darwinism absorbed from statist political theory and peddled as science. As a descriptor for human behaviour, the principle of mutual aid established a background condition of sociability that explained the origin and development of moral systems and the environmental factors that influenced ethics and struggles for justice. Kropotkin's concept of evolution was unashamedly materialist and he rejected Huxley's distinction between nature and ethics and his recourse to theology to explain the development of moral sentiments. Yet if Malatesta intended to suggest a correspondence with the historical or dialectical materialisms of Marxism, the criticism was unfounded. Kropotkin diverged from the deadening official Marxism of the Social Democratic Federation (SDF) as well as Bax's nuanced Hegelian philosophy. His rejection of Marxism amounted to more than empty rhetoric. The interplay of forces that prompted individuals to act in different ways was irreducible to single causes and unpredictable. And while

Kropotkin was convinced that anarchist communism best supported the expression of the ethics of mutual aid, just as he thought statism was destructive of it, he was a communist because he also defended the principle of individual sovereignty. As his Czech followers put it: 'individualism was marked as the philosophical – and communism as the economic side of anarchy.'[23] Separating the two, as Tucker's individualism did, offered no protection against the monopolising tendencies of capitalism, a point that Tucker eventually acknowledged.[24] Kropotkin's critique of Marxism was that it deduced principles of socialism from a philosophical method that lacked empirical support. The local conditions that shaped real economies, and that Kropotkin and Reclus understood to be fundamental to global harmony, appeared to be glossed over. Aware that his political vision stood on a crowded ideological thoroughfare, Kropotkin adopted an anarchist approach in order to show the feasibility of anarchism and to demonstrate how anarchist communist alternatives could be furthered by direct action. Rather than squeeze out space for the will, as Malatesta argued, this politics was fired by a lack of certainty as much as it was by hope.

Kropotkin argued that the freedom that anarchy promised demanded the abandonment of the institutions and practices that emerged as a result of European colonisation. The character of the freedom that anarchy promoted was illustrated in his critique of prisons, which he treated as microcosms of the state. The superintendents charged with overseeing prisoners were mini-autocrats. Each was 'a king in his dominions' able to 'rob his inmates', 'submit them to the most horrible punishments', 'torture the children of convicts' and have killed any convict parent who dared to complain.[25] Prisons bred social divisions that were not only legitimated by the state but that also mirrored the power relations that the state cemented. Those given authority abused power 'like all those who hold power in their hands'. Corrupted by the institutional framework, warders became 'petty and vexatious persecutors of the prisoners',[26] simultaneously developing 'a certain brotherhood, or rather *esprit de corps*' based on 'command and compliance'. Slavish labour practices, as central to prison life as work was to capitalism, were extraordinarily and outrageously degrading. Prisoners, Kropotkin argued, were set tasks to satisfy the 'base revenge of ... society' and 'compelled to work, not because somebody wants one's work, but merely to be punished'.[27] Even so, prison schemes simultaneously promoted the morally improving effects of work, demonising anyone who had the strength to resist as indolent and asocial. In this regard, prisons were more like prototypes for the state rather than its miniature. It was possible to imagine how the dystopia Kropotkin described from his reading of the 'bulky literature' on the prison system may one day extend beyond the prison walls:

> [T]he greatest admiration is bestowed precisely on those systems which have obtained the results of discipline with the least possible number of warders. The ideal of our prisons would be a thousand automatons, rising and working, eating and going to bed, by electric currents transmitted to them by a single warder.[28]

Serving as centres for a type of sociological conditioning that were designed to instil submission and crush insubordination, prisons were inherently repressive.[29] As Oscar Wilde put it, the aim of the prison system was 'not only to form habits, but to *force* them, to reorder the character of the inmates and make them ideal Victorian subjects'.[30] Prisons enforced moral codes based on an unthinking adherence to authority, habitually punishing offenders in order to uphold the principle while acquiescing to the causes of its contravention. Practices that were as often as not linked to impoverishment as to desire were routinely criminalised. Referring to Kropotkin's work, Charlotte Wilson, the co-founder of *Freedom*, estimated that in 1912 in the region of 85 to 90 per cent of women's prisons were populated by women convicted of prostitution.[31] Thus the coerciveness of the methods of socialisation was linked to the rigidity of the moral values that rulers sought to instil. Prison, Wilde argued, 'concentrated and perfected the moral system implicit in the ideology of class society. It served as an institutional embodiment of the Protestant Ethic.'[32]

It is difficult to deny the optimistic cast of the anarchist solutions Kropotkin offered in response to this analysis of slavery and imprisonment. His expectation was that ordinary people had the capacity to resolve complex social problems through their direct interactions. As prison was a metaphor for the state, so too was its abolition a descriptor for anarchy. Freedom, Kropotkin argued, was *the possibility of action without being influenced in those actions by the fear of punishment by society*'. He realised, however, that the abandonment of institutionalised power would not result in absolute liberty or licence. On the contrary, Kropotkin's negative conception of liberty as freedom from slavery described a condition of freedom where individuals were never perfectly free.

Anarchy was integral to freedom's realisation just as private property and the state were embedded in non-anarchists' accounts of liberty. In real life, however, this perfect idea was always compromised by social relationships. Partnerships, families, small associations and social institutions imposed restrictions that were potentially enslaving: 'man is *never free*', Kropotkin observed.[33] The *Spirit of Revolt* was written with the same restrictions in mind. Because human animals were sociable and cohered in societies that constructed rules, norms and social practices, members of those societies were always subject to internal and external constraints. Children were raised in a cultural milieu and absorbed the habits established by previous generations, often unthinkingly. In *Mutual Aid*, Kropotkin accepted that the patriarchal family was institutionalised in mutual-aid societies. He also acknowledged that the emergence of national folk traditions, which he celebrated, had cemented customary laws. The 'sentence-finders' appointed in village communities to settle issues of wrongdoing were 'versed in the songs, triads, sagas, etc., by means of which law was perpetrated in memory'. The retention of the law through folk traditions 'became a sort of art, a "mystery," carefully transmitted in certain families from generation to generation'.[34] His conclusion was that '[n]o society is possible without certain principles of morality generally recognised'.[35] Anarchist societies were no exception.

Kropotkin defended anarchy on the grounds that individuals were not good enough to exercise authority and should not, therefore, be given the power to do so. This view also chimed with Wilde's. 'What is inhuman in modern life is officialdom. Authority is as destructive of those who exercise it as it is to those on whom it is exercised,' Wilde argued.[36] Yet while anarchists left 'to each the right to act as he thinks best', and denied 'the right of society to punish any one, in any way, for any anti-social act which he may have committed', they did 'not forego our own capacity to love what seems to us good and to hate what seems to us bad'.[37] Similarly, while freedom required intellectual and economic well-being or, as Kropotkin put it, freedom from 'the threat of hunger', it did not bring freedom from judgement: free individuals would not have to adjust their behaviours in anticipation of censure 'except when it comes from a friend'.[38]

There were important judgements that free people would have to make about the nature of transgression. One of the pressing issues that the nascent science of criminology had revealed was the prevalence of mental health problems among prisoners. Would anarchy provide a cure? Kropotkin's default was to think in terms of mutual aid and he proposed the introduction of systems of care to help the vulnerable, the alienated and those inhabiting the 'borderland where man loses control over his actions'.[39] The conditions that bred Luccheni, Elizabeth of Austria's assassin, would be eradicated by the movement towards anarchy. Yet resisting the medicalisation of crime just as he opposed the criminalisation of those suffering from mental illness,

Kropotkin did not deny that free people would have to confront this issue. It was possible, too, to imagine wilful disobedience and resistance in anarchist societies, even where the ethics of mutual aid were habituated. What he called firm will or responsibility meant that free people tailored their behaviours from a regard for others, not that they would accept unquestioningly established moral rules. His point was that where norms were challenged and harms done, will and responsibility were not grounds for the attribution of guilt or blame. The general principle was that instances of transgression should be negotiated through compassion and solidarity. Indeed, preferring to leave the certainties of individual accountability to the state, he blurred the boundaries between what may be regarded as wrong, foolhardy and mad. The "'ideal madman whom the law creates," and the only one whom the law is ready to recognize as irresponsible for his acts, is as rare as the ideal "criminal" whom the law insists on punishing'.[40]

Although anarchist communists argued that the tendency of individualism towards economic protectionism was the point at which they parted company with Stirner, it was this conception of freedom as social interdependence that, for Kropotkin, explained their fundamental incompatibility. Kropotkin did not present community as the "'goal" of history'. Nor did he 'aspire to community', as Stirner accused his various opponents. Yet Kropotkin was unable to 'renounce every hypocrisy of community', as Stirner put it, and he did not share Stirner's aspiration for '*one-sidedness*'. Kropotkin accepted what Stirner called 'the most comprehensive commune, "human society," ' as a fact. From his perspective, Stirner's desire to 'seek in others only means and organs which we may use as our property' wrongly suggested a degree of autonomy that was simply unachievable.[41] Even if Kropotkin thought Stirner's egoism attractive (which he did not), he argued that freedom was the ability to change social norms by resistance, using the principle of freedom from slavery as the benchmark for wilful action. Freedom was about recognising interdependence not seeking independence. Being free did not mean being released from social ties and obligations, or asserting uniqueness through egoistic actions, as if those social ties did not or should not exist.

While the unity that Malatesta ascribed to Kropotkin was far more complex than the critique implies, the last criticism, that Kropotkin's science was mechanistic and deterministic, wrongly collapsed the sociological tendencies that Kropotkin believed detectable with the aid of science with the social 'laws' that he repeatedly dismissed as ideological dogmas. Kropotkin used geography to ground this analysis and this led him to trace the historic shifts affecting nineteenth-century politics to the French Revolution. The mainstreaming of revolutionary principles in sets of institutions that were conceived in order to contain their emancipatory force had given birth to the radical political and cultural currents that engulfed Europe, challenging the colonising, monopolising energies of the state and capitalism. Nihilism was one example of the Revolution's impact. Similarly, the 1871 Paris Commune was a defining moment in modern history because it rekindled the Revolution's spirit and expressed it in a new, radical organisational form. Kropotkin had a proclivity to use the Revolution as a reference point for nineteenth-century movements and ideas. His comparison of Lenin with Robespierre was one example. Moreover, he also used the Revolution to forecast the likely evolution of states. In 1898 he outlined both the tendency from local to international revolution and the differential 'character' that national revolutions were likely to take. Being 'in the state that France was fifty years ago', Germany would republicanise, as France had done in 1848. Russia would 'make her revolution of 1789'. France, Spain and Italy would embark on 'a new phase of human development'.[42] In 1920 he confirmed the rightness of this prediction. Russia was going through a transformation equivalent to the revolution of 1639–1648 in Britain and 1789–94 in France.[43] Yet this was not a stage of development, such as Kropotkin associated with Marxism. The difference was twofold. On the one hand, the motive forces of the predicted shifts were multiple, not principally economic. On the other, the outcome of change was largely dependent on prevailing local conditions, not the progress of history itself. Geography showed how cultural movements, from Christianity to the Enlightenment, extended across the globe, with new technologies and systems of knowledge migrating from their source to all parts of the world. Revolutionary aspirations were no different, but both the speed of change and the impacts were variable. Kropotkin's comment to Dr Steffen that the 1905 revolution had forever ruled out the possibility of the revival of Russian autocracy *in the forms it had before* and the emergence of *imperialist forms and spirit which parliamentary rule has taken in Germany*, smacked of patriotism and in retrospect perhaps looked naive.[44] However, it reflected Kropotkin's view that the Russian counterpart to the French Revolution would yield very different results:

[T]he fact is that the Russian (especially the Great Russian) worker and peasant are imbued with that spirit and carry on the *artel* principle into every nook of their lives – not because they are the best men. They do so simply because the village-community has not yet been wrecked by the State, and they carry on into industrial life the spirit of the institution which makes the essence of the agricultural life of the nation.[45]

Kropotkin may have believed that everything in the world had causes and effects, but that hardly supported Malatesta's contention that his science was therefore mechanistic or that it squeezed out the possibility of variation. It was this very possibility that maintained Kropotkin's anarchism, eventually driving him into an oppositional camp. There is a world of philosophy between Kropotkin's anarchism and contemporary anarchist theory. But Malatesta's inflection distorted and vulgarised his work, presenting an interpretation that ripped the heart out of anarchist science.

Reviewing the Classical Anarchist Tradition

The principle aims of this book were to rescue Kropotkin from the framework of classical anarchism and to explain the politics that led him to support the Entente powers in 1914. The two objectives were to open up more space for serious engagement with the history of anarchist ideas and to offer an alternative to the ideological, exclusionary accounts of anarchism that the invention of the classic tradition has helped to stimulate.

The emergence of classical anarchism and Kropotkin's place in it is set out in the first part of the study. Two dominant narratives have been promoted: in their keenness to disassociate anarchism from revolutionary violence, leading new anarchists turned Kropotkin into a poster-boy for a type of non-violent, gradualist politics that overplayed and distorted the role that evolution played in his work and helped create a philosophy that could be detached from practice. Removing the wedge that new anarchists placed between Kropotkin-brand anarchism and Bakuninism, post-anarchists fastened on a dubious account of science to mount a critique of grand narratives, essentialism and utopianism. The shakiness of the application of the classical model to Kropotkin's political thought is discussed in the conclusions to the second and third parts of the study. Neither the new anarchist nor the post-anarchist renderings of Kropotkin's evolutionary theory, his understanding of science, his theory of change or his idea of the state bear close scrutiny. Kropotkin thought that the world was knowable and that knowledge advanced through a process of continual revision. But he also thought that the world could be re-imagined and that its remodelling was achievable by the application of science. He was a scientist, not a metaphysician and an empiricist not a rationalist but he was also a utopian, not a realist. Nihilism shaped Kropotkin's thinking, tailoring science to the achievement of anarchist goals where the removal of fear enabled individuals to investigate a plethora of questions that statism repressed. Rather than root anarchy in a conception of human nature, he grounded it in resistance.

Kropotkin's view was that flawed, ordinary people were capable of taking responsibility for their actions and negotiating their differences without recourse to institutionalised systems of law. This is not an unproblematic view, as the discussion of wilfulness indicates, but the questions that it raises are quite different from those associated with the thesis of natural goodness. Kropotkin addressed two questions: how to overcome habits of servility and re-build institutions for self-government and how to channel revolutionary passions in an anarchist direction. In doing so, he proposed a set of strategies for change and outlined what he considered to be practical organisational principles – decentralised federation, communism, integrated economics, cooperation, direct action, individual sovereignty. The model of anarchy that emerged was a self-regulating condition, harmonious in this regard, but it was not a static or finished order.

Anarchy, like the state, described a kind of social order that might be realised through the adoption of particular practices. Just as it was possible to imagine the further growth of the state, it was also possible to envisage its dismemberment through the stimulation of multiple processes of federation. Kropotkin's account of the European state's development was designed to expose the impermanence of statist institutions and the structural inequalities that abstract political philosophy systematically airbrushed from the analysis of justice, rights and obligation. Both arguments underlined the feasibility and desirability of self-ordering systems. His description of the colonising and monopolising processes inherent in statism explained why territorialisation and bordering could only ever serve as sources of permanent global instability, adding to the normative force of this critique.

Kropotkin's decision to back the Entente in 1914 is often treated as an aberration of his political thought. That Kropotkin's analysis of European history and politics and his estimation of the war's likely outcomes were controversial is hardly a matter of debate. At the outbreak of the war he advocated a response that was not only anti-liberal and anti-pacifist, but also at odds with mainstream anarchist internationalism. Nevertheless, his break with the bulk of the anarchist movement in 1914 is explicable in terms of his anarchism: Kropotkin was not simply out of step with the idea 'no war but the class war', he rejected it. The state was an instrument of class exploitation, but it also imposed the values of particular religious, cultural, ethnic and gendered elites on diverse groups and it cemented social relationships that were based on domination and slavery, typically in the name of freedom. As an anti-militarist Kropotkin was anti-imperialist and anti-capitalist but he supported the right of self-defence to resist imperialism and colonisation. Distinguishing war from violence, he rejected humanitarian intervention as militaristic and advocated direct action as an anti-war strategy. When confronted with the reality of war and the failure of revolutionary direct action to resist it, he supported the campaign against Germany as an anti-militarist and anti-coloniser.

Kropotkin's vilification sweeps his inconvenient deviation from anarchist norms under the carpet and also conceals the divergent ways in which concepts of internationalism and militarism, class, capitalism and solidarity were understood.

The break-up of the First International and the emergence of syndicalism and the Russian revolution all revealed significant differences between revolutionary socialists who shared the same languages. Sensitive to these commonalities, Kropotkin made strenuous efforts to clarify the theoretical distance between anarchism and social democracy. In the British context, his contact with Bax highlighted the possibilities for confusion and the nature of the disagreement. Both were immersed in a common stock of European ideas, from August Comte to Lewis Morgan and Henry Maine. Both were drawn towards evolutionary theory to propound an idea of socialist ethics. Both, moreover, regarded nihilism as the model for this ethics. Yet, as he intimated to Bax on a walk from Croyden to Leatherhead, these ideas played out in ways that were antithetical to anarchism when read through a Marxist lens.[1] Kropotkin's complaint, which chimes with post-anarchist objections to 'classical' theory, pinpointed the commitment to the materialist conception of history as the crucial point of divergence.

The role that Kropotkin assigned to political theory as a central part of action reflected his view that revolutionary cultures were shaped by prevailing currents of ideas. Cahm observes that Kropotkin described 'socialists who wanted to leave all discussion of theory on one side, so as to concentrate on united action to prepare for revolution' as 'dishonest'.[2] Their refusal signalled an attempt to garner support for political ideals that they were unwilling to make explicit for fear of rejection. If anarchists wanted to shape resistance politics and remain wedded to the principle of self-emancipation, it was imperative that their ideas were clearly expressed and well understood. Championing an anti-theoretical stance, in the name of anarchism, was simply nonsensical because it only helped non-anarchists and anti-anarchists fill the void and seize the imagination of oppressed groups.[3]

Judging Kropotkin's stance on the war by the standards of one interpretative position assumes a uniformity of view that his approach to political thought contests. It imposes a conceptual homogeneity in the name of legitimate anarchist politics in the same way that the analysis of classical anarchism turns nineteenth-century anarchists into Enlightenment theorists and Manicheans. Challenging Kropotkin's designation as a classical anarchist not only offers new avenues for the analysis of his thought it also provides an opportunity to consider the value of the model itself.

New anarchism is rightly associated with inventive and distinctive literatures and practices. Post-anarchism has similarly generated important and insightful critiques. But the lenses that leading writers in these currents have used to examine Kropotkin are woefully distorting. While Kropotkin's place in the classical tradition is said to be representative rather than exhaustive, the mismatch between his political thought and the classical descriptor raises questions about its general value: what remains of classical anarchism if one of its chief exponents turns out to be something other than the model allows? Post-anarchist analysis of historical anarchism has been subject to a number of important critiques.[4] Yet as Nathan Jun notes, the 'helpful caricature of anarchism' is 'used again and again to play up the alleged novelty of postmodernism'[5] and the classical model survives largely intact. The impasse Jun observes evokes the theoretical gridlock that Carole Pateman confronted in her critique of Joseph Schumpeter's model of classical democracy. In her intervention into his debate she argued 'critics, too ... tend to accept the characterisation of the "classical" theory by the writers whom they are criticising, and like them, tend to present a composite model of that theory'. Her view was that *the notion of a "classical theory of democracy" is a myth*. For as long as 'the myth of a "classical" theory continues', she argued, the 'views and the nature of the theories of the earlier writers' will be 'persistently misrepresented'. 'Only when the myth has been exposed can the question be tackled of whether the normative revision of democracy is justified or not.'[6] Pateman's critique may equally be applied to classical anarchism. The post-war construction of classical anarchism and Kropotkin's elevation within this tradition was generated by a specific politics but the invention of the tradition bears a resemblance to Schumpeter's approach to democracy and his treatment of the 'eighteenth-century theory'. The myth of classical anarchism similarly warps and distorts analysis of historical thought and the pigeonholing of generations of anarchists by the invention of this tradition is a barrier to the examination of anarchist political ideas.

The tendency towards the ideological framing of Kropotkin's political thought is similarly disfiguring. Although Kropotkin was not solely responsible for the articulation of anarchist communism, he is rightly identified as a leading exponent of this current of thought. In the *Encyclopaedia Britannica* entry on anarchism he described his threefold aims: 'to prove that communism – at least partial – has more chances of being established than collectivism'; 'that free, or anarchist-communism is the only form of communism that has any chance of being accepted in civilised societies' and 'to indicate how, during a revolutionary period, a large city ... could organise itself on the lines of free communism'.[7] As a communist Kropotkin argued that it was right to assess the practical implications of other theoretical positions and to subject proposals to critique. Individualist anarchist doctrines were faulty, in his view, as his engagement with Stirner and Tucker shows. Even so, Kropotkin adopted communism as a solution to a problem of organisation not as a foundational commitment. And there is an important difference between Kropotkin or analysts like Zenker or later, Irving Horowitz, who organised anarchists into particular schools in an effort to analyse currents within the anarchist movement, and more recent analysts who have variously devised measures to determine membership of anarchist traditions or elevated culturally and geographically located practices to demonstrate an apparent shift from time-bound ideology to movement-orientated politics. Rather than apply tests for ideological inclusion Kropotkin recognised the family resemblances between groups who worked within anarchist frameworks: Tucker was an adversary, but an anarchist all the same. Stirner's abstract egoism resulted in his neglect of sociability, yet he, too, was as much an anarchist as Nettlau, whose response to syndicalism Kropotkin dubbed individualist or philosophical. Equally, Kropotkin advocated anarchist involvement in syndicalism because he recognised the compatibility of revolutionary unionism with anarchism and the possibilities that it offered for anarchist propagandising. Unionism was not an article of faith. Unions were mass organisations of disadvantaged groups, counterparts to the rural workers' land movements, whose self-emancipation anarchists wanted to support.

Kropotkin defined anarchism in different ways. In 1894, he suggested that it variously described mode of action, a utopia, a social theory, a way of thinking or reasoning about the world, a critical theory and a way of comprehending the totality of nature.[8] Anarchism's distinctive core, he argued sometime later, was 'both a philosophical and a practical principle which signified that the whole of life of human societies, everything from daily individual relationships between people to broader relationships between races across oceans, could and should be reformulated'.[9] Kropotkin's aversion to scientific laws made him wary of labelling anarchism a synthetic philosophy, since this was the name given to Herbert Spencer's unified system of knowledge. Overcoming his reservations, he adopted the term because it captured the diversity of the social and cultural movements he associated with anarchism. The synthesis Kropotkin had in mind was structured by what he called the " 'No State," or "No Authority" ' principle.[10] This made Proudhon anarchism's first theorist and the anti-authoritarians in the First International its first advocates. Kropotkin understood anarchism historically, as Marie Fleming also argued: 'a movement that had developed in response to specific social-economic grievances'.[11] Yet the synthetic approach enabled Kropotkin to take a broader perspective on anarchist history and the future of anarchist philosophies. Because it described a way of thinking about the world, anarchism chimed with the most significant developments in modern science – evolutionary biology, quantum physics, astronomy – in modern culture – Ibsen, Zola, Tolstoy – and in philosophy – Darwin, Guyau, Comte. Using the same logic, Kropotkin was able to trace a history of non-European and pre-Christian anarchistic doctrines and resistance movements that dovetailed with the anarchist movements that emerged in nineteenth-century Western Europe. Similarly, because anarchism described a mode of action, Kropotkin held that it was rooted in the spontaneous action of social movements while maintaining that the people involved in those movements were not necessarily or even typically anarchist. As a synthetic philosophy anarchism provided a focal point for a spectrum of ideas, highlighting the commonalities that spoke to anarchist aspirations and providing a distinctive theoretical and practical politics, distinguishable from liberalism, syndicalism, mutualism and Marxism, to support their achievement.

Kropotkin's willingness to defend anarchism's scope reflected his understanding of global change. The cultural shifts and complex patterns and movements he saw in geography allowed him to locate the origins of anarchism precisely, while also setting its emergence in a global history of change. At the same time, Kropotkin was also philosophically wedded to the anarchism's non-sectarian progression. His friend William Morris set himself the task of 'making socialists'. Kropotkin's ambition was not to make anarchists but to create the conditions in which diverse groups and individuals could live anarchistically. He told Marie Goldsmith that it was it was impossible to 'convert everyone to anarchism'. In any case, anarchists appreciated that 'not everyone is of the same mind'.[12] Although he linked the realisation of communism to a particular ethics, he imagined that anarchism would provide a home for conservatives as well as socialists and people of faith as well as atheists. Cross-cutting global networks of mutual aid tempered localism but Kropotkin's commitment was internationalist. Turning anarchism into a sect or seeking to determine who was or was not genuinely anarchist would likely undermine this strategy, alienating anarchists from potential sympathisers.

It is interesting to speculate on the ways that Kropotkin might imagine his legacy in prevailing forms of anarchism. His approach to the past was to highlight the continuities and discontinuities of thought, explaining significant innovations with reference to political contingencies.

Adaptation was central to Kropotkin's anarchism. His admiring critique of Proudhon was not trumpeted as the start of a new wave but as the defence of anarchist principles in changed political contexts. Looking at anarchism's third wave, he would be surprised to find that he has been consigned to the past, described as an outmoded sage and a theorist who has had his time. 'Bad timing it is to grow old!' he wrote to Marsh in 1895.[13] He was then in his early fifties and his health was about to decline. By the standards of the *Appeal to the Young*, however, Kropotkin remained as youthful as he had ever been. The shape of things to come, he argued, was in the hands of those who had the power to mould the material world by choosing to act ethically in ways that challenged the social, political and economic forces that affected to control it. The *Appeal* was addressed to students, but the young were really the young at heart who refused to stop pushing the alternatives.

Notes

Introduction

1. Marie Fleming, *Geography of Freedom*, p. 23.
2. Paul Eltzbacher, *Anarchism*.
3. Michael Schmidt and Lucien van der Walt, *Black Flame*.

Chapter 1

1. Richard Day, *Gramsci is Dead*, pp. 16–17, 93–4.
2. Eltzbacher, *Anarchism*.
3. George Woodcock, *Anarchism*. In 2004 Colin Ward noted that Peter Marshall's *Demanding the Impossible* was likely to overtake Woodcock's book in global sales, but that it had probably been 'the most widely read book on the subject in the world'. Foreword to *Anarchism*.
4. Eltzbacher, p. 207. For a critique of Eltzbacher's attempt to capture a 'putative anarchist tradition' see Fleming, *Geography of Freedom*, p. 24.
5. Süreyyya Evren and Ruth Kinna (eds), *Anarchist Developments in Cultural Studies*, pp. 212–40.
6. Eltzbacher identified William Godwin, Max Stirner, P.-J. Proudhon, Mikhail Bakunin, Benjamin Tucker and Leo Tolstoy as the other six. Woodcock relegated Tucker to a supporting role, including him in his chapter 'Various traditions' but otherwise followed Eltzbacher's choices.
7. Woodcock, *Anarchism*, p. 221.
8. Day, *Gramsci is Dead*, p. 16.
9. Simon Critchley, *Infinitely Demanding*, p. 148.
10. Paul McLaughlin, *Anarchism and Authority*, p. 10.
11. McLaughlin's introductory chapter, 'Defining anarchism', examines the negative components of this construction.
12. James J. Martin, *Men against the State*, p. 281.
13. Ernst Victor Zenker, *Anarchism*, p. 173.
14. *The Times*, Monday 31 January 1921.
15. Subrata Mukherjee and Sushila Ramaswamy (eds), *Prince Peter Kropotkin*, p. xiii.
16. Marshall, *Demanding the Impossible*, p. 320.
17. Lee Alan Dugatkin, *The Prince of Evolution*; Graham Purchase, *Evolution and Revolution*.
18. Max Nettlau, 'Peter Kropotkin at work', in Joseph Ishill (ed.), *Peter Kropotkin*, p. 13.
19. Errico Malatesta, 'The most greatly humane man', in Ishill (ed.), *Peter Kropotkin*, p. 39.

20. Errico Malatesta, 'Peter Kropotkin', *Freedom Bulletin*, 12 July 1931.

21. D. L. Sills (ed.), *International Encyclopedia of the Social Sciences*, vol. 8, p. 464.

22. Brian Morris, *The Anarchist Geographer*, p. 18.

23. J. Scott Keltie, 'Peter Kropotkin, Geographer, Explorer, Mutualist', in *Centennial Expressions on Peter Kropotkin, 1842–1942 by Pertinent Thinkers*, p. 5.

24. Federico Ferretti 'The correspondence between Elisée Reclus and Pëtr Kropotkin as a source for the history of geography', p. 217. Reclus's separate development of the concept of mutual aid is discussed in Rob Knowles, *Political Economy from Below*, pp. 212–15.

25. See Iain McKay's *Mutual Aid*.

26. Pablo Servigne, 'Qu'a-t-on appris sur l'entraide depuis Kropotkine?', p. 54.

27. Woodcock, *Anarchism*, pp. 205–6.

28. Ibid. p. 221.

29. Eltzbacher, p. 1.

30. Woodcock, *Anarchism*, p. 7.

31. George Woodcock, *Anarchy or Chaos*, p. 19.

32. George Woodcock, *Anarchism and Anarchists*, p. 41.

33. Adam Buick, 'What Marx should have said to Kropotkin'; Schmidt and van der Walt, *Black Flame*, pp. 17–19.

34. Samuel Clark argues that anti-statism fails to capture adequately the unity of anarchist traditions. See *Living Without Domination*, p. 10. Fleming rejects the idea of a tradition; see *Geography of Freedom*, pp. 23–4. Fleming disputed the point with Woodcock who defended anti-statism as a defining feature of anarchism in order to distinguish it from what he considered to be rival forms of socialism.

35. Woodcock, *Anarchy or Chaos*, p. 47.

36. Colin Ward, *Anarchy in Action*, p. 4.

37. Carissa Honeywell, *A British Anarchist Tradition*; Matthew Adams, *Kropotkin, Read and the Intellectual History of British Anarchism*.

38. Woodcock, *Anarchy or Chaos*, p. 46.

39. For a discussion of Woodcock's contribution to the development of the anarchist canon, see Süreyyya Evren and Ruth Kinna 'George Woodcock', pp. 45–61.

40. Woodcock, *Anarchism,* p. 145.

41. Robert Cutler, *The Basic Bakunin*; Robert M. Cutler 'Bakunin and the psychobiographers'. See also Jon Bekken, 'Bakunin and the historians'.

42. Maurice Paléologue, 'Deux Précurseurs de Bolshévisme', p. 62.

43. Stephen Osofsky gives a comprehensive listing of testimonials in *Peter Kropotkin*, pp. 19–22.

44. 'Earnest Adddress by Anna Strunsky', *San Francisco Call*, 11 October 1904.

45. Louise H. Williams, 'Prince Kropotkin's philosophy in the light of today', p. 441.

46. Victor Robinson, 'Comrade Kropotkin', p. 111.

47. Nicholas Walter, 'The scientific revolutionary', p. 280. Oscar Wilde's appreciation is in *De Profundis*, p. 934. For other tributes, see Tom Swan, *Kropotkin*; Havelock Ellis, *Kropotkin*.

48. George Woodcock and Ivan Avakumović, *The Anarchist Prince*, p. 439.

49. Colin MacInnes, 'Eve's children', p. 288.

50. Alexander Grey, *The Socialist Tradition*, p. 362.

51. G. D. H. Cole, *A History of Socialist Thought: Marxism and Anarchism 1850–1890*, vol. 2, p. 351.

52. George Lichtheim, *A Short History of Socialism*, pp. 146–7.

53. Woodcock, *Anarchism*, p. 151.

54. Ibid. p. 171.

55. Paul Avrich, *The Russian Anarchists*, pp. 26–7.

56. On Nechaev see Paul Avrich, *Bakunin and Nechaev*.

57. 'Switzerland', *The Times*, 10 August 1881.

58. Richard T. Ely, *Recent American Socialism*, p. 6.

59. Richard T. Ely, *French and German Socialism in Modern Times*, p. 187.

60. For Haymarket, see Dave Roediger and Franklin Rosemont (eds), *Haymarket Scrapbook*; for the anarchist peril, see Nhat Hong, *The Anarchist Beast*.

61. *The Spectator*, 17 July 1886, p. 961.

62. Haia Shpayer-Makov, 'The reception of Peter Kropotkin in Britain, 1886–1917', pp. 373–90.

63. Edith Sellers, 'Our most distinguished refugee', p. 537.

64. 'Foreign view of anarchism', *Sacramento Daily Union*, 13 November 1898.

65. Paul H. Douglas, 'Proletarian political theory', in Charles Edward Merriam and Harry Elmber Barnes (eds), *A History of Political Theories*, p. 203.

66. Marshall, *Demanding the Impossible*, p. 631.

67. Hermia Oliver, *The International Anarchist Movement in Late Victorian London*, p. 152.

68. Henry Seymour, *The Two Anarchisms*.

69. Oliver, *International Anarchist Movement*, p. 153.

70. Kathy E. Ferguson, 'Toward a new anarchism', pp. 39–57.

71. Herbert Read in David Goodway (ed.), *A One Man Manifesto*, p. 124.

72. David Stafford, 'Anarchists in Britain today', in David Apter and James Joll (eds), *Anarchism Today*, p. 91; Herbert Read, 'Pragmatic anarchism', pp. 54–61.

73. Stafford, 'Anarchists', p. 92. Landauer's remark is in 'Weak statesmen, weaker people!', in Gabriel Kuhn, *Gustav Landauer, Revolution and Other Writings*, p. 214.

74. Read, 'Pragmatic anarchism', p. 55.

75. David Apter, 'The old anarchism and the new – some comments', in Apter and Joll (eds), *Anarchism Today*, p. 8.

76. Read, *One Man Manifesto*, p. 124.

77. Woodcock, *Anarchism and Anarchists*, p. 57; Giovanni Baldelli, *Social Anarchism*, pp. 11–68.

78. For a discussion of anarchism and counter-community, see Sharif Gemie, 'Counter-community', pp. 349–67.
79. Daniel Cohn-Bendit, *Obsolete Communism*, p. 111.
80. Jerry Rubin, *Scenarios of the Revolution*, p. 89.
81. Woodcock and Avakumović, *The Anarchist Prince*, p. 329.
82. Victor Mūnoz, 'A chronology of Peter Kropotkin', in *Anarchists*, trans. Scott Johnson, p. 15.
83. Lewis Mumford, *The Culture of Cities*, pp. 9, 340.
84. Bookchin refers to Kropotkin and William Morris in *Post-Scarcity Anarchism*, p. 37.
85. Murray Bookchin, *The Ecology of Freedom*, p. 241.
86. Bookchin, *Ecology of Freedom*, p. viii.
87. Roel van Duyn, *Message of a Wise Kabouter*, p. 48.
88. Friedrich Engels, 'Introduction', in Karl Marx, *Class Struggles in France*.
89. Woodcock, *Anarchism and Anarchists*, p. 95.
90. Ibid. p. 55.
91. Bookchin, 'Post-scarcity anarchism', p. 13.
92. Edward Carpenter, *My Days and Dreams*, p. 218.
93. Nicholas Walter, 'About anarchism', in Howard Ehrlich, Carol Ehrlich, David de Leon and Glenda Morris (eds), *Reinventing Anarchy*, p. 62.
94. William O. Reichert, 'Toward a new understanding of anarchism', p. 865.
95. Paul Goodman, *The Black Flag of Anarchism*, p. 6.
96. Paul Goodman, 'Kropotkin at this moment', p. 126.
97. Rudolf de Jong, 'Provos and Kabouters', in Apter and Joll (eds), *Anarchism Today*, pp. 177–9.
98. Eric Hobsbawm, *Revolutionaries*, p. 82.

Chapter 2

1. Landauer, in Kuhn, *Revolution and Other Writings*, p. 303; emphasis in original.
2. Eltzbacher, *Anarchism*, p. 1.
3. Woodcock and Avakumović, *The Anarchist Prince*; Martin Miller, *Kropotkin*; Caroline Cahm, *Kropotkin and the Rise of Revolutionary Anarchism 1872–1886*.
4. David Stafford, *From Anarchism to Reformism*, p. 66.
5. Kropotkin to Georges Herzig, 9 March 1909, Wintsch papers, IISH. Kropotkin's account of the Bern demonstration appears in *Memoirs of a Revolutionist*, p. 273. For an account of the demonstration and the genesis of propaganda by the deed, see Stafford, *From Anarchism to Reformism*, pp. 80–3.
6. Nunzio Pernicone, *Italian Anarchism, 1864–1892*, p. 120.
7. Miller, *Kropotkin*, p. 167.
8. See Woodcock and Avakumović, *The Anarchist Prince*, pp. 368–70.
9. Kropotkin, *Memoirs*, p. 329.
10. Ibid. p. 262.

11. Fleming, *Geography of Freedom*, pp. 11, 137–8.
12. Cahm, *Kropotkin and the Rise of Revolutionary Anarchism 1872–1886*, p. 1.
13. Cahm, *Kropotkin and the Rise of Revolutionary Anarchism 1872–1886*, p. 64.
14. John Quail, *The Slow Burning Fuse*, p. 59.
15. Kropotkin, 'Anarchism', in R. N. Baldwin (ed.), *Kropotkin's Revolutionary Pamphlets*, p. 284.
16. Guy Aldred, *Socialism and Parliament*, pt 1, p. 47.
17. Woodcock and Avakumović, *The Anarchist Prince*, pp. 200, 252.
18. Barry C. Johnson (ed.), *Tea and Anarchy!*, p. 65.
19. James Hulse, *Revolutionists in London*, p. 52.
20. See, for example, R. B. Fowler, 'The anarchist tradition of political thought'.
21. For example, Irving Horowitz (ed.), *The Anarchists*.
22. See, for example, William O. Reichert, 'Anarchism, freedom, and power', pp. 139–49.
23. John Clark's *The Anarchist Moment* is an exception.
24. Robert Paul Wolff, *In Defense of Anarchism*.
25. Rudolf Rocker, *Anarcho-Syndicalism*, pp. 16–17; Nicholas Walter, 'About anarchism', in Howard Ehrlich, Carol Ehrlich, David de Leon and Glenda Morris (eds), *Reinventing Anarchy*, p. 43; Apter 'The old anarchism and the new', in Apter and Joll (eds), *Anarchism Today*, p. 2.
26. Alan Ritter, 'Anarchism and liberal theory in the nineteenth century', pp. 37–66.
27. Alan Ritter, *Anarchism*, p. 10. G. C. Macallum's essay 'Negative and positive freedom' was originally published in *Philosophical Review*, 76, pp. 312–34. For a critique of this approach, see Benjamin Franks, 'Anarchism and Analytic Philosophy' in Ruth Kinna (ed.), *Continuum Companion to Anarchism*, pp. 50–71.
28. Critchley, *Infinitely Demanding*, p. 93.
29. George Crowder, *Classical Anarchism*, p. 4.
30. Ibid. p. 30.
31. Ibid. p. 150.
32. Albeit tempered by his reading of Marie Fleming's critique. Crowder, *Classical Anarchism*, pp. 1–2.
33. Woodcock, *Anarchism*, pp. 205–6.
34. David Miller, *Social Justice*, p. 230.
35. Ibid. p. 212.
36. Ibid. p. 210.
37. David Miller, 'The neglected (II) – Kropotkin', p. 338.
38. Miller, *Social Justice*, p. 211.
39. Crowder, *Classical Anarchism*, p. 36; emphasis in original.
40. Ibid. p. 165.
41. Ibid. p. 184.
42. Ibid. p. 185.

43. Ibid. p. 185.

44. Nicholas Walter, in David Goodway (ed.), *The Anarchist Past and Other Essays*, p. 27.

45. Walter, *The Anarchist Past*, p. 28.

46. Woodcock, *Anarchism and Anarchists*, p. 45

47. Gabriel Kuhn, 'Global anarchism and Asia', in Hiraru Tanaka, Masaya Hiyazaki and Chilharu Yamanaka (eds), *Global Anarchism*, p. 150.

48. Gordon, *Anarchy Alive!*, pp. 30, 31.

49. Ibid. p. 25.

50. Ibid. p. 13.

51. For a discussion of utopianism in anarchist political culture, see the essays in Part V of Davis and Kinna (eds), *Anarchism and Utopianism*, pp. 207–75.

52. Gordon, in Davis and Kinna (eds), *Anarchism and Utopianism*, p. 266.

53. Gordon, *Anarchy Alive!*, p. 42

54. Saul Newman, 'Anarchism, poststructuralism and the future of radical politics', p. 3. As Süreyyya Evren and Duane Rousselle argue, Saul Newman has been identified as 'the representative' of post-anarchism, although his approach to the revision of anarchist theory is idiosyncratic. Süreyyya Evren and Duane Rousselle, *Post-anarchism*, p. 7.

55. Gabriel Kuhn, 'Anarchism, postmodernity, and poststructuralism', in Randall Amster, Abraham DeLeon, Luis A. Fernandez, Anthony J. Nocella, II and Deric Shannon (eds), *Contemporary Anarchist Studies*, p. 20.

56. Newman, 'Anarchism, poststructuralism and the future of radical politics', p. 16.

57. Saul Newman, *From Bakunin to Lacan*, p. 173.

58. For Lewis Call's similar critique, see *Postmodern Anarchism*, pp. 14–21.

59. Ibid. p. 16.

60. Newman, 'Anarchism, poststructuralism and the future of radical politics', p. 13.

61. Benjamin Franks, *Rebel Alliances*, pp. 13, 17–18.

62. Ibid. p. 101.

63. Ibid. p. 114.

64. Cindy Milstein, *Anarchism and Its Aspirations*, p. 68.

65. Honeywell, *British Anarchist Tradition*, p. 140.

66. Colin Ward, 'Temporary Autonomous Zones'.

67. Matthew Wilson, *Rules without Rulers*, pp. 15–18.

68. Chris Wilbert and Damian F. White (eds), *Autonomy, Solidarity, Possibility*, p. x.

69. Saul Newman, *The Politics of Postanarchism*, pp. 163, 176.

70. Schmidt and van der Walt, *Black Flame*, pp. 6–7.

71. Ibid. pp. 14, 18.

72. Brian Morris, *Kropotkin*, p. 70.

73. Ibid. pp. 276–7.

74. Ibid. p. 272.

75. Ibid. p. 277.

76. Schmidt and van der Walt, *Black Flame*, p. 170.

Conclusion to Part 1

1. Woodcock and Avakumović, *The Anarchist Prince*, p. 200.
2. Ibid. p. 297.
3. Newman, *Politics of Postanarchism*, pp. 40–1.
4. Ibid. pp. 46–7.
5. Jean Grave, *Mémoires d'un Anarchiste (1854–1920)*, p. 144.

Introduction to Part 2

1. Cahm, *Kropotkin*, p. 97.
2. Kropotkin, 'Must we occupy ourselves with an examination of the ideal of a future system?', in Miller (ed.), *P. A. Kropotkin*, pp. 47–116; see also Miller's comments pp. 12–17.
3. Miller, *Kropotkin*, ch. 5.
4. Kropotkin, *Memoirs*, p. 213.
5. Miller, *Kropotkin*, pp. 93, 109.
6. Kropotkin, *Memoirs*, p. 214.
7. Sergey V. Saytanov, *The Argumentation of Peter Kropotkin's Anarcho-refomism in His Social-political and Anarchist Views (According to Russian Materials)*.
8. Haia Shpayer-Makov, 'The reception of Peter Kropotkin in Britain, 1886–1917', p. 381.
9. 'Personalities', *The Feilding Star Oroua and Kiwitea Counties Gazette*, 25 January 1913.
10. Miller, *Kropotkin*, pp. 133, 156, 164.
11. *Hansard* 1803–2005, Aliens Bill, HC Deb 29 March 1904, vol. 132, cc. 987–95.
12. Constance Bantman, *The French Anarchists in London, 1880–1914*, p. 62.
13. Pietro di Paola, *The Knights Errant of Anarchy*, p. 207.
14. Miller, *Kropotkin*, p. 203.
15. Thomas B. Eyges, *Beyond the Horizon*, p. 103.
16. Kropotkin, *Memoirs*; Kropotkin, *Ideals and Realities in Russian Literature*.
17. Richard Morgan, 'The interplay of politics and science in the making of Petr Kropotkin's modern anarchism'.
18. Peter Kropotkin, 'Elisée Reclus: Obituary', from the *Geographical Journal* for September 1905, pp. 337–43.

Chapter 3

1. Peter Kropotkin, *Ethics: Origin and Development*, pp. 9, 11.
2. For a discussion of the historical context, science, sociology and anarchism of mutual aid, see Ruth Kinna, 'Mutual aid in historical context'; Michael Glassman, 'Mutual aid theory and human development'; John Hewetson, 'Mutual aid and social evolution'; Iain McKay, 'Mutual aid'.

3. Kropotkin to Brandes, 29 May 1896, *Correspondance de Georg Brandes Lettres Choisies et Annotées par Paul Krüger II, L'angleterre et la Russie*, p. 117.

4. Stepniak was exposed for this killing, which he committed in 1878, by 'Z', 'Anarchists'. The article, which identified Stepniak as an assassin, is discussed in Barry Johnson, *Olive and Stepniak*, pp. 1–18.

5. The black propaganda is discussed in *Nihilism As It Is, Being Stepniak's Pamphlets*, p. 7. For the activities of the society, see Barry Hollingsworth, 'The Society of Friends of Russian Freedom'.

6. 'Anarchism according to Stepniak', *Freedom*, January–February 1893.

7. Kropotkin, *Ethics*, p. 262.

8. 'Letter to Max Nettlau', trans. Paul Sharkey, in Iain McKay, *Direct Struggle against Capital*, p. 151; emphasis in original.

9. For a discussion, see Kinna, 'Kropotkin's theory of mutual aid', pp. 268–70.

10. Max Nettlau, *A Short History of Anarchism*, p. 222.

11. Allan Antliff, 'Revolutionary seer for a post-industrial age', in John Moore and Spencer Sunshine (eds), *I am not a Man, I am Dynamite!*, pp. 44–5.

12. Max Baginski 'Stirner'; emphasis in the original.

13. Georg Brandes wrote to Nietzsche that he was 'a little hurt' at 'the off-hand and impetuous pronouncements against such phenomena as socialism and anarchism in your works'. He directed Nietzsche to Kropotkin, with whom he also corresponded. Nietzsche was apparently not persuaded that his anarchism 'is no stupidity' and never responded to Brandes' suggestion. *Friedrich Nietzsche*, p. 67.

14. di Paola, *The Knights Errant*, pp. 89, 104.

15. Jean Maitron identifies illegalism as a distinctive phase in French anarchist history separate from propaganda by the deed. *Ravachol et les Anarchistes*.

16. Grave, *Mémoires d'un Anarchiste*, p. 357.

17. For a discussion of the development of propaganda by the deed, see Marie Fleming, 'Propaganda by the deed', pp. 1–23; Z. Ivianksy, 'Individual terror', pp. 43–63; David Novak, 'Anarchism and individual terrorism', pp. 176–84. For the history of anarchist violence and the international response it provoked see, Richard Bach Jensen, *The Battle against Anarchist Terrorism*.

18. Johnson, *Tea and Anarchy!*, p. 138.

19. Kropotkin to Brandes, *Correspondance*, pp. 129–33.

20. Kropotkin to Nannie Dryhurst, 30 November 1893, BL Add. MS 46362 ff. 23–7; emphasis in original.

21. Woodcock and Avakumović, *The Anarchist Prince*, p. 248.

22. See, for example, 'On anarchy' and 'Thou shalt not kill', in David Stephens (ed.), *Government is Violence*, pp. 68–70, 72–6.

23. Cahm, *Kropotkin and the Rise of Revolutionary Anarchism 1872–1886*, p. 100.

24. Fleming, *Geography of Freedom*, pp. 130–6, 161–2.

25. Kropotkin's *Memoirs* was published in 1899; *Ideals and Realities in Russian Literature*, based on a series of lectures that Kropotkin delivered in 1901, was first published in 1905.

26. Petr Alekseevich Kropotkin, 'Máterials, printed and MS., on the emancipation of women in Russia, collected and annotated by Prince P. A. Kropotkin 1842–1921' (1891–1907), BL General Reference Collection 1884. a.11.

27. Kropotkin, *Memoirs*, pp. 210–11; emphasis in original.

28. A. Brückner, *A Literary History of Russia*, p. 322.

29. Ivan Turgenev, 'Hamlet and Don Quixote', pp. 93, 95, 107.

30. Kropotkin, *Memoirs*, p. 282; reproduced in *Ideals and Realities*, pp. 105–6.

31. Kropotkin, *Memoirs*, p. 210.

32. Ibid. p. 282.

33. Kropotkin, *Ideals and Realities*, p. 108.

34. Kropotkin, *Memoirs*, p. 210.

35. Kropotkin, *Ideals and Realities*, p. 108.

36. Kropotkin, *Memoirs*, p. 282.

37. Joseph Frank, 'Dostoevsky and Russian nihilism: A context for *Notes from Underground*', p. 18.

38. Kropotkin, *Ideals and Realities*, p. 290.

39. Ibid. p. 107.

40. Ibid. p. 293.

41. Ibid. p. 85.

42. Franco Venturi, *Roots of Revolution*, p. 327.

43. Kropotkin, *Ideals and Realities*, p. 228; *Memoirs*, p. 208.

44. Kropotkin, 'The Russian Revolutionary Party', in Miller (ed.), *P. A. Kropotkin*, p. 135.

45. Kropotkin, *Ideals and Realities*, p. 102.

46. Sergei Stepniak, 'Terrorism in Russia and terrorism in Europe', p. 325

47. Emma Goldman, *Living My Life*, vol. I, pp. 27–8.

48. Venturi, *Roots of Revolution*, p. 326.

49. G. B. Arnaudo, *Il Nihilismo*, pp. 2, 85. The recommendation was made by Mme. Novikov, reported by W. T. Stead, *The MP for Russia*, p. 332.

50. Fritz Cunliffe-Owen, 'Russian nihilism', p. 2.

51. See Avrich, *Bakunin and Nechaev*. Kropotkin gives an account of Nechaev in *In French and Russian Prisons*, pp. 108–13.

52. A full English translation of the *Catechism* was published in Michael Confino (ed.), *Daughter of a Revolutionary, Natalie Herzen and the Bakunin-Nechayev Circle*, pp. 221–30.

53. Cathy Porter, *Fathers and Daughters*, p. 88.

54. Oscar Wilde, *Vera; or, The Nihilists*; George Rowell, 'The truth about Vera', pp. 94–100.

55. George Kennan, *Siberia and the Exile System*, vol. 2, p. 172.

56. Perovskaya shot to fame as one of the plotters involved in the assassination of Alexander II and through being the only woman to be executed for her part in the killing. Vera Zasulich came to public attention when

she was acquitted of the attempted assassination in 1878 of Trepov, the governor of St Petersburg.

57. John Page Hopps, 'Nihilisms and socialisms of the world', p. 273.

58. Frances Miriam Reed, 'Oscar Wilde's Vera; Or, the nihilist', pp. 163–77.

59. Karl Blind, 'Conspiracies in Russia under the Reigning Czar', p. 134.

60. Edward Lawrence Levy, 'Russian nihilism'. A paper read before the members of the Alliance Literary and Debating Society, 1881, p. 25.

61. John Baker Hopkins, *Nihilism Its Words and Deeds*, pp. 26, 32–3.

62. Anon., *The Breakup of Nihilists in Russia*.

63. Reed, 'Oscar Wilde's Vera; Or, the nihilist', pp. 163–4.

64. Bakunin makes an appearance in the last third of the book. He is reliant on the good services of Vladimir the hero, who renounces nihilism for liberalism.

65. Mark Eastwood, *Within an Ace*, pp. 33, 144–8.

66. Woodcock and Avakumović, *The Anarchist Prince*, p. 149.

67. Quoted in Ibid. p. 258. Woodcock and Avakumović suggest that Kropotkin's apparently stunted sexual development coloured his attitudes to women, and issues of liberation, pp. 171–2. Bonnie Haaland argues that Goldman's novel contribution to anarchism rested on her synthesis of Kropotkin and Ibsen. She not only accepts Woodcock's evaluation but also by-passes Kropotkin positive assessment of Ibsen's work. Haaland, *Emma Goldman*, ch. 1.

68. For an account of the burdens on rural women, see Richard Stites, *The Women's Liberation Movement in Russia*, pp. 160–1.

69. Kropotkin, 'Emancipation of Women', f. 20; emphasis in original.

70. Ibid. f. 27

71. Kropotkin, *Memoirs*, pp. 186, 216; BL. 1884 a.11 f.27.

72. Kropotkin, *Ideals and Realities*, p. 294.

73. Kropotkin, *Memoirs*, p. 209.

74. Ibid. p. 185.

75. Kropotkin, 'Emancipation of women', f.17; emphasis in original.

76. Ibid. ff. 27–8; emphasis in original.

77. Kropotkin, *Memoirs*, p. 196.

78. Ibid. p. 210.

79. Nikolai Chernyshevksy, *What is to be Done?*, pp. 74–5.

80. Kropotkin, *French and Russian Prisons*, p. 89.

81. This is Alejandro de Acosta's critique of Emile Armand, 'Critical comments on "Revolutionary Sexualism" ', in *Individualist Anarchism*, pp. 116–23.

82. Sergei Stepniak, *Underground Russia*, pp. 8–9.

83. Princess Alexandra Kropotkin, 'Pleasant memories of Bernard Shaw', p. 23.

84. See, for example, the reviews by G. K. Chesterton and A. B. Walkley in T. F. Evans (ed.), *Shaw*, pp. 98–101, 10–115.

85. Kropotkin to Marsh, August 23, 1903, Alfred Marsh papers, IISH; emphasis in original.

86. Kropotkin to George Bernard Shaw, 23 August 1903, BL Add. MS 50514 ff. 113–16; emphasis in original.

87. G. B. Shaw to H. G. Wells, December 7, 1916 in Dan H. Laurence (ed.), *Bernard Shaw Collected Letters 1911–1925*, p. 439; emphasis in original.

88. Alexandra Kropotkin, 'Pleasant memories', p. 27.

89. Kropotkin, *Memoirs*, p. 186.

90. Peter Kropotkin, 'La Nécessité de la Révolution', in *Paroles d'un Révolté*, p. 23.

91. Kropotkin, 'Emancipation of women', f.18.

92. Kropotkin, *Memoirs*, p. 281.

93. Peter Kropotkin, *Anarchist Morality*, pp. 6–7.

94. Ibid. p. 22; emphasis in original.

95. H. M. Hyndman, *The Record of an Adventurous Life*, p. 266.

96. Sandy McFarlane, 'An appeal to the young', *Justice*, 23 March 1895.

97. Kropotkin, *Memoirs*, p. 286.

98. Ibid. p. 284.

99. Peter Kropotkin, 'Aux Jeunes Gens', *Paroles*, pp. 43–75. The English was published as a sixteen-page pamphlet in London by William Reeves (n.d), and the same text appears in Baldwin, *Revolutionary Pamphlets*, pp. 261–82.

100. Kropotkin, *Appeal to the Young*, p. 15.

101. Ibid. p. 280.

102. Ibid. p. 277.

103. Ibid. p. 274.

104. Ibid. pp. 271, 277.

105. Ibid. p. 274.

106. Kropotkin, 'Aux Jeunes Gens', *Paroles*, p. 75.

107. Kropotkin, *Appeal to the Young*, pp. 281–2.

108. Ibid. p. 282.

109. Ibid. p. 274.

110. Ibid. p. 276.

111. Ibid. p. 261.

112. Kropotkin, *Memoirs*, p. 209.

113. Kropotkin, *Appeal to the Young*, p. 276.

114. Ibid. p. 278.

115. Brian Morris argues that there is no possible accommodation. *The Politics of Community*, pp. 30–1. For a reading of the affinities between anarchism and Nietzsche, see Christos Iliopoulos, 'Nietzsche and anarchism, an elective affinity and a Nietzschean reading of the December '08 revolt in Athens'.

116. Keith Ansell-Pearson, *Introduction to Nietzsche as a Political Thinker*, p. 200.

117. Kropotkin, *Ethics*, p. 12; emphasis in original.

118. Michael Allen Gillespie, *Nihilism before Nietzsche*, p. 161; Justin Clemens and Chris Feik, 'Nihilism, tonight …' in Keith Ansell-Pearson and Diane Morgan (eds), *Nihilism Now!*

119. For a discussion of *Notes from Underground*, identified as a key text for Nietzsche's thinking, see C. A. Miller, 'Nietzsche's "discovery" of Dostoevsky', pp. 202–57.

120. Brückner, *A Literary History of Russia*, p. 402.

121. Kropotkin, *Ideals and Realities*, p. 168.

122. Following Joseph Frank, 'Nihilism and *Notes from Underground*', pp. 1–33.

123. Moritz Kaufman, 'Nihilism in Russia', p. 913.

124. Ibid. p. 913.

125. Cunliffe-Owen, 'Russian nihilism', pp. 1–2.

126. Kropotkin, *Memoirs*, p. 208.

127. Ibid. p. 208.

128. Albert Fouillée, 'The ethics of Nietzsche and Guyau', p. 19; emphasis in original.

129. Robin Aizlewood, 'Berdiaev and Chaadaev, Russia and feminine passivity', in Peter I Barta (ed.), *Gender and Sexuality in Russian Civilisation*, p. 131.

Chapter 4

1. Kropotkin, *Memoirs*, p. 205.

2. Kropotkin gave a fuller account of Russian history from the ninth century in Donald McKenzie Walllace, Prince Kropotkin, C. Mijatovich and J. D. Bourchier, *A Short History of Russia and the Balkan States*, chs 10–16.

3. Peter Kropotkin, 'The present crisis in Russia', p. 720.

4. Ibid.

5. Kropotkin, 'The Russian Revolutionary Party', p. 656.

6. Ibid. p. 657.

7. Peter Kropotkin, *The Great French Revolution*, p. 431.

8. Paul Avrich, *The Russian Anarchists*, p. 10.

9. Peter Kropotkin, 'The Russian peasantry', *Newcastle Daily Chronicle*, 7 February 1882.

10. Kropotkin, 'La Question Agraire', *Paroles*, p. 148.

11. Sergei Stepniak, *The Russian Peasantry*, p. 114. Dessiatines are Russian units of measurement: one unit is equivalent to 10,800 square metres.

12. David Saunders, *Russia in the Age of Reaction and Reform, 1801–1881*, p. 242.

13. Kropotkin, *French and Russian Prisons*, p. 179.

14. S. L. Hoch, 'On good numbers and bad: Malthus, population trends and peasant standard of living in late imperial Russia'; S. L. Hoch, 'Famine, disease and mortality patterns in the parish of Borshevka, Russia, 1830–1912', pp. 357–68.

15. Kropotkin, 'The London Jews' Meeting', *Newcastle Daily Chronicle*, 9 February 1882.

16. Peter Kropotkin, 'Russian schools and the Holy Synod', pp. 519–27.

17. Kropotkin, *Memoirs*, p. 175.

18. Saunders, *Russia*, pp. 255, 266.

19. Peter Kropotkin, *The Terror in Russia*, p. 7.
20. Kropotkin, 'The Russian peasantry'.
21. Kropotkin, *Memoirs*, pp. 124–5.
22. Peter Kropotkin, 'The Revolutionary Party of Russia', *Newcastle Daily Chronicle*, 12 October 1881.
23. Peter Kropotkin, *Le Procès Solovieff: La Vie D'un Socialiste Russe; La Vérité Sur Les Exécutions en Russie Suivie D'une Esquisse Biographique Sur Sophie Perowskaya*.
24. Kropotkin, 'La Question Agraire', *Paroles*, p. 143.
25. Peter Kropotkin, 'Finland', *The Anarchist Library*, 2009 [1885], p. 2.
26. Kropotkin, *Memoirs*, p. 131.
27. Alex Prichard, *Justice, Order and Anarchy*, ch. 3.
28. Kropotkin, 'Finland', pp. 2, 14.
29. Ibid. p. 3.
30. Saunders, *Russia*, p. 181.
31. Kropotkin, 'Finland', pp. 2–17.
32. Kropotkin, *Russia and the Balkan States*, pp. 64, 69.
33. Kropotkin, 'Finland'.
34. Stepniak, *The Russian Peasantry*, pp. 121–5.
35. Peter Kropotkin, 'Russian administration', *Newcastle Daily Chronicle*, 18 January 1882.
36. Kropotkin, 'The London Jews' Meeting'.
37. Kropotkin to Augustin Hamon, 19 June 1891, IISH.
38. Derek Offord, *The Russian Revolutionary Movement in the 1880s*, pp. 45–6.
39. Erich E. Haberer, *Jews and Revolution in Nineteenth Century Russia*, pp. 60–1.
40. Kropotkin, 'The London Jews' Meeting'.
41. Kropotkin, 'The Russian Revolutionary Party', p. 667.
42. Robert M. Cutler, *The Basic Bakunin*, p. 22.
43. Peter Kropotkin, 'Le Gouvernement Représentatif', *Paroles,* p. 169.
44. Mikhail Bakunin, *Statism and Anarchy*, p. 142.
45. S. V. Utechin, *Russian Political Thought*, pp. 125–7, 141.
46. Ibid. pp. 103–5, 114–15.
47. Susan Buck-Morss, 'Hegel and Haiti', p. 842.
48. Bakunin, *God and the State*, ch. II.
49. Emma Goldman, 'Anarchism', in Alix Kates Shulman (ed.), *Red Emma Speaks*, p. 54.
50. Quoted in Lewis Perry, *Radical Abolitionism*, p. 5.
51. Leo Tolstoy, 'The slavery of our times', in Stephens (ed.), *Government is Violence,* pp. 129, 136.
52. Kropotkin, 'Communism and anarchy', in McKay (ed.), *Direct Struggle against Capital*, p. 638.
53. Kropotkin, *Ethics,* pp. 109, 127.
54. Kropotkin, 'Le Gouvernement Représentatif', p. 182.
55. Ibid. p. 183.
56. Ibid. pp. 209–11.

57. Peter Kropotkin, 'Les Droits Politiques', *Paroles,* p. 39.

58. Ibid. p. 35.

59. Kropotkin, 'Le Gouvernement Représentatif', pp. 202–9.

60. Kropotkin, 'La Loi et L'Autorité', *Paroles*, pp. 213–35.

61. Kropotkin to Mrs. Dryhurst, 30 November 1893, BL Add. MS 46362 ff. 23–7.

62. Kropotkin, 'Le Gouvernement Représentatif', p. 199.

63. Ibid. p. 211.

64. Peter Kropotkin, 'La Commune de Paris', *Paroles*, p. 141.

65. Reclus, *Ouvrier, Prends La Machine!*; Fleming, *Geography of Freedom*, p. 146.

66. Fleming, *Geography of Freedom*, pp. 144–6; Gustav Landauer, *For Socialism*, pp. 74–83.

67. Woodford McClellan, *Revolutionary Exiles*, pp. 60–3. Kropotkin, *Ideals and Realities*, pp. 267–8.

68. Woodcock and Avakumović, *The Anarchist Prince*, p. 89.

69. Kropotkin, *Memoirs*, pp. 126–54, 169–72; 'The orography of Asia'; 'The desiccation of Eur-Asia'; Kropotkin includes a discussion of desiccation in his 'Recent Science' article for *The Nineteenth Century*, 35, 1894, pp. 141–56.

70. Ferretti, 'Elisée Reclus and Pëtr Kropotkin', pp. 216–22.

71. Geoffrey Parker, *Western Geopolitical Thought in the Twentieth Century*, pp. 157, 181.

72. Richard Peet, 'For Kropotkin', p. 42.

73. Morris, *The Politics of Community*, p. 123.

74. Adam Goodwin, 'Evolution and anarchism in international relations', pp. 417–37.

75. Kropotkin, *Ethics*, p. 44.

76. A. J. Fielding, 'What geographers ought to do'.

77. Robyn Roslak, *Neo-Impressionims and Anarchism in Fin-de-Siècle France*, p. 99.

78. Peter Kropotkin, 'What geography ought to be', p. 942.

79. Ibid. p. 943.

80. Kropotkin, *Memoirs*, pp. 80–1.

81. Lucian Ashworth, 'Realism and the spirit of 1919', p. 283.

82. Holger H. Herwig, 'Geopolitik', in Colin S. Gray and Geoffrey Sloan (eds), *Geopolitics, Geography and Strategy*, p. 220.

83. Gerry Kearns, 'The Political Pivot of Geography', pp. 337–46. See also Simon Springer, 'Anarchism!', pp. 1,605–24.

84. Geoffrey Sloan, 'Sir Halford J. Mackinder', in Gray and Sloan (eds), *Geopolitics, Geography and Strategy,* pp. 17–18.

85. Ashworth, 'Realism and the spirit of 1919', p. 286.

86. Ferretti, 'Elisée Reclus and Pëtr Kropotkin', p. 11.

87. Kearns, 'The political pivot of geography', pp. 337–46. Adam Goodwin also draws on *Mutual Aid* to discuss social theorising in international relations, 'Evolution and anarchism in international relations', pp. 417–37.

88. Sloan, 'Sir Halford J. Mackinder', p. 16.

89. Peter Kropotkin, 'La Décomposition des États', *Paroles*, p. 11.
90. Élisée Reclus, *Nouvelle Géographie Universelle La Terre Et Les Hommes*, VI *L'Asie Russe*, p. 283.
91. Ernest Renan, 'What is a nation?'.
92. Kropotkin, 'Finland', p. 3.
93. Kropotkin, 'Letter to Maria Isidine Goldsmith', trans. Paul Sharkey, in McKay (ed.), *Direct Struggle against Capital*, p. 142.
94. Umut Özkirimili, *Theories of Nationalism*, p. 35.
95. Peter Kropotkin, *Mutual Aid*, p. 137.
96. Kropotkin, 'Finland', p. 11.
97. Fleming, *Geography of Freedom*, p. 137. Ferretti notes that Kropotkin was Reclus's 'most important' collaborator on this volume. 'Elisée Reclus and Pëtr Kropotkin', p. 4.
98. John Breuilly, *Nationalism and the State*, p. 6.
99. Özkirimili, *Nationalism*, p. 36.
100. Reclus, *Nouvelle Géographie*, p. 32.
101. Peter Kropotkin, 'La Guerre', *Paroles*, pp. 80–3.
102. Kropotkin, 'La Décomposition des États', p. 11
103. Kropotkin, 'La Guerre', p. 83.
104. Ibid. pp. 80–1.
105. Ibid. p. 84.
106. Ibid. p. 83.
107. Peter Kropotkin, 'L'Ordre', *Paroles*, pp. 101–4.
108. Kropotkin, 'Anarchists and the French Revolution', *Freedom*, December 1903.
109. Philippe Forêt, 'Climate change'; Philippe Forêt, 'Challenges to fieldwork before 1914 and today', in Marcus Hall and Patrick Kupper (eds) 'Crossing mountains', pp. 9–18.
110. Ellsworth Huntington, *Civilization and Climate*.
111. Kropotkin, 'What geography ought to be', p. 949.
112. For Reclus's views, see John Clark and Camille Martin (eds), *Anarchy, Geography, Modernity*, pp. 36–7.
113. Reclus, *Nouvelle Géographie*, pp. 36–7.
114. Peter Kropotkin, 'La Loi et L'Autorité', *Paroles*, p. 221.
115. Kropotkin, *Mutual Aid*, p. 260.
116. Kropotkin, *Ethics*, p. 17.
117. Kropotkin, 'What geography ought to be', p. 943.
118. Ibid. p. 943.
119. Kropotkin, 'La commune', pp. 114–15.
120. Peter Kropotkin, 'The great Siberian Railway', pp. 146–54.
121. Kropotkin, *Ethics*, pp. 116–17.
122. Kropotkin, 'La Situation', *Paroles*, p. 4.
123. Mark Leier, *Bakunin. The Creative Passion*, p. 290.
124. Mikhail Bakunin, *The Paris Commune and the Idea of the State*.
125. Bakunin, *The Paris Commune and the Idea of the State*, p. 2.
126. Peter Kropotkin, 'La Commune de Paris', *Paroles*, pp. 123–4.

127. Ibid. p. 139.
128. Bakunin, *The Paris Commune*, p. 2.
129. Kropotkin, 'La Commune de Paris', p. 120.
130. Bakunin, *The Paris Commune*, p. 2.
131. Kropotkin, 'La Commune de Paris', p. 121.
132. Ibid. pp. 134–5.
133. Ibid. p. 117.
134. Kropotkin, *Memoirs*, pp. 171, 172.
135. Kropotkin, 'What geography ought to be', p. 948.
136. Ibid. p. 955.
137. Ibid. p. 941.
138. Ibid. p. 946.
139. Kropotkin, 'La Loi et L'Autorité', pp. 215–17.
140. Kropotkin, 'La Commue de Paris', p. 120.
141. Utechin, *Russian Political Thought*, p. 87; Kropotkin, *Ideals and Realities*, pp. 266–70.
142. Kropotkin, 'On the teaching of physiography', p. 2.
143. Kropotkin, 'What geography ought to be', p. 952.
144. Kropotkin, 'Finland', p. 14.
145. Kropotkin, *The Terror in Russia*, pp. 2, 75.

Conclusion to Part 2

1. Kropotkin, *Memoirs*, p. 290.
2. Dominique Miething, 'Overcoming the preachers of death: Gustav Landauer's reading of Friedrich Nietzsche'.
3. Newman, *Politics of Postanarchism*, p. 162 and a fuller discussion in *Postanarchism* (forthcoming, Polity Press).
4. Kropotkin, *Memoirs*, p. 157.
5. Gabriel Kuhn with Siegbert Wolf, 'Introduction', in *Revolution and Other Writings*, pp. 32–3.
6. Kropotkin, *Modern Science and Anarchism*, p. 39.
7. Ivan Turgenev, *Fathers and Sons*, trans. Rosemary Edmonds, pp. 40, 36.
8. Kropotkin, 'The anarchist principle', trans. James Bar Bowen, in McKay (ed.), *Direct Struggle against Capital*, p. 199.
9. Kropotkin, 'Anarchist action in the revolution', in McKay (ed.), *Direct Struggle against Capital*, p. 572; emphasis in original.
10. Turgenev, *Fathers and Sons*, p. 39.
11. Kropotkin, 'Letter to Maria Isidine Goldsmith', in McKay (ed.), *Direct Struggle against Capital*, p. 145.
12. Kropotkin, *Modern Science and Anarchism*, p. 40.
13. Vincent Barnett, *A History of Russian Economic Thought*, p. 11.
14. Kropotkin, *Memoirs*, pp. 273–4.
15. Ibid. p. 274.
16. George Bernard Shaw, *The Perfect Wagnerite*.

17. Victor Dave, *Michel Bakounine et Karl Marx*, p. 1.
18. Kropotkin, Manuscript of the article 'Bakunin' published in *Freedom*, 1905, IISH Nettlau collection 2672
19. Ibid.
20. Cutler, *The Basic Bakunin*, p. 21.
21. Kropotkin, 'Le Gouvernement Représentif', *Paroles*, pp. 186, 188–9.
22. Kropotkin, 'Economic expedients', trans. Paul Sharkey, in McKay (ed.), *Direct Struggle against Capital*, p. 248.
23. Ibid. p. 250.
24. Kropotkin, 'Local action', in Nicholas Walter and Heiner Becker (eds), *Act for Yourselves*, p. 42.
25. Kropotkin, 'A general view', in Walter and Becker (eds), *Act for Yourselves*, pp. 75–80.
26. Eric Hobsbawm, *Nations and Nationalism since 1780*, pp. 34–5.
27. Dave, *Michel Bakounine et Karl Marx*, p. 2.
28. Bakunin, *The Paris Commune and the Idea of the State*, p. 2.
29. Élisée Reclus, 'Progress', in Clark and Martin (eds), *Anarchy, Geography, Modernity*, p. 220.
30. Kropotkin, 'Le Gouvernement Représentif', p. 203.
31. Kropotkin, 'Bakunin', Nettlau 2672; emphasis in original.
32. James R. Lehning, *European Colonialism since 1700*, p. 219.
33. Kropotkin, 'Are we good enough?', in Walter and Becker (eds), *Act for Yourselves*, p. 84.
34. Robert Bartlett, *The Making of Europe*.
35. Maia Ramnath, *Decolonizing Anarchism*, p. 21.
36. Kropotkin, *Modern Science and Anarchism*, pp. 59–62.
37. C. V. Wedgewood, *The Thirty Years War*, p. 32.
38. Hobsbawm, p. 35; emphasis in original.
39. Bernard Kampffmeyer, 'Anarchism and the European equilibrium'.
40. Kropotkin to Brandes, 29 May 1896, p. 118.
41. Carole Pateman and Charles Mills, 'Contract and social change', in *Contract and Domination*, pp. 14–15.
42. Georg Brandes, 'Preface', in *Memoirs of a Revolutionist*, p. xi.
43. Kropotkin, 'The Russian Revolutionary Party', p. 662.

Introduction to Part 3

1. Alfredo Bonnano, 'Introduction', in *The Conquest of Bread*, p. 11.
2. Matthew Adams, 'Formulating an Anarchist Sociology'.
3. Kropotkin, *Memoirs*, pp. 157–8.
4. Ibid. pp. 172; emphasis in original.
5. Ibid. pp. 286–7.
6. Ibid. p. 286.
7. Kropotkin, 'L'Esprit de Révolte', *Paroles*, pp. 275–9.
8. C. Alexander McKinley, *Illegitimate Children of the Enlightenment*, p. 58.

9. Matthew Adams, 'Kropotkin', pp. 56–81.

10. Kropotkin, 'Enemies of the people', in McKay (ed.), *Direct Struggle against Capital*, pp. 291–2.

11. Kropotkin, *The Great French Revolution*, p. 7.

12. Ibid. p. 11.

13. Ibid. pp. 11–12.

14. Ibid. pp. 487–8.

15. Ibid. pp. 11–12.

16. Ibid. p. 9.

17. Kropotkin, 'Communist-anarchism', in Walter and Becker (eds), *Act for Yourselves*, p. 99.

18. Kropotkin, *Modern Science and Anarchism*, p. 43.

19. Kropotkin, 'Insurrections and revolution', in McKay (ed.), *Direct Struggle against Capital*, p. 551.

20. Kropotkin, 'The death of the new international', trans. Paul Sharkey, in McKay (ed.), *Direct Struggle against Capital*, p. 338.

21. G. D. H. Cole, *A History of Socialist Thought*, vol. 3, pt 1, *The Second International 1889–1914*, p. 26.

22. 'Socialist party politics at Zurich', *Freedom*, August 1893.

23. Wilhelm Liebknecht, 'Our congress', *Justice*, 29 August 1896.

24. 'Report of the Holborn Town Hall Meeting', supplement to *Freedom*, August–September 1897.

25. Kropotkin to Marsh, 30 December 1898, IISH Marsh papers; emphasis in original.

26. Ibid.

27. Kropotkin, 'Politics and socialism', in McKay (ed.), *Direct Struggle against Capital*, p. 374; emphasis in original.

28. Kropotkin, 'Trade unionism and parliamentarism', trans. Paul Sharkey, in McKay (ed.), *Direct Struggle against Capital*, p. 385.

29. Kropotkin, 'Preface' in *Words of a Rebel*, trans. Nicholas Walter, in McKay (ed.), *Direct Struggle against Capital*, p. 546.

Chapter 5

1. For a modern re-statement, see Paul Blackledge, 'The struggle for freedom and democracy', in Alex Prichard, Ruth Kinna, Saku Pinta and David Berry (eds), *Libertarian Socialism*, pp. 17–34, and for a critique, Iain McKay, 'Libertarian socialism'.

2. Editorial, 'An anarchist messiah', *Justice*, 14 November 1896.

3. Ruth Kinna, 'Anarchism, individualism and communism', in Prichard, Kinna, Pinta and Berry (eds), *Libertarian Socialism*, pp. 35–56.

4. Engels to Laura Lafargue, 4 May 1891, *Correspondence of Friedrich Engels and Paul and Laura Lafargue, vol. 3, 1891–1895*, trans. Yvonne Kapp, p. 58.

5. Alfred Hitchcock, *The 39 Steps* (Gaumont-British, 1935).

6. H. Pearce, 'Scientific Socialism v. Revolutionary Syndicalism', *Justice*, 25 January 1913.

7. A. P. Hazell, 'Two schools of socialism', *Justice*, 9 February 1895.

8. For a discussion, see Ruth Kinna, 'Anarchism and the politics of utopia', in Davis and Kinna (eds), *Anarchism and Utopianism*, pp. 221–40.

9. Kropotkin to Bernard Kampffmeyer, 14 December 1909, IISH Kleine Korrespondenz.

10. J. Robins, 'Plechanoff answered', *The Torch*, 18 April 1895. Robins was responding to George Pleckanov [Plechanoff], *Anarchism and Socialism*.

11. Kropotkin to Guillaume 23 December 1902, 5 May 1903, IISH Nettlau collection 2700.

12. Varlaam Cherkesov [W. Tcherkesov], 'Socialism or democracy', *Supplement to Freedom*, July 1895.

13. Kropotkin, 'Glimpses into the labour movement in this country, 1886–1907', in Walter and Becker (eds), *Act for Yourselves*, pp. 116–17.

14. Kropotkin, *Modern Science and Anarchism*, p. 49.

15. Matthew Adams, 'Rejecting the American model', pp. 147–73.

16. Kropotkin, *Memoirs*, p. 278.

17. Ibid. p. 276.

18. Kropotkin, *The Place of Anarchism in Socialistic Evolution*, p. 12.

19. Kropotkin describes Fourier's scheme in *Modern Science and Anarchism*, pp. 57–60.

20. Dennis Hardy, *Alternative Communities in Nineteenth Century England*, pp. 165–71.

21. Kropotkin, 'Advice to those about to emigrate'; 'Proposed communist settlement'.

22. Kropotkin, 'Communism and anarchy', in McKay (ed.), *Direct Struggle against Capital*, p. 635.

23. Kropotkin, 'Recent science', pp. 934–46; Kropotkin, 'Recent science', *The Nineteenth Century*, 32, 1892, pp. 224–42, especially pp. 224–30.

24. Kropotkin, *Anarchism*, p. 6.

25. Peter Kropotkin, 'Anarchism', in Roger Baldwin (ed.), *Kropotkin's Revolutionary Pamphlets*, p. 284.

26. Karl Marx, 'Afterword to the second German edition', in *Capital*, vol. 1.

27. Kropotkin, 'Bakunin', Nettlau 2672.

28. Kropotkin, *Modern Science and Anarchism*, p. 46; emphasis in original.

29. Kropotkin, 'Are we good enough', in Walter and Becker (eds), *Act for Yourselves*, p. 84; emphasis in original.

30. Kropotkin, 'Edward Bellamy', *Freedom*, July 1898.

31. Kropotkin, *Ethics*, p. 192.

32. Kropotkin, *Modern Science and Anarchism*, p. 46; emphasis in original.

33. Kropotkin, *Memoirs*, p. 286.

34. Kropotkin, *Modern Science and Anarchism*, p. 46.

35. Kropotkin, *Anarchism*, p. 22.

36. Kropotkin, 'Must we occupy ourselves', in Miller (ed.), *P. A. Kropotkin*, p. 47; emphasis in original.

37. Kropotkin, *Modern Science and Anarchism*, p. 41; emphasis in original.

38. Ibid. p. 61.

39. Ya'acov Oved, 'The future society according to Kropotkin', p. 306.

40. Kropotkin, 'The necessity of communism', in Walter and Becker (eds), *Act for Yourselves*, p. 62.

41. Kropotkin, *Fields, Factories and Workshops*, p. 21.

42. Ibid. p. 18.

43. On Ferrer, see 'Manuscript of Kropotkin's speech at the Ferrer Meeting at Memorial Hall, London, October 21, 1909, with corrections by Alfred Marsh', Nettlau collection 2683.

44. Kropotkin, *Fields, Factories and Workshops*, p. 369.

45. Paul Avrich, *The Modern School Movement*, pp. 15–17; Mikhail Bakunin, 'All-round education', in Cutler, *The Basic Bakunin*, pp. 111–25. Kropotkin's correspondence with Robin is in Nettlau 2702.

46. 'The Reformed School, Peter Kropotkin to Francisco Ferrer, founder of new review *L'Ecole Rénovée*', *Freedom*, June 1908; emphasis in original.

47. Kropotkin, *Fields, Factories and Workshops*, p. 378.

48. Kropotkin, *Ethics*, p. 305.

49. Kropotkin, *French and Russian Prisons*, p. 315.

50. Kropotkin, *The Conquest of Bread*, pp. 155–66; *Fields, Factories and Workshops*, p. 405.

51. Kropotkin, *The State*, pp. 22–3.

52. Kropotkin, *Fields, Factories and Workshops*, p. 408.

53. Kropotkin, *Modern Science and Anarchism*, p. 75.

54. Kropotkin, *Conquest of Bread*, p. 221.

55. Kropotkin, *Modern Science and Anarchism*, pp. 75, 78.

56. David Golemboski, 'Proudhon on the social dimensions of labor'.

57. Kropotkin, *Anarchism Its Philosophy and Ideal*, p. 15; emphasis in original.

58. Kropotkin, *Modern Science and Anarchism*, p. 78; 'Syndicalism and anarchism', in McKay (ed.), *Direct Struggle against Capital*, p. 405; emphasis in original.

59. Kropotkin, 'Proposed communist settlement'.

60. Kropotkin, *The State*, p. 21.

61. Kropotkin, *Fields, Factories and Workshops*, p. 23; emphasis in original.

62. Ibid. p. 21.

63. Kropotkin, 'Proposed communist settlement'.

64. Kropotkin, *Mutual Aid*, pp. 279–83.

65. Knowles, *Political Economy from Below*, p. 239.

66. Kropotkin, *Fields, Factories and Workshops*, p. 19.

67. Ibid. p. 23.

68. Peter Ryley, *Making another World Possible*, p. 43.

69. Kropotkin, *Fields, Factories and Workshops*, p. 19.

70. James Glyn Ford, *Prince Peter Kropotkin and the Channel Islands*.

71. Kropotkin, 'Foreword', in Thomas Smith, *French Gardening*.

72. Kropotkin to Kampffmeyer, 20 September 1903, IISH Kleine Korrespondenz.

73. Kropotkin, *Fields, Factories and Workshops*, p. 361; emphasis in original.

74. Ibid. p. 49; emphasis in original.

75. Ibid. p. 251.

76. Varlaam Cherkesov [W. Tcherkesoff], *Concentration of Capital*, pp. 12–13.
77. Robert Blatchford, *Merrie England*, p. 11; 'South Island notes', *Maoriland Worker*, 24 December 1913.
78. C. V. Drysdale, *Can Everyone be Fed?*
79. Kropotkin, *Mutual Aid*, p. 219.
80. Iain McKay, *Mutual Aid*.
81. Glassman, 'Mutual aid theory and human development', pp. 391–412; Kinna, 'Kropotkin's theory of mutual aid', pp. 259–83.
82. Kropotkin, 'Must we occupy ourselves?', in Miller (ed.), *P. A. Kropotkin*, p. 54.
83. Kropotkin, 'The coming anarchy', p. 161.
84. Kropotkin, *Wars and Capitalism*.
85. Kropotkin, 'Postscript to words of a rebel', in McKay (ed.), *Direct Struggle against Capital*, p. 587.
86. George Esenwein, *Anarchist Ideology and the Working Class Movement in Spain, 1868–1898*, p. 147; Max Nettlau, *A Short History of Anarchism*, pp. 195–203.
87. Kropotkin, *Conquest of Bread*, p. 216.
88. Kropotkin, *Modern Science and Anarchism*, p. 63.
89. Kropotkin, 'The first work of the revolution'; 'The necessity of communism', in Walter and Becker (eds), *Act for Yourselves*, pp. 57, 63.
90. 'The 1880 congress of the Jura Federation', in Daniel Guérin, *No Gods, No Masters*, vol. 2, p. 283.
91. Kropotkin, *Modern Science and Anarchism*, pp. 49, 53.
92. Ibid. p. 63.
93. Ibid. pp. 52–3.
94. Kropotkin, 'Must we occupy ourselves?', in Miller (ed.), *P. A. Kropotkin*, pp. 49–52.
95. Kropotkin, 'Communist-anarchism', in Walter and Becker (eds), *Act for Yourselves*, p. 97.
96. 'Kropotkin as mock bourgeois radical', *Justice*, March 1904, Nettlau 2690.
97. For a discussion, see Buick, 'What Marx should have said to Kropotkin'.
98. Kropotkin, *Modern Science and Anarchism*, p. 70.
99. Golemboski, p. 20.
100. Kropotkin, *Conquest of Bread*, pp. 226–35.
101. Kropotkin, *Anarchism*, p. 14.
102. 'Anarchy and communism', in Daniel Guérin, *No Gods, No Masters*, p. 295.
103. Kropotkin, *Conquest of Bread*, p. 220; emphasis in original.
104. Kropotkin, *Modern Science and Anarchism*, p. 71.
105. Kropotkin, 'A few thoughts about the essence of anarchism', in McKay (ed.), *Direct Struggle against Capital*, p. 203; emphasis in original.
106. Gustav Landauer, 'Tucker's revelation', in Kuhn, *Gustav Landauer*, p. 249.
107. 'Anarchy and communism', in Guérin, *No Gods, No Masters*, p. 295.
108. Kropotkin, *Anarchism*, pp. 9, 15.

109. Ibid. p. 14.

110. Ibid. p. 15.

111. Ryley, *Making another World Possible*, pp. 100–1.

112. Victor Yarros, *Anarchism*, p. 22.

113. Wendy McElroy, *The Debates of Liberty*, p. 4.

114. John Henry Mackay, *The Anarchists*, p. 105.

115. Kropotkin, *Modern Science and Anarchism*, p. 35.

116. Kropotkin, 'Anarchism', in Baldwin (ed.), *Kropotkin's Revolutionary Pamphlets*, p. 288.

117. Kropotkin, *The State,* pp. 28; 30; emphasis in original.

118. Kropotkin, 'Recent science', *The Nineteenth Century*, 1892, p. 230.

119. Kropotkin, *Anarchism*, pp. 3–4.

120. Thomas Hobbes, *Leviathan,* p. 115.

121. Kropotkin, *French and Russian Prisons*, p. 59.

122. Ibid. pp. 62–3, 178, 206–8.

123. Ibid. pp. 169, 293, 333.

124. Kropotkin, 'Prisons and their moral influence on prisoners', in Baldwin (ed.), *Kropotkin's Revolutionary Pamphlets*, p. 225.

125. Kropotkin, 'Prisons', in Baldwin (ed.), *Kropotkin's Revolutionary Pamphlets*, p. 225.

126. Kropotkin, *Modern Science and Anarchism*, pp. 65–6; emphasis in original.

127. Kropotkin, 'Anarchism', in Baldwin (ed.), *Kropotkin's Revolutionary Pamphlets*, p. 296.

128. Kropotkin, *Modern Science and Anarchism*, p. 50.

129. Kropotkin, 'Anarchism', p. 293.

130. Kropotkin, *Organised Vengeance Called 'Justice'*, p. 9.

131. Kropotkin, 'Lyon Anarchist Trial of 1883', trans. Nicholas Walter, in McKay (ed.), *Direct Struggle against Capital*, p. 112.

132. Kropotkin, 'Communism and anarchy', in McKay (ed.), *Direct Struggle against Capital*, p. 639; emphasis in original.

133. Kropotkin, 'Anarchists and trade unions', in MacKay, *The Anarchists*, p. 390.

134. Matthew Adams, 'Formulating an anarchist sociology'.

135. William M. Dugger, 'Veblen and Kropotkin on human evolution', pp. 971–85.

136. Kropotkin, 'The birth of conscience "the morality of nature"', in *The Meaning of Modern Life*, p. 1.

137. Kropotkin, 'The morality of nature', p. 407.

138. Tim Gray, 'Herbert Spencer's liberalism – from social statics to social dynamics', in Richard Bellamy (ed.), *Victorian Liberalism*, pp. 110–30.

139. Kropotkin published a series of articles in *The Nineteenth Century* examining natural selection and functional adaptation to environmental conditions: 'Recent science', 32, 1892, pp. 1,007–14 [1002–20]; 'Recent science', 35, 1894, pp. 685–88 [673–91]; 'Recent science', 50, 1901, pp. 423–38 [417–38]; 'The theory of evolution and mutual aid', 67, 1910, pp. 86–107; 'The direct action of environment on plants', 68,

1910, pp. 58–77; 'Response of the animals to their environment', 68, 1910, pp. 856–66; 'The response of the animals to their environment', 68, 1910, pp. 1,047–59; 'Inheritance of acquired characters', 71, 1912, pp. 511–30; 'Inherited variation in plants', 76, 1914, pp. 816–36; 'Inherited variation in animals', 78, 1915, pp. 1124–44; 'The direct action of environment and evolution', 85, 1919, pp. 70–89. This body of work is discussed by Michael Confino and Daniel Rubinstein, 'Kropotkin Savant', pp. 243–302.

140. Kropotkin to Herzig, 29 April 1911, IISH Jean Wintsch papers.

141. Kropotkin, *Ethics*, p. 150.

142. Ibid. p. 35. The question of definition is discussed in Joanna Bourke, *What It Means to the Human, Reflections from 1791 to the Present*.

143. Kropotkin, *Ethics*, pp. 32–6, 50–61.

144. Kropotkin, *Mutual Aid*, p. 111.

145. Kropotkin, *Anarchist Morality*, p. 13.

146. Elie Reclus, *Primitive Folk*, pp. x–xi. Kropotkin refers to the book in his *Memoirs*, p. 328; Kropotkin, *Mutual Aid*, p. 102; Kropotkin, *Ethics*, p. 66.

147. Kropotkin, *Ethics*, p. 36; Kropotkin, *Mutual Aid*, pp. 101–3.

148. Kropotkin, *Ethics*, p. 11.

149. Kropotkin, 'The ethical need of the present day', p. 210.

150. Kropotkin, *Ethics*, pp. 144–5.

151. Ibid. pp. 127–8.

152. Ibid. pp. 216–17.

153. Ibid. p. 28; emphasis in original.

154. Ibid. p. 30.

155. Ibid. p. 272.

156. Ibid. p. 31.

157. Keith Ansell-Pearson, 'Morality and the philosophy of life in Guyau and Bergson', p. 63.

158. Dario Padovan, 'Social morals and ethics of nature', p. 493; emphasis in original.

159. Kropotkin, *Ethics*, p. 24.

160. Kropotkin, *Anarchist Morality*, p. 29.

161. John Price, *Postman's Park*.

162. Kropotkin, *Anarchist Morality*, p. 5.

163. Frank, 'Dostoevsky and Russian nihilism', p. 140.

164. Kropotkin, *Anarchist Morality*, p. 22.

165. Kropotkin, 'Letter to Max Nettlau', trans. Paul Sharkey, in McKay (ed.), *Direct Struggle against Capital*, p. 153.

166. Kropotkin, 'Must we occupy ourselves', in Miller (ed.), *P. A. Kropotkin*, p. 71.

167. Wolfi Landstreicher, *Willful Disobedience*.

168. Kropotkin, *Conquest of Bread*, p. 235.

169. Kropotkin, *Ethics*, p. 85.

170. Kropotkin, *The State*, p. 25.

171. Kropotkin, *Ethics*, p. 79; emphasis in original.
172. Kropotkin, *Anarchism*, pp. 18, 28.
173. Kropotkin, *Ethics*, p. 272. For Proudhon's view, see Prichard, *Justice, Order and Anarchy*, ch. 5; emphasis in original.
174. Kropotkin, *The State*, p. 41.

Chapter 6

1. Rosa Luxemburg, *The Junius Pamphlet*.
2. Woodcock and Avakumović, *The Anarchist Prince*, p. 219
3. Ibid. p. 230.
4. Woodcock, *Anarchism*, p. 199.
5. Woodcock and Avakumović, *The Anarchist Prince*, p. 245.
6. Woodcock, *Anarchism*, pp. 199–200.
7. Kropotkin to Herzig, 9 March 1909, 12 May 1909, IISH Wintsch.
8. Pernicone, *Italian Anarchism*, pp. 190–4. A translation of the full resolution appears in Cahm, *Kropotkin and the Rise of Revolutionary Anarchism 1872–1886*, p. 158.
9. Jensen, *The Battle against Anarchist Terrorism*, p. 17.
10. Cahm, *Kropotkin and the Rise of Revolutionary Anarchism 1872–1886*, p. 160.
11. Ibid. pp. 153, 176.
12. Kropotkin, 'Le Gouvernement Révolutionnaire'; 'Tous Socialistes', *Paroles*, pp. 245–65, 267–73.
13. Kropotkin, 'L'Esprit de Révolte', *Paroles*, p. 289.
14. Ibid. p. 290.
15. Ibid. p. 284.
16. Ibid. p. 284.
17. Ibid. p. 288.
18. Kropotkin, 'Anarchist action in the revolution', trans. Paul Sharkey, in McKay (ed.), *Direct Struggle against Capital*, p. 573.
19. André Reszler, 'Peter Kropotkin and his vison of anarchist aesthetics', p. 56.
20. Renate Poggioli, *The Theory of the Avant-Garde*, p. 9.
21. Kropotkin, *Un Siècle D'Attente 1789–1889*, pp. 4, 25.
22. Kropotkin, 'Must we occupy ourselves', p 83.
23. Kropotkin, *Anarchist Morality*, p. 16.
24. Kropotkin, *Anarchism*, p. 29.
25. Kropotkin, *French Revolution*, p. 452.
26. Olindo Malagodi, 'The psychology of anarchist conspiracies', pp. 88–9.
27. Cesare Lombroso, 'Illustrative studies in criminal anthropology', p. 336.
28. Michael Schwab, 'A convicted anarchist's reply to Professor Lombroso', p. 520.
29. Kropotkin, 'Prisons: Universities of crime', in McKay (ed.), *Direct Struggle against Capital*, p. 262.

30. Kropotkin, *French and Russian Prisons*, p. 336; emphasis in original.
31. Ibid. pp. 324–33.
32. Ibid. p. 323.
33. Kropotkin, *Anarchist Morality*, p. 17; emphasis in original.
34. Yarros, *Anarchism*, p. 13.
35. Kropotkin, 'Communism and anarchy', in McKay (ed.), *Direct Struggle against Capital*, p. 641.
36. Kropotkin, *Anarchist Morality*, pp. 22–3; emphasis in original.
37. Stites, *The Women's Liberation Movement in Russia*, p. 272.
38. Kropotkin, 'The Russian revolution and anarchism', trans. Josephien van Kessel, in McKay (ed.), *Direct Struggle against Capital*, p. 474.
39. Kropotkin, *Anarchist Morality*, p. 23; emphasis in original.
40. Kropotkin, 'Anarchist action in the revolution', pp. 568, 570.
41. Kropotkin, '1848–1871' in McKay (ed.), *Direct Struggle against Capital*, p. 430.
42. Kropotkin, 'The Great French Revolution', p. 839.
43. Kropotkin, '1848–1871', in McKay (ed.), *Direct Struggle against Capital*, p. 429.
44. Ibid. p. 431.
45. Ibid. p. 431.
46. Kropotkin, 'The Great French Revolution', p. 839.
47. Kropotkin, 'Anarchist action in the revolution', pp. 574–5.
48. Stirner, *The Ego and Its Own*, pp. 91, 107, 323; emphasis in original.
49. Kropotkin, 'Workers' organisation', trans. James Bar Bowen, in McKay (ed.), *Direct Struggle against Capital* p. 303.
50. Kropotkin, *Anarchist Morality*, p. 10.
51. Ibid. p. 10.
52. Ibid. p. 27.
53. Ibid. p. 32.
54. Ibid. p. 19; emphasis in original.
55. Ibid. p. 33; emphasis in original.
56. Ibid. p. 27
57. Kropotkin, 'Communism and anarchy', in McKay (ed.), *Direct Struggle against Capital*, p. 633.
58. Kropotkin, *Anarchist Morality*, p. 26.
59. Vladimir D. Bonch-Bruevich, 'Conversation with Lenin', in Miller (ed.), *P. A. Kropotkin*, p. 327.
60. Kropotkin, *Anarchist Morality*, p. 20.
61. Kropotkin, *The State*, p. 31.
62. Kropotkin, *Anarchism*, p. 25.
63. Kropotkin, *The State*, p. 41.
64. Kropotkin, *Anarchist Morality*, pp. 29–30; emphasis in original.
65. Stirner, *The Ego and Its Own*, p. 196; emphasis in original.
66. Kropotkin, 'Communism and anarchy', in McKay (ed.), *Direct Struggle against Capital*, p. 639.

67. Kropotkin, *Modern Science and Anarchism*, p. 87.

68. Kropotkin, '1848–1871', in McKay (ed.), *Direct Struggle against Capital*, p. 436.

69. D. Novak (ed.), 'An unpublished essay on Leo Tolstoy by Peter Kropotkin', pp. 19–20.

70. Kropotkin, 'Co-operation', *Freedom*, January 1897; emphasis in original.

71. Kropotkin, 'Anarchist action in the revolution', in McKay (ed.), *Direct Struggle against Capital*, p. 577.

72. Kropotkin, 'Are we good enough?', in Walter and Becker (eds), *Act for Yourselves*, p. 85.

73. Kropotkin, *Modern Science and Anarchism*, p. 87.

74. Kropotkin, 'Preface to words of a rebel', in McKay (ed.), *Direct Struggle against Capital*, p. 583.

75. Kropotkin, '1848–1871', in McKay (ed.), *Direct Struggle against Capital*, p. 429.

76. Kropotkin, 'Co-operation', *Freedom*, December 1896.

77. Kropotkin, 'Syndicalism and anarchism', in McKay (ed.), *Direct Struggle against Capital*, p. 408.

78. Ernest Belfort Bax, 'The materialistic doctrine of history', in *Essays in Socialism New and Old*, pp. 17, 18.

79. Ibid. p. 19.

80. Kropotkin, 'Co-operation', *Freedom*, December 1896.

81. Kropotkin, 'Anarchism and syndicalism', in McKay (ed.), *Direct Struggle against Capital*, p. 408.

82. Kropotkin, 'Politics and socialism', in McKay (ed.), *Direct Struggle against Capital*, p. 375.

83. Kropotkin, *Anarchism*, p. 27; emphasis in original.

84. Ibid. p. 27.

85. Kropotkin, *Memoirs*, p. 328.

86. Kropotkin, *Conquest of Bread*, p. 71.

87. Kropotkin, 'Postscript to words of a rebel', in McKay (ed.), *Direct Struggle against Capital*, 584; emphasis in original.

88. Marcel van der Linden and Wayne Thorpe, 'The rise and fall of revolutionary syndicalism', in van der Linden and Thorpe (eds), *Revolutionary Syndicalism*, p. 5; Schmidt and van der Walt, *Black Flame*, pp. 153–8.

89. Kropotkin, 'The workers' movement in Spain', trans. Paul Sharkey, in McKay (ed.), *Direct Struggle against Capital*, pp. 297–300.

90. Kropotkin, 'Anarchists and trade unions', in McKay (ed.), *Direct Struggle against Capital*, p. 392.

91. Schmidt and van der Walt, *Black Flame*, pp. 124–6.

92. Kropotkin, *Mutual Aid*, pp. 264–7.

93. Ibid. pp. 269–70; 'Syndicalism and anarchism', in McKay (ed.), *Direct Struggle against Capital*, p. 404.

94. Kropotkin, 'Syndicalism and anarchism', in McKay (ed.), *Direct Struggle against Capital*, p. 404; 'Trade unionism and parliamentarism', trans.

Paul Sharkey, in McKay (ed.), *Direct Struggle against Capital*, pp. 384–5; emphasis in original.

95. Rudolf Rocker, *Anarcho-Syndicalism*.
96. Kropotkin, 'Syndicalism and anarchism', in McKay (ed.), *Direct Struggle against Capital*, p. 403.
97. Kropotkin, 'Anarchists and trade unions', in McKay (ed.), *Direct Struggle against Capital*, p. 392; 'Syndicalism and anarchism', in McKay(ed.), *Direct Struggle against Capital*, p. 411.
98. Kropotkin to Herzig, 23 February 1906, IISH Wintsch.
99. Kropotkin, 'Commemoration of the Chicago martyrs', in McKay (ed.), *Direct Struggle against Capital*, p. 344.
100. On Nettlau, see Bert Altena, 'A networking historian', in Bert Altena and Constance Bantman (eds), *Reassessing the Transnational Turn*, p. 69.
101. Kropotkin to Jean Grave, 3 July 1902.
102. Kropotkin, 'Anarchists and trade unions', in McKay (ed.), *Direct Struggle against Capital*, p. 391.
103. Kropotkin 'Letter to Alexander Berkman', in McKay (ed.), *Direct Struggle against Capital*, p. 401; emphasis in original.
104. Schmidt and van der Walt, *Black Flame*, pp. 182–3.
105. Malatesta, address to the International Anarchist Congress, Amsterdam, 26–31 August 1907.
106. Kropotkin, 'Syndicalism and anarchism', in McKay (ed.), *Direct Struggle against Capital*, p. 407.
107. Kropotkin, 'Preface', in *How We Shall Bring about the Revolution*', in McKay (ed.), *Direct Struggle against Capital*, pp. 556–62.
108. Kropotkin to Grave, 14 December 1910; 22 December 1910.
109. Kropotkin, 'L'Action Des Masses & L'Individu', *La Révolte*, 24–30 May 1890.
110. Kropotkin, 'Commemoration of the Chicago martyrs', in McKay (ed.), *Direct Struggle against Capital*, p. 344.
111. Kropotkin to Jean Grave, 3 July 1902.
112. Rocker, *Anarcho-Syndicalism*, p. 51.
113. Malatesta, address to the International Anarchist Congress.
114. Kropotkin, 'Workers' organisations', in McKay (ed.), *Direct Struggle against Capital*, p. 309.
115. Malatesta, *Anarchy*, pp. 17–18.
116. Ibid. p. 14.
117. Kropotkin, '1848–1871', in McKay (ed.), *Direct Struggle against Capital*, p. 435.
118. Kropotkin, 'Anarchists and trade unions', in McKay (ed.), *Direct Struggle against Capital*, p. 391.
119. Kropotkin, 'Letter to French and British trade union delegates', in McKay (ed.), *Direct Struggle against Capital*, p. 360.
120. Kropotkin to Grave, 20 August 1911; emphasis in original.
121. 'The Railway Strike and its Background', *The Times*, 19 August 1911.

122. Kropotkin, 'Workers' organisation', in McKay (ed.), *Direct Struggle against Capital*, p. 310.

123. Kropotkin, 'Politics and socialism', in McKay (ed.), *Direct Struggle against Capital*, p. 377.

124. Kropotkin, *Anarchism*, p. 28.

125. Kropotkin, 'La Leçon que nous donne l'Italie', *Almanach Illustré De La Révolution*, p. 12; emphasis in original.

126. Kropotkin to Herzig, 23 Februrary 1906.

127. Kropotkin, 'La Révolution en Russie', *Almanach Illustré de la Révolution*, pp. 9–15.

128. Kropotkin, 'The revolution in Russia', in McKay (ed.), *Direct Struggle against Capital*, p. 457. In Kropotkin's draft 'The revolution in Russia' it has emphasis in original. IISH Nettlau 2722.

129. *Freedom*, November 1901.

130. Kropotkin, 'Letter to French and British trade union delegates', in McKay (ed.), *Direct Struggle against Capital*, p. 361.

131. Kropotkin, 'The workers' movement in Spain', in McKay (ed.), *Direct Struggle against Capital*, p. 298.

132. Kropotkin, 'Ist May 1891', trans. Paul Sharkey, in McKay (ed.), *Direct Struggle against Capital*, p. 333.

133. Kropotkin, 'The Russian Revolution and anarchism', trans. Josephien van Kessel, in McKay (ed.), *Direct Struggle against Capital*, p. 476.

134. Kropotkin, 'La Leçon que nous donne l'Italie', p. 10; emphasis in original.

135. Kropotkin, 'Trade unionism and parliamentarism', trans. Paul Sharkey, in McKay (ed.), *Direct Struggle against Capital*, p. 385–6.

136. Kropotkin, 'Syndicalism and anarchism', in McKay (ed.), *Direct Struggle against Capital*, p. 409.

137. For a discussion, see H. Tudor and J. M. Tudor, *Marxism and Social Democracy*.

138. Kropotkin, 'La Democratie Sociale Allemande et E. Bernstein', *Les Temps Nouveaux*, 27 January 1900.

139. Kropotkin to Marsh, 15 October 1901, IISH Marsh.

140. Kropotkin, 'Socialism and anarchism', in McKay (ed.), *Direct Struggle against Capital*, p. 411.

141. Kropotkin, 'Postscript to words of a rebel', in McKay (ed.), *Direct Struggle against Capital*, p. 589.

142. Letter to Steffen, in Miller (ed.), *P. A. Kropotkin*, pp. 309–16.

143. Kropotkin, 'Prince Kropotkin's farewell', *The Times*, 8 June 1917.

144. Malatesta, 'Anarchists have forgotten their principles', *Freedom*, November 1914.

145. Kropotkin, *Wars and Capitalism*, p. 6.

146. Ibid. p. 9.

147. Kropotkin to Brandes, 31 March 1904, p. 183.

148. Kropotkin, 'L'Alliance Franco-Russe', *Les Temps Nouveaux*, 18 February 1899.

149. Kropotkin, 'Une Lettre de Kropotkine', *La Libertaire*, 22 July 1921, Nettlau 2710.

150. Kropotkin, 'La Guerre Russo-Japonaise', *Les Temps Nouveaux*, 5 March 1904.

151. Kropotkin, *Modern Science and Anarchism*, p. 83.

152. Kropotkin, 'The Russian Revolution and anarchism', in McKay (ed.), *Direct Struggle against Capital*, p. 463.

153. Kropotkin, 'L'Alliance Franco-Russe'.

154. Kropotkin, 'Co-operation', *Freedom*, December 1896.

155. Kropotkin, 'Caesarism', *Freedom*, June 1899.

156. Ibid.

157. Kropotkin, 'Antimilitarisme et Révolution', *Les Temps Nouveaux*, 4 November 1905.

158. Letter to Steffen, p. 310.

159. Malatesta, 'Anarchists have forgotten their principles'.

160. Kropotkin to Herzig, 3 June 1913.

161. Kropotkin to Maria Isidine Goldsmith, 11 May 1897, in MacKay, *The Anarchists*, p. 138.

162. Ibid. p. 145.

163. Kropotkin to Herzig, 3 June 1913, IISH.

164. Kropotkin to Maria Isidine Goldsmith, in MacKay, *The Anarchists*, p. 140.

165. Kropotkin, *Anarchist Morality*, p. 21.

166. Kropotkin, 'La Guerre Russo-Japonaise'.

167. Kropotkin, *Wars and Capitalism*, pp. 14–15.

168. Kropotkin, *French Revolution*, p. 323.

169. Kropotkin, 'La Guerre Russo-Japonaise'.

170. Kropotkin, *Great French Revolution*, pp. 416–19.

171. Guglielmo Ferrero, *Militarism, A Contribution To the Peace Crusade*, pp. 48–51.

172. Harriet Anderson, *Utopian Feminism*, p. 127.

173. C. K. Ogden and Mary Sargant Florence, *Militarism versus Feminism*, pp. 55–140.

174. Guy Aldred, 'Militarism and revolution', in *Essays in Revolt*, p. 3.

175. Kropotkin, 'Antimilitarisme et Révolution'.

176. Errico Malatesta, 'Pro-government Anarchists', *The Blast*, p. 109.

177. On Butler's anarchistic leanings see Ryley, *Making another World Possible*, pp. 51–60. Butler likened the Boer's attitude towards the indigenous African people to white supremacism in the southern states of America and believed British imperialism was a lesser evil, defending intervention against the Boers in these terms in *Native Races and the War*. See Jane Jordan, *Josephine Butler*, p. 283.

178. Kropotkin, 'Message to the Workers of the Western World', in MacKay, *The Anarchists*, p. 488.

179. Kropotkin, 'The Russian Revolution and anarchism', in McKay (ed.), *Direct Struggle against Capital*, p. 463.

180. *Manifesto of the Sixteen*, trans. Shawn P. Wilbur.
181. Kropotkin to Domela Nieuwenhuis, 3 October 1916, IISH Nettlau 208/279
182. Letter to Steffen, in Miller (ed.), *P. A. Kropotkin*, pp. 315–16.
183. Kropotkin to May Morris, 23 March 1917, BL Add. Ms. 45347 ff. 144–5; emphasis in original.

Conclusion to Part 3

1. Malatesta, 'Kropotkin: Recollections', *Freedom Bulletin*, 12, July 1931.
2. Ibid.
3. David Miller, 'The neglected (II) – Kropotkin', p. 338.
4. Alfredo Bonnano, 'Introduction', in *The Conquest of Bread*, p. 12.
5. Newman, *Politics of Postanarchism*, n. 1 p. 14.
6. Kropotkin, 7 January 1915, IISH Nettlau 2706; emphasis in original.
7. A. F. Pollard, 'The superstition of the state', *Times Literary Supplement*, 18 July 1918, p. 329.
8. Kropotkin, 'The Lena atrocities', *The Anarchist*, 17 May 1912.
9. Woodcock and Avakumović, *The Anarchist Prince*, p. 400.
10. Camille Berneri, *Peter Kropotkin*, p. 17.
11. Kropotkin, 'Message to the workers of the Western world', in McKay (ed.), *Direct Struggle against Capital*, p. 489.
12. Kropotkin, 'Russian Schools and the Holy Synod', p. 527.
13. Kropotkin, 'Message to the workers of the Western World', in McKay (ed.), *Direct Struggle against Capital*, p. 489.
14. Ibid. p. 489.
15. Reclus, 'The feeling for nature in modern society', in Clark and Martin (eds), *Anarchy, Geography, Modernity*, pp. 103–12.
16. Morris, *Kropotkin*, ch. 4.
17. Kropotkin, 'Syndicalism and anarchism', in McKay (ed.), *Direct Struggle against Capital*, p. 410.
18. Kropotkin, *Conquest of Bread*, pp. 152–3.
19. Kropotkin, *Memoirs*, p. 95.
20. Mumford, *The Culture of Cities*, p. 442.
21. Uri Gordon, *Anarchy Alive!* p. 114.
22. Roslak, *Neo-Impressionism*, p. 103.
23. Lenka Anna Rovná, 'Peter Kropotkin and his influence on Czech anarchism', p. 67.
24. Benjamin Tucker, 'Postscript', in 'State socialism and anarchism', in C. L. S. (ed.), *Selections from the Writings of Benjamin R. Tucker*, pp. 17–18.
25. Kropotkin, *French and Russian Prisons*, p. 168.
26. Ibid. p. 333.
27. Ibid. p. 315.
28. Ibid. p. 325.
29. Ibid. pp. 293–4.
30. Kristian Williams, ' "A criminal with a noble face" '; emphasis in original.

31. Helen Blagg and Charlotte Wilson, *Women and Prisons*, p. 13.
32. Williams, ' "A criminal with a noble face" '.
33. Kropotkin, 'Communism and anarchy', in McKay (ed.), *Direct Struggle against Capital*, p. 639; emphasis in original.
34. Kropotkin, *Mutual Aid*, pp. 124, 158.
35. Kropotkin, 'The coming anarchy', p. 162.
36. Oscar Wilde, 'To the editor of the *Daily Chronicle*', 27 May 1897, in Merlin Holland and Rupert Hart-Davis (eds), *The Complete Letters of Oscar Wilde*, p. 848.
37. Kropotkin, *Anarchist Morality*, p. 25.
38. Kropotkin, 'Communism and anarchy', in McKay (ed.), *Direct Struggle against Capital*, p. 639.
39. Kropotkin, *French and Russian Prisons*, p. 350.
40. Ibid. p. 348.
41. Stirner, *The Ego and Its Own*, p. 311; emphasis in original.
42. Kropotkin, '1848–1871', in McKay (ed.), *Direct Struggle against Capital*, p. 432.
43. Kropotkin, 'Message to the workers of the Western world', in McKay (ed.), *Direct Struggle against Capital*, p. 487.
44. Kropotkin, 'Letter to Steffen', in Miller (ed.), *P. A. Kropotkin*, p. 315.
45. Kropotkin, 'Co-operation', *Freedom*, December 1896.

Reviewing the Classical Anarchist Tradition

1. Bax, *Reminiscences and Reflexions of a Mid and Late Victorian*, pp. 42–4.
2. Cahm, *Kropotkin and the Rise of Revolutionary Anarchism 1872–1886*, p. 175.
3. Letter to Maria Goldsmith, p. 142.
4. Jesse Cohn and Shawn P. Wilbur, 'What's wrong with postanarchism?'
5. Nathan Jun, *Anarchism and Political Modernity*, p. xiii.
6. Carole Pateman, *Participation and Democratic Theory*, p. 17.
7. Kropotkin, 'Anarchism', in McKay (ed.), *Direct Struggle against Capital*, p. 173.
8. Kropotkin, 'Les Temps Nouveaux: Conférence Faite à Londres', *La Révolte*, Paris, 1894.
9. Kropotkin, 'The anarchist principle', in McKay (ed.), *Direct Struggle against Capital*, pp. 197–8.
10. Ibid. pp. 197–8.
11. Fleming, *Geography of Freedom*, p. 23.
12. 'Letter to Marie Isidine Goldsmith', in McKay (ed.), *Direct Struggle against Capital*, p. 145.
13. Kropotkin to Marsh, 27 July 1895.

Bibliography

Archive and manuscript material

International Institute of Social History

Augustin Hamon papers

Kleine Korrespondenz (from the archives of the Sozialdemokratische Partei Deutschlands)

Alfred Marsh papers

Max Nettlau Collection: Peter Kropotkin papers; Domela Nieuwenhuis papers

Jean Wintsch – *Le Réveil*

British Library

Petr Alekseevich Kropotkin, 'Máterials, printed and MS., on the emancipation of women in Russia, collected and annotated by Prince P. A. Kropotkin 1842–1921' (1891–1907), BL General Reference Collection 1884. a.11.

Correspondence with Nannie Dryhurst. Miscellaneous Letters and Papers. Add. MS 46362 ff. 23–27.

Correspondence George Bernard Shaw. Western Manuscripts Vol. VII BL Add. MS 50514 ff. 113–16.

Correspondence May Morris. Western Manuscripts Vol. X BL Add. MS 45347 ff. 144–5.

Institute Français d'Histoire Sociale/Archives nationales, Pierrefitte-sur-Seine

Fonds Grave, Jean (14 AS 184/b) correspondence Kropotkin.

Newspapers

Freedom

Justice

The Times

Kropotkin: Anthologies

Baldwin, Roger (ed.), *Kropotkin's Revolutionary Pamphlets* (New York: Dover, 1970).

McKay, Iain (ed.), *Direct Struggle against Capital: A Peter Kropotkin Anthology* (Edinburgh and Oakland: AK Press, 2014).

Miller, Martin (ed.), *P. A. Kropotkin: Selected Writings on Anarchism and Revolution* (Cambridge, MA: MIT Press, 1970).

Walter, Nicholas and Heiner Becker (eds), *Act for Yourselves* (London: Freedom Press, 1988).

Kropotkin: Books and Pamphlets

Le Procès Solovieff: La Vie D'un Socialiste Russe (Geneva: Imp. Jurassienne, 1879).

La Vérité Sur Les Exécutions en Russie Suivie D'une Esquisse Biographique Sur Sophie Perowskaya (Geneva: Edition du Révolté, 1881).

Paroles d'un Révolté, nouvelle édition (Paris: Librairie Marpon et Flammarion, n.d. [1885]).

In French and Russian Prisons (London: Ward and Downey, 1887).

Anarchist Morality, 8th edn (London: Freedom Press, n.d. [1898]).

Anarchism: Its Philosophy and Ideal (London: Freedom Press, 1907 [1898]).

Fields, Factories and Workshops: Or, Industry Combined with Agriculture and Brain Work with Manual Work, new edn (London: Thomas Nelson and Sons, 1912 [1898]).

Memoirs of a Revolutionist (London: Folio, 1978 [1899]).

Mutual Aid. A Factor of Evolution (Boston: Extending Horizons Books, n.d. [1902]).

Organised Vengeance Called 'Justice' (London: Freedom Library, 1902).

The State: Its Historic Role (London: Freedom, 1943 [1903]).

The Conquest of Bread (London: Chapman and Hall, 1906).

The Terror in Russia (London: Gresham Press, 1909).

Modern Science and Anarchism (London: Freedom, 1912).

Wars and Capitalism (London: Freedom, 1914).

Ideals and Realities in Russian Literature (New York: Alfred A. Knopf, 1916 [1905]).

The Great French Revolution, 2 vols (New York: Vanguard Press, 1927 [1909]).

Ethics Origin and Development, Louis S. Friedland and Joseph R. Piroshnikoff (trans) (New York: Benjamin Blom, 1968).

Kropotkin: Articles and Journalism

'The Revolutionary Party of Russia', *Newcastle Daily Chronicle*, 12 October 1881.

'Russian administration', *Newcastle Daily Chronicle*', 18 January 1882.

'The Russian peasantry', *Newcastle Daily Chronicle*, 7 February 1882.

'The Russian Revolutionary Party', *Fortnightly Review*, 31, 1882, pp. 654–71.

'Finland: A rising nationality', *The Nineteenth Century*, 17, 1885, pp. 527–46, *The Anarchist Library*, 2009, pp. 2–17, <https://archive.org/details/al_Petr_Kropotkin_Finland_A_Rising_Nationality_a4> (last accessed 3 March 2015).

'What geography ought to be', *The Nineteenth Century*, 18, 1885, pp. 940–58.

The Place of Anarchism in Socialistic Evolution, Address delivered in Paris, Henry Glasse (trans.) (London: William Reeves, 1886).

'The coming anarchy', *The Nineteenth Century*, 22, 1887, pp. 149–252.

'L'Action Des Masses & L'Individu', *La Révolte*, 24–30 May, 1890.

'Recent science', *The Nineteenth Century*, 32, 1892, pp. 1,002–20.

'Advice to those about to emigrate', *Freedom,* March 1893.

'On the teaching of physiography', from *The Geographical Journal* (London: William Clowes & Sons, 1893).

Un Siècle D'Attente 1789–1889 (Paris: Publications de La Révolte, 1893).

'Les Temps Nouveaux: Conférence Faite à Londres', *La Révolte*, Paris, 1894.

'Recent science', *The Nineteenth Century*, 35, 1894, pp. 141–56.

'Recent science', *The Nineteenth Century*, 35, 1894, pp. 673–91.

'Proposed communist settlement: A new colony for Tyneside or Wearside', *Newcastle Daily Chronicle*, 16 February 1895.

'The great Siberian Railway', *The Geographical Journal*, 5, 1895, pp. 146–54.

'Co-operation: A reply to Herbert Spencer', *Freedom*, December 1896.

'Co-operation: A reply to Herbert Spencer', part II, *Freedom*, January 1897.

'Edward Bellamy', *Freedom*, July 1898.

'Caesarism', *Freedom*, June 1899.

'L'Alliance Franco-Russe', *Les Temps Nouveaux*, 18 February 1899.

'Recent science: Meteorites and comets', *The Nineteenth Century*, 46, 1899, pp. 934–46.

'La Democratie Sociale Allemande et E. Bernstein', *Les Temps Nouveaux*, 27 January 1900.

'The present crisis in Russia', *North American Review*, 172, 1901, pp. 711–23.

'Recent science', *The Nineteenth Century*, 50, 1901, pp. 417–38.

'Russian schools and the Holy Synod', *North American Review*, 174, 1902, pp. 518–27.

'Anarchists and the French Revolution', *Freedom*, December 1903.

'The desiccation of Eur-Asia', *The Geographical Journal*, 23, 1904, pp. 722–34.

'The ethical need of the present day', *The Nineteenth Century*, 56, 1904, pp. 207–26.

'La Guerre Russo-Japonaise', *Les Temps Nouveaux*, 5 March 1904.

'The orography of Asia', *The Geographical Journal*, 23, 1904, repr. London: William Claves & Son, 1904.

'Antimilitarisme et Révolution', *Les Temps Nouveaux*, 4 November 1905.

'Elisée Reclus: Obituary', from the *Geographical Journal* for September 1905 (London: William Claves), pp. 337–43.

'La Leçon que nous donne l'Italie', in *Almanach Illustré De La Révolution* (Paris: Paul Delesalle, 1905), pp. 9–12.

'The morality of nature', *The Nineteenth Century*, 57, 1905, pp. 407–26.

'The birth of conscience "The morality of nature"', in Charles F. Horne, (ed. foreword, introductions and notes) *The Meaning of Modern Life* (New York: The National Alumni, 1907), pp. 1–12.

'La Révolution en Russie', in *Almanach Illustré de la Révolution* (Paris: La Publication Sociale, 1907), pp. 9–15.

'Foreword', in Thomas Smith, *French Gardening* (London: Joseph Fels & Utopian Press, 1909), pp. v–x.

'The direct action of environment on plants', *The Nineteenth Century*, 68, 1910, pp. 58–77.

'Response of the animals to their environment', *The Nineteenth Century*, 68, 1910, pp. 856–66.

'The response of the animals to their environment', *The Nineteenth Century*, 68, 1910, pp. 1,047–59.

'The theory of evolution and mutual aid', *The Nineteenth Century*, 67, 1910, pp. 86–107.

'Inheritance of acquired characters: Theoretical difficulties', *The Nineteenth Century*, 71, 1912, pp. 511–30.

'The Lena Atrocities', *The Anarchist*, 17 May 1912.

'The direct action of environment and evolution', *The Nineteenth Century*, 85, 1919, pp. 70–89.

'Inherited variation in plants', *The Nineteenth Century*, 76, 1914, pp. 816–36.

'Inherited variation in animals', *The Nineteenth Century*, 78, 1915, pp. 1,124–44.

Other Works

Anon., *The Breakup of Nihilists in Russia: Female Nihilists* (London: F. and P. Broemel, 1885).

Adams, Matthew, 'Kropotkin: Evolution, revolutionary change and the end of history', *Anarchist Studies*, 19, 2011, pp. 56–81.

Adams, Matthew, 'Rejecting the American model: Peter Kropotkin's radical communalism', *History of Political Thought*, 35(1), 2014, pp. 147–73.

Adams, Matthew, *Kropotkin, Read and the Intellectual History of British Anarchism: Between Reason and Romanticism* (Basingstoke: Palgrave/Macmillan, 2015).

Adams, Matthew, 'Formulating an anarchist sociology: Peter Kropotkin's reading of Herbert Spencer', *Journal of the History of Ideas*, 77(1), forthcoming.

Aizlewood, Robin, 'Berdiaev and Chaadaev, Russia and feminine passivity', in Peter I. Barta (ed.), *Gender and Sexuality in Russian Civilisation* (London: Routledge, 2001), pp. 121–39.

Aldred, Guy, *Militarism and Revolution* (London: Bakunin Press, 1909).

Aldred, Guy, *Socialism and Parliament*, pt 1, 3rd edn (Glasgow: Strickland Press, 1942 [1923]).

Altena, Bert, 'A networking historian', in Bert Altena and Constance Bantman (eds), *Reassessing the Transnational Turn: Scales of Analysis in Anarchist Studies* (London: Routledge, 2015), pp. 62–79.

Anderson, Harriet, *Utopian Feminism: Women's Movements in fin-de-siècle Vienna* (New Haven and London: Yale University Press, 1992).

Ansell-Pearson, Keith, *Introduction to Nietzsche as a Political Thinker* (Cambridge: Cambridge University Press, 1994).

Ansell-Pearson, Keith and Diane Morgan (eds), *Nihilism Now! Monsters of Energy* (Basingstoke: Macmillan, 2000).

Ansell-Pearson, Keith, 'Morality and the philosophy of life in Guyau and Bergson', *Continental Philosophy Review*, 47, 2014, pp. 59–85.

Antliff, Allan, 'Revolutionary seer for a post-industrial age', in John Moore and Spencer Sunshine (eds), *I am not a Man, I am Dynamite! Friedrich Nietzsche and the Anarchist Tradition* (Brooklyn: Autonomedia, 2004), pp. 40–8.

Apter, David E., 'The old anarchism and the new – some comments', in David Apter and James Joll (eds), *Anarchism Today* (London: Macmillan, 1971), pp. 1–13.

Apter, David and James Joll (eds), *Anarchism Today* (London: Macmillan, 1971).

Arnaudo, G. B., *Il Nihilismo* (Turin: Francesco Casnova, 1879).

Ashworth, Lucian, 'Realism and the spirit of 1919: Halford Mackinder, geopolitics and the reality of the League of Nations', *European Journal of International Relations*, 17, 2010, pp. 289–301.

Avrich, Paul, *Bakunin and Nechaev* (London: Freedom Press, 1974).

Avrich, Paul, *The Russian Anarchists* (Oakland and Edinburgh: AK Press, 2005 [1967]).

Avrich, Paul, *The Modern School Movement: Anarchism and Education in the United States* (Edinburgh and Oakland: AK Press, 2006 [1980]).

Baginski, Max, 'Stirner: "The ego and his own" ', *Mother Earth*, 2: 3, 1907, pp. 142–51, <http://dwardmac.pitzer.edu/Anarchist_Archives/goldman/ME/mev2n3.html> (last accessed 3 March 2015).

Bakunin, Michael, *God and the State* (New York: Mother Earth Publishing, 1916 [1882]), <https://www.marxists.org/reference/archive/bakunin/works/godstate/> (last accessed 3 March 2015).

Bakunin, Michael, *The Paris Commune and the Idea of the State* (London: CIRA, 1971).

Bakunin, Michael, *Statism and Anarchy*, Marshall Shatz (ed.) (Cambridge: Cambridge University Press, 1990 [1873]).

Baldelli, Giovanni, *Social Anarchism* (Chicago and New York: Aldine Altherton, 1971).

Bantman, Constance, *The French Anarchists in London, 1880–1914. Exile and transnationalism in the first globalisation* (Liverpool: Liverpool University Press, 2013).

Barnett, Vincent, *A History of Russian Economic Thought* (London: Routledge, 2005).

Bartlett, Robert, *The Making of Europe: Conquest, Colonization and Cultural Change, 950–1350* (Harmondsworth: Penguin, 1993).

Bax, Ernest Belfort, *Essays in Socialism New and Old* (London: E. Grant Richards, 1907).

Bax, Ernest Belfort, *Reminiscences and Reflexions of a Mid and Late Victorian* (New York: Augustus M. Kelley, 1967).

Bernard Shaw, George, 'The Perfect Wagnerite. A commentary on the Niblung's Ring', in *Major Critical Essays* (Harmondsworth: Penguin, 1986 [1898]), pp. 177–304.

Bekken, Jon, 'Bakunin and the historians', *Libertarian Labor Review*, 13, 1992, pp. 30–2, <http://www.syndicalist.org/archives/llr1–13/13i.shtml> (last accessed 6 June 2015).

Berneri, Camille, *Peter Kropotkin: His Federalist Ideas* (Sheffield: Pirate Press, n.d. [1942]).

Blackledge, Paul, 'The struggle for freedom and democracy: Marxism, anarchism and the problem of human nature', in Alex Prichard, Ruth Kinna, Saku Pinta and David Berry (eds), *Libertarian Socialism: Politics in Black and Red* (Basingstoke: Palgrave/Macmillan, 2012), pp. 17–34.

Blagg, Helen and Charlotte Wilson, *Women and Prisons* (London: The Fabian Society, 1912).

Blatchford, Robert, *Merrie England* (London: Journeyman Press, 1977 [1893]).

Blind, Karl, 'Conspiracies in Russia under the reigning czar', *Contemporary Review*, 36, 1879, pp. 120–47.

Bonnano, Alfredo, 'Introduction', in Peter Kropotkin, *The Conquest of Bread* (London: Elephant Editions, 1985), pp. 7–15.

Bookchin, Murray, *The Ecology of Freedom* (Palo Alto: Cheshire Books, 1982).

Bookchin, Murray, *Post-Scarcity Anarchism*, 3rd edn (Edinburgh and Oakland: AK Press, 2004).

Bourke, Joanna, *What it Means to the Human: Reflections from 1791 to the Present* (London: Virago, 2011).

Brandes, Georg, 'Preface', in Peter Kropotkin, *Memoirs of a Revolutionist* (London: Swan Sonnenschein & Co. Ltd, 1906), pp. ix–xvi.

Brandes, Georg, *Friedrich Nietzsche* (New York: Macmillan, 1915).

Brandes, Georg, *Correspondance de Georg Brandes Lettres Choisies et 'Annotées par Paul Krüger II, L'angleterre et la Russie* (Copenhagen: Rosenkilde Og Bagger, 1956).

Breuilly, John, *Nationalism and the State*, 2nd edn (Manchester: Manchester University Press, 1995).

Brückner, A., *A Literary History of Russia*, Ellis H. Minns (ed.), H. Havelock (trans.) (London and Leipzig: T. Fisher Unwin, 1908).

Buck-Morss, Susan, 'Hegel and Haiti', *Critical Inquiry*, 26, 2000, pp. 821–65.

Buick, Adam, 'What Marx should have said to Kropotkin', *Socialist Standard*, 1 June 2006 [1994], <http://socialiststandardmyspace.blogspot.co.uk/2006/06/what-marx-should-have-said-to-kropotkin.html> (last accessed 3 March 2015).

Cahm, Caroline, *Kropotkin and the Rise of Revolutionary Anarchism 1872–1886* (Cambridge: Cambridge University Press, 2002).

Call, Lewis, *Postmodern Anarchism* (Lanham: Lexington Books, 2002).

Carpenter, Edward, *My Days and Dreams: Being: Autobiographical Notes* (London: George Allan and Unwin, 1916).

Centennial Expressions on Peter Kropotkin 1842–1942 by Pertinent Thinkers (Los Angeles: Rocker Publications Committee, 1942).

Cherkesov, Varlaam [W. Tcherkesov], 'Socialism or democracy: What is Socialism?', *Supplement to Freedom*, July 1895.

Cherkesov, Varlaam [W. Tcherkesoff], *Concentration of Capital* (London: Freedom, 1911), pp. 12–13.

Chernyshevksy, Nikolai, *What is to be Done?*, Michael R. Katz (trans.) (Ithaca and London: Cornell University Press, 1989 [1863]).

C. L. S. (ed.), *Individual Liberty, Selections from the Writings of Benjamin R. Tucker* (New York: Vanguard Press, 1926) <https://mises.org/library/individual-liberty> (last accessed 28 June 2015).

Clark, John, *The Anarchist Moment: Reflections on Culture, Nature and Power* (Montreal: Black Rose Books, 1984).

Clark, John and Camille Martin (eds), *Anarchy, Geography, Modernity. Selected Writings of Elisée Reclus* (Oakland: PM Press, 2013).

Clark, Samuel, *Living without Domination: The Possibility of an Anarchist Utopia* (Aldershot: Ashgate, 2007).

Cohn, Jesse and Shawn P. Wilbur, 'What's wrong with postanarchism?', Anarchist Studies, 31 August 2003, <http://theanarchistlibrary.org/library/jesse-cohn-and-shawn-wilbur-what-s-wrong-with-postanarchism> (last accessed 25 March 2015).

Cohn-Bendit, Daniel, *Obsolete Communism: The Left-Wing Alternative*, Arnold Pomerans (trans.) (London: Andre Deutsch, 1968).

Cole, G. D. H., *A History of Socialist Thought*, vol. 3, pt 1, *The Second International 1889–1914* (London: Macmillan, 1967).

Cole, G. D. H., *A History of Socialist Thought: Marxism and Anarchism 1850–1890*, vol. 2 (London, Macmillan, 1954).

Confino, Michael (ed.), *Daughter of a Revolutionary, Natalie Herzen and the Bakunin-Nechayev Circle*, Hilary Sternberg and Lydia Bott (trans) (LaSalle: Library Press, 1973).

Confino, Michael and Daniel Rubinstein, 'Kropotkin Savant. Vingt-cinq lettres inédites de Pierre Kropotkine à Marie Goldsmith 27 juillet 1901–9 juillet 1915', *Cahiers du Monde russe et soviétique*, XXXIII, 1992, pp. 243–302.

Critchley, Simon, *Infinitely Demanding* (London: Verso, 2008).

Crowder, George, *Classical Anarchism: The Political Thought of Godwin, Proudhon, Bakunin, and Kropotkin* (Oxford: Clarendon, 1991).

Cunliffe-Owen, Fritz, 'Russian nihilism', *The Nineteenth Century*, 7, 1880, pp. 1–2.

Cutler, Robert, *The Basic Bakunin: Writings 1869–1871* (Buffalo: Prometheus Books, 1992).

Cutler, Robert, 'Bakunin and the psychobiographers: The anarchist as mythical and historical object', *Klio*, 2010 (No. 2), pp. 115–24, <http://www.robertcutler.org/bakunin/pdf/ar09klio.pdf> (last accessed 3 March 2015).

Dave, Victor, *Michel Bakounine et Karl Marx* (Paris: édition de l'Humanité Nouvelle, 1900).

Davis, Laurence and Ruth Kinna (eds), *Anarchism and Utopianism* (Manchester: Manchester University Press, 2009).

Day, Richard, *Gramsci is Dead. Anarchist Currents in the Newest Social Movements* (London and Toronto: Pluto/Between the Lines, 2005).

de Acosta, Alejandro, 'Critical Comments on "Revolutionary Sexualism"', in *Individualist Anarchism: Writings by Emile Armand* (Austin: Pallaksch Press, 2012), pp. 116–23.

de Jong, Rudolf, 'Provos and Kaboubters', in David Apter and James Joll (eds), *Anarchism Today* (London: Macmillan, 1971), pp. 164–80.

di Paola, Pietro, *The Knights Errant of Anarchy: London and the Italian Anarchist Diaspora (1880–1917)* (Liverpool: Liverpool University Press, 2013).

Douglas, Paul H., 'Proletarian political theory', in Charles Edward Merriam and Harry Elmber Barnes (eds), *A History of Political Theories: Recent Times Essays on Contemporary Developments in Political Theory* (New York: Macmillan, 1932), pp. 200–15.

Drysdale, C. V., *Can Everyone be Fed? A Reply to Prince Kropotkin* (London: The Malthusian League, 1913).

Dugatkin, Lee Alan, *The Prince of Evolution: Peter Kropotkin's Adventures in Science and Politics* (CreateSpace, 2011).

Dugger, William M., 'Veblen and Kropotkin on human evolution', *Journal of Economic Issues*, 18, 1984, pp. 971–85.

Eastwood, Mark, *Within an Ace. A Story of Russian Nihilism*, 5th edn (London: Digby and Long, n.d.).

Ellis, Havelock, *Kropotkin: A Tribute* (New Jersey: Oride Press, 1963).

Eltzbacher, Paul, *Anarchism: Seven Exponents of the Anarchist Philosophy*, James J. Martin (ed.), Steven T. Byington (trans.) (London: Freedom Press, 1960).

Ely, Richard T., *French and German Socialism in Modern Times* (New York: Harper & Bootles, 1883).

Ely, Richard T., *Recent American Socialism* (Baltimore: John Hopkins University, 1885).

Engels, Friedrich, 'Introduction', in Karl Marx, *Class Struggles in France*, 1895, <http://www.marxists.org/archive/marx/works/1850/class-struggles-france/intro.htm> (last accessed 3 March 2015).

Esenwein, George, *Anarchist Ideology and the Working Class Movement in Spain, 1868–1898* (Oxford: University of California Press).

Evans, T. F. (ed.), *Shaw: The Critical Heritage* (London: Routledge & Kegan Paul, 1976).

Evren, Süreyyya and Ruth Kinna (eds), *Anarchist Developments in Cultural Studies: Blasting the Canon* (New York: Punctum Books, 2013).

Evren, Süreyyya and Ruth Kinna, 'Unscientific Survey. 7 Sages of Anarchism', in Süreyyya Evren and Ruth Kinna (eds), *Anarchist Developments in Cultural Studies: Blasting the Canon* (New York: Punctum Books, 2013), pp. 211–41.

Evren, Süreyyya and Ruth Kinna, 'George Woodcock: The ghostwriter of anarchism', *Anarchist Studies*, 23, 2015, pp. 45–61.

Eyges, Thomas B., *Beyond the Horizon. The Story of a Radical Emigrant* (Boston: Group Free Society, 1944), <http://archive.org/stream/beyhorizon00eyge/beyhorizon00eyge_djvu.txt> (last accessed 3 March 2015).

Ferguson, Kathy E., 'Toward a new anarchism', *Crime, Law and Social Change*, 7, 1973, pp. 39–57.

Ferrero, Guglielmo, *Militarism, A Contribution To the Peace Crusade* (Boston: L.C. Page & Company, 1902).

Ferretti, Federico, 'The correspondence between Elisée Reclus and Pëtr Kropotkin as a source for the history of geography', *Journal of Historical Geography*, 37, 2011, pp. 216–22.

Fielding, A. J., 'What geographers ought to do: The relationship between thought and action in the life and works of P.A. Kropotkin', *University of Sussex Research Papers in Geography*, 1980, pp. 1–14.

Fleming, Marie, 'Propaganda by the deed: Terrorism and anarchist theory in late nineteenth-century Europe', *Terrorism: An International Journal*, 4, 1980, pp. 1–23.

Fleming, Marie, *The Geography of Freedom. The Odyssey of Elisée Reclus* (Montreal: Black Rose, 1988).

Ford, James Glyn, *Prince Peter Kropotkin and the Channel Islands*, Guernsey Historical Monograph no. 19 (St Peter Port: Toucan Press, 1979).

Forêt, Philippe, 'Climate change: A challenge to the geographers of colonial Asia', *French Network for Institutes of Advanced Study*, 2013, <http://rfiea.fr/en/articles/climate-change-challenge-geographers-colonial-asia> (last accessed 3 March 2015).

Forêt, Philippe, 'Challenges to fieldwork before 1914 and today: Adaptation, omission, rediscovery', in Marcus Hall and Patrick Kupper (eds), 'Crossing mountains: The challenges of doing environmental history', *Rachel Carson Center Perspectives*, 2014, 4, pp. 9–18, <http://www.environmentandsociety.org/sites/default/files/2014_i4_foret_0.pdf> (last accessed 3 March 2015).

Fouillée, Albert, 'The ethics of Nietzsche and Guyau', *International Journal of Ethics*, 13 1902, pp. 13–27.

Fowler, R. B., 'The anarchist tradition of political thought', *Western Political Quarterly*, 25, 1972, pp. 738–52.

Frank, Joseph, 'Nihilism and *Notes from Underground*', *The Sewanee Review*, 69, 1961, pp. 1–33.

Frank, Joseph, 'Dostoevsky and Russian nihilism: A context for *Notes From Underground*', (PhD thesis, University of Chicago, 1960).

Franks, Benjamin, *Rebel Alliances: The Means and Ends of Contemporary British Anarchisms* (Edinburgh and Oakland: AK Press and Dark Star, 2006).

Franks, Benjamin, 'Anarchism and analytic philosophy', in Ruth Kinna (ed.), *Continuum Companion to Anarchism* (New York: Continuum, 2009), pp. 50–71.

Gemie, Sharif, 'Counter-community: An aspect of anarchist political culture', *Journal of Contemporary History*, 29, 1994, pp. 349–67.

Gillespie, Michael Allen, *Nihilism before Nietzsche* (Chicago and London: University of Chicago Press, 1996).

Glassman, Michael, 'Mutual aid theory and human development: Sociability as primary', *Journal for the Theory of Social Behaviour*, 30, 2000, pp. 391–412.

Goldman, Emma, *Living My Life*, vol. I (New York: Dover Publications, 1970).

Goldman, Emma, 'Anarchism: What it really stands for', in Alix Kates Shulman (ed.), *Red Emma Speaks. The selected speeches and writings of the anarchist and feminist Emma Goldman* (London: Wildwood House, 1979 [1911]), pp. 47–63.

Golemboski, David, 'Proudhon on the social dimensions of labor', *Social Science Research Network*, 2013, pp. 1–27 <http://papers.ssrn.com/sol3/papers.cfm?abstract_id=2300902> (last accessed 3 March 2015).

Goodman, Paul, *The Black Flag of Anarchism* (Corinth: Black Mountain Press, 1968).

Goodman, Paul, 'Kropotkin at this moment', *Anarchy*, 99, 1969, pp. 124–8.

Goodwin, Adam, 'Evolution and anarchism in international relations: The challenge of Kropotkin's biological ontology', *Millennium Journal of International Studies*, 39, 2010, pp. 417–37.

Gordon, Uri, *Anarchy Alive! Anti-Authoritarian Politics from Practice to Theory* (London: Pluto, 2008).

Grave, Jean, *Mémoires d'un Anarchiste (1854–1920)* (Paris: Éditions du Sextant, 2009).

Gray, Tim, 'Herbert Spencer's liberalism – from social statics to social dynamics', in Richard Bellamy (ed.), *Victorian Liberalism. Nineteenth-century Political Thought and Practice* (London and New York: Routledge, 1990), pp. 110–30.

Grey, Alexander, *The Socialist Tradition: Moses to Lenin* (London: Longmans, 1943).

Guérin, Daniel, *No Gods, No Masters*, 4 vols, Paul Sharkey (trans.) (Oakland and Edinburgh: AK Press, 2005).

Haaland, Bonnie, *Emma Goldman. Sexuality and the Impurity of the State* (Montreal: Black Rose, 1993).

Haberer, Erich E., *Jews and Revolution in Nineteenth Century Russia* (Cambridge: Cambridge University Press, 1995).

Hansard 1803–2005, Aliens Bill, HC Deb 29 March 1904, vol. 132, cc987–95, <http://hansard.millbanksystems.com/commons/1904/mar/29/aliens-bill> (last accessed 3 March 2015).

Hardy, Dennis, *Alternative Communities in Nineteenth Century England* (London: Longman, 1979).

Hazell, A. P., 'Two schools of socialism: Scientific and humanitarian', *Justice*, 9 February 1895.

Herwig, Holger H., 'Geopolitik: Haushofer, Hitler and Lebensraum', in Colin S. Gray and Geoffrey Sloan (eds), *Geopolitics, Geography and Strategy* (London and Portland: Frank Cass, 1999), pp. 218–41.

Hewetson, John, 'Mutual aid and social evolution', *Anarchy*, 55, 1965, pp. 257–70.

Hobbes, Thomas, *Leviathan,* Richard Flathman and David Johnston (eds) (New York: W. W. Norton, 1997 [1651]).

Hobsbawm, Eric, *Revolutionaries* (London: Quartet, 1977).

Hobsbawm, Eric, *Nations and Nationalism since 1780. Programme, Myth, Reality,* 2nd edn (Cambridge: Canto, 1992).

Hoch, S. L., 'On good numbers and bad: Malthus, population trends and peasant standard of living in late Imperial Russia', *Slavic Review,* 53, 1994, pp. 41–75.

Hoch, S. L., 'Famine, disease and mortality patterns in the parish of Borshevka, Russia, 1830–1912', *Population Studies,* 52, 1998, pp. 357–68.

Holland, Merlin and Rupert Hart-Davis (eds), *The Complete Letters of Oscar Wilde* (London: Fourth Estate, 2000).

Hollingsworth, Barry, 'The Society of Friends of Russian Freedom: English liberals and Russian socialists, 1890–1917', *Oxford Slavonic Papers,* 3, 1970, pp. 45–64.

Honeywell, Carissa, *A British Anarchist Tradition: Herbert Read, Alex Comfort and Colin Ward* (New York: Continuum, 2011).

Hong, Nhat, *The Anarchist Beast: The Anti-Anarchist Crusade in Periodical Literature (1884–1906)* (Minneapolis: Soil of Liberty, n.d.).

Hopkins, John Baker, *Nihilism Its Words and Deeds* (London: Diprose and Bateman, 1881 [1879]).

Hopps, John Page, 'Nihilisms and socialisms of the world', *Contemporary Review,* 58, 1890, pp. 271–82.

Horowitz, Irving (ed.), *The Anarchists* (New York: Dell Publishing, 1964).

Hulse, James, *Revolutionists in London: A Study of Five Unorthodox Socialists* (Oxford: Clarendon Press, 1970).

Huntington, Ellsworth, *Civilization and Climate* (New Haven: Yale University Press, 1915).

Hyndman, H. M., *The Record of an Adventurous Life* (London: Macmillan & Co., 1911).

Iliopoulos, Christos, 'Nietzsche and anarchism, an elective affinity and a Nietzschean reading of the December '08 revolt in Athens' (PhD thesis, Loughborough University, 2013).

Ishill, Joseph (ed.), *Peter Kropotkin: The Rebel, Thinker and Humanitarian. Tributes and Appreciations* (Berkeley Heights: Free Spirit Press, 1923).

Ivianksy, Z., 'Individual terror: Concept and typology', *Journal of Contemporary History,* 12, 1977, pp. 43–63.

Jensen, Richard Bach, *The Battle against Anarchist Terrorism. An International History, 1878–1934* (Cambridge: Cambridge University Press, 2014).

Johnson, Barry C. (ed.), *Olive and Stepniak: The Bloomsbury Diary of Olive Garnett 1893–1895* (London: Bartletts Press, 1993).

Johnson, Barry C. (ed.), *Tea and Anarchy! The Bloomsbury Diary of Olive Garnett 1890–1893* (London: Bartletts Press, 1989).

Joll, James, 'Anarchism – a living tradition', in David Apter and James Joll (eds), *Anarchism Today* (London: Macmillan, 1971), pp. 212–25.

Jordan, Jane, *Josephine Butler* (London: John Murray, 2001).

Jun, Nathan, *Anarchism and Political Modernity* (London and New York: Continuum, 2012).

Kampffmeyer, Bernard, 'Anarchism and the European equilibrium', *The Torch*, August 1894.

Kapp, Yvonne (ed.), *Correspondence of Friedrich Engels and Paul and Laura Lafargue, vol. 3, 1891–1895*, trans. Yvonne Kapp (Moscow: Foreign Languages Publishing House, n.d.).

Kaufman, Moritz, 'Nihilism in Russia', *Contemporary Review*, 38, 1880, pp. 913–31.

Kearns, Gerry, 'The political pivot of geography', *The Geographical Journal*, 170, 2004, pp. 337–46.

Keltie, J. Scott, 'Peter Kropotkin, Geographer, Explorer, Mutualist', in *Centennial Expressions on Peter Kropotkin 1842–1942 by Pertinent Thinkers* (Los Angeles: Rocker Publications Committee, 1942), pp. 4–6.

Kennan, George, *Siberia and the Exile System*, 2 vols (New York: Century, 1891).

Kinna, Ruth, 'Kropotkin's theory of mutual aid in historical context', *International Review of Social History,* 40, 1995, pp. 259–83.

Kinna, Ruth, 'Anarchism, individualism and communism: William Morris's critique of anarcho-communism', in Alex Prichard, Ruth Kinna, Saku Pinta and David Berry (eds), *Libertarian Socialism: Politics in Black and Red* (Basingstoke: Palgrave/Macmillan, 2012), pp. 35–56.

Knowles, Rob, *Political Economy from Below. Economic Thought in Communitarian Anarchism, 1840–1914* (New York and London: Routledge, 2004).

Kropotkin, Princess Alexandra, 'Pleasant memories of Bernard Shaw', *The American Mercury,* 1951, pp. 23–9, <http://www.unz.org/Pub/AmMercury-1951jan–00023> (last accessed 3 March 2015).

Kuhn, Gabriel, *Gustav Landauer, Revolution and Other Writings. A Political Reader* (Oakland: PM Press, 2010).

Kuhn, Gabriel, 'Global anarchism and Asia', in Hiraru Tanaka, Masaya Hiyazaki and Chilharu Yamanaka (eds), *Global Anarchism: Past, Present and Future – New Anarchism in Japan* (Kansai: Association for Anarchism Studies, 2014), pp. 150–3.

Kuhn, Gabriel, 'Anarchism, postmodernity, and poststructuralism', in Randall Amster, Abraham DeLeon, Luis A. Fernandez, Anthony J. Nocella, II and Deric Shannon (eds), *Contemporary Anarchist Studies: An introductory anthology of anarchy in the academy* (London: Routledge, 2009), pp. 18–25.

Landauer, Gustav, *For Socialism*, David J. Parent (trans.) (St Louis: Telos Press, 1978 [1911]).

Landstreicher, Wolfi, *Willful Disobedience* (n.p.: Ardent Press, 2009).

Laurence, Dan H. (ed.), *Bernard Shaw Collected Letters 1911–1925* (London: Max Reinhardt, 1985).

Lehning, James R., *European Colonialism since 1700* (Cambridge: Cambridge University Press, 2013).

Leier, Mark, *Bakunin. The Creative Passion: A Biography* (New York: Seven Stories, 2006).

Levy, Edward Lawrence, 'Russian nihilism'. A paper read before the members of the Alliance Literary and Debating Society (1881).

Lichtheim, George, *A Short History of Socialism* (London: Flamingo, 1983).

Liebknecht, Wilhelm, 'Our congress', *Justice*, 29 August 1896.

Lombroso, Cesare, 'Illustrative studies in criminal anthropology. III. The physiognomy of the anarchists', *The Monist*, 1, 1890, pp. 336–43.

Luxemburg, Rosa, *The Junius Pamphlet: The Crisis of German Social Democracy* (New York: Socialist Publication Society, 1919), <https://archive.org/details/crisisingermanso00luxeiala> (last accessed 3 March 2015).

Macallum, G. C., 'Negative and positive freedom', *Philosophical Review*, 76, 1967, pp. 312–34.

McClellan, Woodford, *Revolutionary Exiles. The Russians in the First International and the Paris Commune* (London: Frank Cass, 1979).

McElroy, Wendy, *The Debates of Liberty: An Overview of Individualist Anarchism, 1881–1908* (Lanham and Oxford: Lexington Books, 2003).

McFarlane, Sandy, 'An appeal to the young', *Justice*, 23 March 1895.

MacInnes, Colin, 'Eve's children', *New Statesman*, 7, 1962, p. 288.

Mackay, John Henry, *The Anarchists: A Picture of Civilization at the Close of the Nineteenth Century*, George Schumm (trans.) (Boston: Benjamin R. Tucker, 1891).

McKay, Iain, 'Libertarian socialism: Beyond anarchism and Marxism?', Anarchists Writers, 28 February 2014, <http://anarchism.pageabode.com/anarcho/libertarian-socialism-beyond-anarchism-marxism> (last accessed 3 March 2015).

McKay, Iain, *Mutual Aid: An Introduction and Evaluation*, 27 May 2008, <http://anarchism.pageabode.com/anarcho/mutual-aid-an-introduction-and-evaluation> (last accessed 3 March 2015).

McKenzie Walllace, Donald, Prince Kropotkin, C. Mijatovich and J. D. Bourchier *A Short History of Russia and the Balkan States* (London: The Encyclopaedia Britannica Co., 1914).

McKinley, C. Alexander, *Illegitimate Children of the Enlightenment. Anarchist and the French Revolution 1880–1914* (New York: Peter Lang, 2006).

McLaughlin, Paul, *Anarchism and Authority: A Philosophical Introduction to Classical Anarchism* (Aldershot: Ashgate, 2007).

Maitron, Jean, *Ravachol et les Anarchistes* (Paris: Gallimard, 1992).

Malagodi, Olindo, 'The psychology of anarchist conspiracies', *The Westminster Review*, 147, 1897, pp. 87–91.

Malatesta, Errico, *Anarchy* (London: Freedom, 1909).

Malatesta, Errico, 'The Most Greatly Humane Man', in Joseph Ishill (ed.), *Peter Kropotkin: The Rebel, Thinker and Humanitarian. Tributes and Appreciations* (Berkeley Heights: Free Spirit Press, 1923), pp. 38–9.

Malatesta, Errico, 'Peter Kropotkin: Recollections and criticisms by one of his old friends', *Freedom Bulletin*, 12 July 1931.

Malatesta, Errico, 'Pro-government anarchists', *The Blast*, 15 May 1916, p. 109, repr. *The Blast* (Edinburgh and Oakland: AK Press, 2005).

Malatesta, Errico, 'Anarchists have forgotten their principles', *Freedom*, November 1914, <http://dwardmac.pitzer.edu/Anarchist_Archives/malatesta/ForgottenPrinciples.html> (last accessed 3 March 2015).

Malatesta, Errico, 'Address to the International Anarchist Congress, Amsterdam 26–31 August 1907', in Maurizio Antonioli, *Anarchism and/or Syndicalism*, <http://www.fdca.it/fdcaen/historical/amsterdam07/5.htm> (last accessed 3 March 2015).

Manifesto of the Sixteen, 1916, Shawn P. Wilbur (trans.), <http://libertarian-labyrinth.blogspot.co.uk/2011/05/manifesto-of-sixteen–1916.html> (last accessed 3 March 2015).

Maoriland Worker, 24 December 1913, <http://paperspast.natlib.govt.nz/cgi-bin/paperspast?a=d&d—W19131224> (last accessed 3 March 2015).

Marshall, Peter, *Demanding the Impossible: A History of Anarchism* (London: HarperCollins, 1992).

Martin, James J., *Men against the State: The Expositors of Individualist Anarchism in America, 1827–1908* (Colorado Springs: Ralph Myles, 1970).

Marx, Karl, 'Afterword to the second German edition', *Capital*, vol. 1, 1873, <https://www.marxists.org/archive/marx/works/1867-c1/p3.htm> (last accessed 3 March 2015).

Miller, C. A., 'Nietzsche's "discovery" of Dostoevsky', *Nietzsche Studien*, 2, 1973, pp. 202–57.

Miller, David, *Social Justice* (Oxford: Clarendon, 1976).

Miller, David, 'The neglected (II) – Kropotkin', *Government and Opposition*, 18, 1983, pp. 319–38.

Miller, Martin, *Kropotkin* (Chicago and London: University of Chicago Press, 1976).

Milstein, Cindy, *Anarchism and Its Aspirations* (Edinburgh and Oakland: AK Press/Institute for Anarchist Studies, 2010).

Morgan, Richard, 'The interplay of politics and science in the making of Petr Kropotkin's modern anarchism' (PhD thesis, University of London, 2014).

Morris, Brian, *Kropotkin. The Politics of Community* (New York: Humanity Books, 2004).

Morris, Brian, *The Anarchist Geographer: An Introduction to the Life of Peter Kropotkin* (Minehead: Genge Press, 2007).

Mukherjee, Subrata and Sushila Ramaswamy (eds), *Prince Peter Kropotkin: His Thoughts and Works* (New Delhi: Deep & Deep Publications, 1998).

Mumford, Lewis, *The Culture of Cities* (London: Secker and Warburg, 1944).

Mũnoz, Victor, *Anarchists: A Biographical Encyclopedia*, Scott Johnson (trans.) (New York: Gordon Press, 1981).

Nettlau, Max, 'Peter Kropotkin at work', in Joseph Ishill (ed.), *Peter Kropotkin: The Rebel, Thinker and Humanitarian. Tributes and Appreciations* (Berkeley Heights: Free Spirit Press, 1923), pp. 12–14.

Nettlau, Max, *A Short History of Anarchism*, Heiner M. Becker (ed.), Ida Pilat Isca (trans.) (London: Freedom Press, 1996).

Newcastle Daily Chronicle, 'The London Jews' meeting: Prince Krapotkine's speech', 9 February 1882.

Newman, Saul, *From Bakunin to Lacan: Anti-Authoritarianism and the Dislocation of Power* (Lanham: Rowman and Littlefield, 2001).

Newman, Saul, *The Politics of Postanarchism* (Edinburgh: Edinburgh University Press, 2011).

Newman, Saul, 'Anarchism, poststructuralism and the future of radical politics', *SubStance*, 36, 2007, pp. 3–19.

Novak, D. (ed.), 'An unpublished essay on Leo Tolstoy by Peter Kropotkin', *Canadian Slavonic Papers*, 3, 1958, pp. 7–26.

Novak, David, 'Anarchism and individual terrorism', *Canadian Journal of Economics and Political Science*, 20, 1954, pp. 176–84.

Offord, Derek, *The Russian Revolutionary Movement in the 1880s* (Cambridge: Cambridge University Press, 1986).

Ogden, C. K. and Mary Sargant Florence, *Militarism versus Feminism. An Enquiry and a Policy Demonstrating that Militarism Involves the Subjection of Women* [1915] repr. in Margaret Kamester and Jo Vellacott (eds), *Militarism versus Feminism Writings on Women and War* (London: Virago, 1987), pp. 55–140.

Oliver, Hermia, *The International Anarchist Movement in Late Victorian London* (London: Croom Helm, 1983).

Osofsky, Stephen, *Peter Kropotkin* (Boston: Twayne Publishers, 1979).

Oved, Ya'acov, 'The future society according to Kropotkin', *Cahiers du Monde russe et soviétique*, XXXIII, 1992, pp. 303–20.

Özkirimili, Umut, *Theories of Nationalism. A Critical Introduction* (London: Palgrave, 2000).

Padovan, Dario, 'Social morals and ethics of nature: From Peter Kropotkin to Murray Bookchin', *Democracy and Nature*, 5, 1999, pp. 485–500.

Palélogue, Maurice, 'Deux Précurseurs de Bolshévisme: Herzen et Bakounine', *Revue Des Deux Mondes*, 44, 1938, p. 62.

Parker, Geoffrey, *Western Geopolitical Thought in the Twentieth Century* (London: Croom Helm, 1985).

Pateman, Carole, *Participation and Democratic Theory* (London: Cambridge University Press, 1977).

Pateman, Carole and Charles Mills, 'Contract and social change. A dialogue between Carole Pateman and Charles W. Mills', in *Contract and Domination* (Cambridge: Polity Press, 2008), pp. 10–34.

Pearce, Harry, 'Scientific socialism v. revolutionary syndicalism', *Justice*, 25 January 1913.

Peet, Richard, 'For Kropotkin', *Antipode: A Radical Journal of Geography*, 7, 1975, pp. 42–3.

Pernicone, Nunzio, *Italian Anarchism, 1864–1892* (Oakland and Edinburgh: AK Press, 2009).

Perry, Lewis, *Radical Abolitionism. Anarchy and the Government of God in Antislavery Thought* (Ithaca and London: Cornell University Press, 1973).

Pleckanov, George [Plechanoff], *Anarchism and Socialism*, Eleanor Marx Aveling (trans.) (Chicago: Charles Kerr, n.d [1895]).

Poggioli, Renate, *The Theory of the Avant-Garde*, Gerald Fitzgerald (trans.) (Cambridge, MA: Belknap Press, 1968).

Pollard, A. F., 'The superstition of the state', *Times Literary Supplement*, 18 July 1918, p. 329.

Porter, Cathy, *Fathers and Daughters: Russian Women in Revolution* (London: Virago, 1976).

Price, John, *Postman's Park: G.F. Watt's Memorial to Heroic Self-Sacrifice* (London: Watts Gallery, 2008).

Prichard, Alex, *Justice, Order and Anarchy: The International Political Theory of Pierre-Joseph Proudhon* (London: Routledge, 2013).

Proudhon, P. -J., *What is Property? An Inquiry into the Principle of Right and of Government*, Benj. R. Tucker (trans.) (London: William Reeves, 1969 [1840]).

Purchase, Graham, *Evolution and Revolution: An Introduction to the Life and Thought of Peter Kropotkin* (Petersham, Australia: Jura Media, 1996).

Quail, John, *The Slow Burning Fuse: The Lost History of British Anarchists* (London: Granada, 1978).

Ramnath, Maia, *Decolonizing Anarchism. An Anti-Authoritarian Account of India's Liberation Struggle* (Oakland and Edinburgh: AK Press/Institute for Anarchist Studies, 2011).

Read, Herbert, 'Pragmatic anarchism', *Encounter,* 30, 1968, pp. 54–61.

Read, Herbert, *A One Man Manifesto*, David Goodway (ed.) (London: Freedom Press, 1994).

Reclus, Elie, *Primitive Folk. Studies in Comparative Ethnography* (London: Walter Scott, 1896).

Reclus, Élisée, *Ouvrier, Prends La Machine! Prends La Terre, Paysan!* (Geneva: Edition du Révolté, 1880).

Reclus, Élisée, *Nouvelle Géographie Universelle La Terre Et Les Hommes*, VI, *L'Asie Russe* (Paris: Librairie Hachette, 1881).

Reed, Frances Miriam, 'Oscar Wilde's Vera; Or, the nihilist: The history of a failed play', *Theatre Survey*, 26, 1985, pp. 163–77.

Reichert, William O., 'Anarchism, freedom, and power', *Ethics*, 79, 1969, pp. 139–49.

Reichert, William O., 'Toward a new understanding of anarchism', *Western Political Quarterly*, 20, 1967, pp. 856–65.

Renan, Ernest, 'What is a Nation?', in Ethan Rundell (trans.), *Qu'est-ce qu'une nation?* (Paris: Presses Pocket, 1992), <http://ucparis.fr/files/9313/6549/9943/What_is_a_Nation.pd> (last accessed 3 March 2015).

Reszler, André, 'Peter Kropotkin and his vision of anarchist aesthetics', *Diogenes*, 78, 1972, pp. 52–63.

Ritter, Alan, 'Anarchism and liberal theory in the nineteenth century', *Bucknell Review*, XIX, 1971, pp. 37–66.

Ritter, Alan, *Anarchism: A Theoretical Analysis* (Cambridge: Cambridge University Press, 1980).

Robins, J., 'Plechanoff answered', *The Torch,* 18 April 1895.

Robinson, Victor, *Lives of the Great Altrurians: Comrade Kropotkin* (New York: The Altrurians, 1908).

Rocker, Rudolf, *Anarcho-Syndicalism* (London: Phoenix Press, n.d. [1938]).

Roediger, Dave and Franklin Rosemont (eds), *Haymarket Scrapbook* (Chicago: Charles H. Kerr Publishing Company, 1986).

Roslak, Robyn, *Neo-Impressionim and Anarchism in Fin-de-Siècle France: Painting, Politics and Landscape* (Aldershot: Ashgate, 2005).

Rousselle, Duane and Süreyyya Evren (eds), *Post-Anarchism: A Reader* (London: Pluto, 2011).

Rovná, Lenka Anna, 'Peter Kropotkin and his influence on Czech anarchism', *Moving the Social*, 50, 2013, pp. 53–79.

Rowell, George, 'The truth about Vera', *Nineteenth Century Theatre*, 21, 1993, pp. 94–100.

Rubin, Jerry, *Scenarios of the Revolution* (London: Jonathan Cape, 1970).

Ryley, Peter, *Making another World Possible. Anarchism, Anti-Capitalism and Ecology in Late 19th and Early 20th Century Britain* (New York and London: Bloomsbury, 2013).

Ryley, Peter, 'Individualist anarchism in late-Victorian Britain', *Anarchist Studies*, 20, 2012, pp. 72–100.

Sacramento Daily Union, 'Foreign views of Anarchism', 13 November 1898, <http://cdnc.ucr.edu/cgi-bin/cdnc?a=d&d=SDU18981113.2.13> (last accessed 3 March 2015).

Saunders, David, *Russia in the Age of Reaction and Reform, 1801–1881* (London: Longman, 1992).

Saytanov, Sergey V., *The Argumentation of Peter Kropotkin's Anarcho-refomism in His Social-political and Anarchist Views (According to Russian Materials)*, Natalia I. Saytanova (trans.) (Moscow: Ontoprint, 2014).

Schmidt, Michael and Lucien van der Walt, *Black Flame. The Revolutionary Class Politics of Anarchism and Syndicalism. Vol 1. Counter-Power* (Oakland and Edinburgh: AK Press, 2009).

Schwab, Michael, 'A convicted anarchist's reply to Professor Lombroso', *The Monist*, 1, 1890, pp. 520–4.

Sellers, Edith, 'Our most distinguished refugee', *Contemporary Review*, 66, 1894, pp. 537–49.

Servigne, Pablo, 'Qu'a-t-on appris sur l'entraide depuis Kropotkine?', *Réfractions*, 23, 2009, pp. 53–63.

Seymour, Henry, *The Two Anarchisms* (London: Proudhon Press, 1894).

Shpayer-Makov, Haia, 'The reception of Peter Kropotkin in Britain, 1886–1917', *Albion: A Quarterly Journal Concerned with British Studies*, 19, 1987, pp. 373–90.

Sills D. L. (ed.), *International Encyclopedia of the Social Sciences*, vol. 8 (London: Macmillan/The Free Press, 1968).

Sloan, Geoffrey, 'Sir Halford J. Mackinder: The Heartland Theory then and now', in Colin S. Gray and Geoffrey Sloan (eds), *Geopolitics, Geography, and Strategy* (London: Frank Cass, 1999), pp. 15–38.

The Spectator, 'Prince Kropotkin's Fanaticism' 17 July 1886, pp. 960–1.

Springer, Simon, 'Anarchism! What geography still ought to be', *Antipode*, 44, 2012, pp. 1, 605–24.

Stafford, David, 'Anarchists in Britain today', in David Apter and James Joll (eds), *Anarchism Today* (London: Macmillan, 1971), pp. 84–104.

Stafford, David, *From Anarchism to Reformism. A Study of the Political Activities of Paul Brousse, 1870–1890* (London: Weidenfeld and Nicolson, 1971).

Stead, W. T., *The MP for Russia: Reminiscences and Correspondence of Olga Novikoff* (London: Andrew Melrose, 1909).

Stephens, David (ed.), *Government is Violence: Essays on Anarchism and Pacifism* (London: Phoenix Press, 1990).

Stepniak, Sergei, 'Terrorism in Russia and terrorism in Europe', *Contemporary Review*, 45, 1884, pp. 325–41.

Stepniak, Sergei, *Underground Russia. Revolutionary Profiles and Sketches from Life*, 3rd edn (London: Smith, Elder & Co., 1890).

Stepniak, Sergei, *Nihilism As It Is, Being Stepniak's Pamphlets* E.L. Voynich (trans.) (London: T. Fisher Unwin, n.d. [1894]).

Stepniak, Sergei, *The Russian Peasantry: Their Agrarian Condition, Social Life and Religion* (London: Forgotten Books, 2013 [1888]).

Stirner, Max, *The Ego and Its Own. The Case of the Individual against Authority*, Steven Byington (trans.) (London: Rebel Press, 1982).

Stites, Richard, *The Women's Liberation Movement in Russia: Feminism, Nihilism and Bolshevism, 1860–1930* (New Jersey: Princeton University Press, 1978).

Strunksy, Anna, 'Earnest address by Anna Strunsky. Prince Kropotkin's work pictured', *San Francisco Call*, 11 October 1904 <http://cdnc.ucr.edu/cgi-bin/cdnc?a=d d=SFC19041011.2.51> (last accessed 3 March 2015).

Swan, Tom, *Kropotkin: The Man and His Message* (London: Freedom 1909).

The Feilding Star Oroua and Kiwitea Counties Gazette, 'Personalities', 25 January 1913, <http://paperspast.natlib.govt.nz/cgi-bin/paperspast?a=d&d=FS19130125.2.6> (last accessed 3 March 2015).

Tudor, H. and J. M. Tudor, *Marxism and Social Democracy: The Revisionist Debate 1896–1898* (Cambridge: Cambridge University Press, 1988).

Turgenev, Ivan, *Fathers and Sons*, Rosemary Edmonds (trans.) (Harmondsworth: Penguin, 1968 [1862]).

Turgenev, Ivan, 'Hamlet and Don Quixote', Moshe Spiegel (trans.), *Chicago Review*, 17, 1965, pp. 92–109.

Utechin, S. V., *Russian Political Thought* (London: J. M. Dent & Sons, 1963).

van der Linden, Marcel and Wayne Thorpe (eds), *Revolutionary Syndicalism: An International Perspective* (Aldershot: Scolar Press, 1990).

van Duyn, Roel, *Message of a Wise Kabouter* (London: Duckworth, 1972).

Venturi, Franco, *Roots of Revolution: A History of the Populist and Socialist Movements in Nineteenth-Century Russia*, Francis Haskell (trans.) (Chicago and London: Chicago University Press, 1983).

Walter, Nicholas, *The Anarchist Past and Other Essays*, David Goodway (ed.) (Nottingham: Five Leaves, 2007).

Walter Nicholas 'The scientific revolutionary', *New Society*, 18, 1971, p. 280.

Walter, Nicholas, 'About anarchism', in Howard Ehrlich, Carol Ehrlich, David de Leon and Glenda Morris (eds), *Reinventing Anarchy* (London: Routledge & Kegan Paul, 1979), pp. 42–63.

Ward, Colin, *Anarchy in Action* (London: Freedom Press, 1982).

Ward, Colin, *Anarchism: A Very Short Introduction* (Oxford: Oxford University Press, 2004).

Ward, Colin, 'Temporary autonomous zones', *Freedom*, 1997, <http://raforum.info/spip.php?article1079&lang=fr> (last accessed 3 March 2015).

Wedgewood, C. V., *The Thirty Years War* (Harmondsworth: Penguin, 1957).

Wilbert, Chris and Damian F. White (eds), *Autonomy, Solidarity, Possibility. The Colin Ward Reader* (Oakland and Edinburgh: AK Press, 2011).

Wilde, Oscar, *Vera; or, The Nihilists* (Milton Keynes: Dodo Press, n.d. [1883]).

Wilde, Oscar, *The Complete Works of Oscar Fingal O'Flahertie Wills Wilde* (London: Collins, 1985).

Williams, Kristian, ' "A criminal with a noble face": Oscar Wilde's encounters with the Victorian gaol', *Perspectives*, 2009, <http://anarchiststudies.mayfirst.org/node/335> (last accessed 3 March 2015).

Williams, Louise H., 'Prince Kropotkin's philosophy in the light of today', *The Hibbert Journal*, 19, 1921, pp. 441–8.

Wilson, Matthew, *Rules without Rulers. The Possibilities and Limits of Anarchism* (Winchester: Zero Books, 2014).

Wolff, Robert Paul, *In Defense of Anarchism* (New York: Harper Torchbooks, 1976 [1970]).

Woodcock, George, *Anarchy or Chaos* (London: Freedom Press, 1944).

Woodcock, George, *Anarchism, A History of Libertarian Ideas and Movements* (Cleveland and New York: Meridian, 1962).

Woodcock, George, *Anarchism and Anarchists* (Kingston, Ontario: Quarry Press, 1992).

Woodcock, George and Ivan Avakumović, *The Anarchist Prince: A Biographical Study of Peter Kropotkin* (New York: Schoken Books, 1971).

Yarros, Victor, *Anarchism: Its Aims and Methods* (Boston: Benjamin R. Tucker, 1887).

'Z', 'Anarchists: Their methods and organisation', *New Review*, X, 1894, pp. 1–16.

Zenker, Ernst Victor, *Anarchism; A Criticism and History of the Anarchist Theory* (New York and London: Knickerbocker Press, 1897).

of women, 66–71
of workers, 120, 129, 172, 173–4
see also slavery
'Emancipation of women' (Kropotkin), 66, 67
Encyclopaedia Britannica, 132, 200
'Enemies of the people' (Kropotkin), 121
Engels, Friedrich, 21, 111, 113, 128, 130, 132
the Enlightenment, 33, 37, 45, 121, 122
Entente powers, 2, 156, 198; *see also* war
Equality (Bellamy), 132
ethics
    and anarchism, 105, 125
    and culture, 98–100
    evolutionary, 147–50, 153, 189
    justice and morality, 150–3, 158–9
    means–ends doctrine, 165–8
    mutual aid, 38, 55, 193
    and nihilism, 71, 75–7, 127–8, 199
    prefiguration, 39
    and revolution, 161
    see also morality
Ethics (Kropotkin), 55, 56–7, 87, 98, 99, 100, 133,
    149–50
'The ethics of Nietzsche and Guyau' (Fouillée), 77
European state system
    development, 89, 93, 98–9, 111–12, 144,
        194, 198
    economic competition, 96–7, 178–9
    and Germany, 113, 115, 179–80
    resistance, 101, 157
    and Russia, 53
    see also state
evolution
    and ethics, 127–8, 147–50, 153, 189
    Kropotkin's theory, 12–13, 25, 31–3, 121, 197
    and revolution, 21–3, 40, 125, 157, 169–70
    social, 98–100, 108–9, 186
    see also mutual aid
exile, 50–2

The Fable of the Bees (Mandeville), 56–7
Farewell Letter (June 1917), 178
fatalism, 32, 130, 185
Fathers and Sons (Turgenev), 60–2, 63, 92, 107
federalism, 113, 156, 188, 198
feminism, 56, 63–71, 77, 105–6, 135, 182; *see also*
    women
Ferguson, Kathy E., 19
Ferrero, Guglielmo, 182
Ferretti, Federico, 12
Fielding, Anthony J., 91–2
Fields, Factories and Workshops (Kropotkin), 20,
    27, 127, 134, 135, 136–8
Finland, 91, 183
'Finland' (Kropotkin), 83, 84, 94, 103
First International, 110, 111–12, 113, 171, 176,
    199, 201
Flaubert, Gustave, 70
Fleming, Marie, 1, 27, 201–2
Foucault, Michel, 32
Fouillée, Albert, 76–7
Fourier, Charles, 20, 127, 131–2, 134, 135, 145
France, 50, 70, 179, 180, 194; *see also* French
    Revolution
Franco-Prussian war, 97, 111, 179–80
Franks, Benjamin, 39
freedom *see* liberty
Freedom (periodical), 26, 69, 123, 131, 175, 178
French and Russian Prisons (Kropotkin), 162, 190–1

French Revolution
    and elite power, 88, 90, 113
    and the middle class, 121–2
    as a reference point, 188, 193–4
    and violent action, 159, 161
    and war, 181, 182, 183, 186–7
From Bakunin to Lacan (Newman), 37

Garnett, Olive, 28
Geddes, Patrick, 20
geography
    and anarchism, 53, 107–8, 202
    heimatskunde and erdkunde, 102–3
    human and physical, 97–9, 101–2
    Kropotkin's contribution, 12, 91–2
    and political theory, 92–7, 101, 193–4
    see also science
Germanophobia, 2, 45, 113, 115, 178, 179–80
Germany
    imperialism, 176–8
    militarism, 156, 179–80, 183
    and the Second International, 123–4, 130–1, 156,
        175–6
    statism, 111–12, 115, 171, 187
'Global anarchism and Asia' (Kuhn), 34
globalisation, 98–9, 101, 108
Godwin, William, 9, 28, 131, 150
Goldman, Emma, 9, 63, 65, 86
Goodman, Paul, 22–3
Gordon, Uri, 35–6, 38, 189
Grave, Jean, 45
The Great French Revolution (Kropotkin), 80, 121–2
Grey, Alexander, 15
Guyau, Jean-Marie, 76–7, 151, 167

Haaland, Bonnie, 65
Haitian Revolution, 86
'Hamlet and Don Quixote' (Turgenev), 61
Hamon, Augustin, 85
harmony, 37, 91–2, 132, 144–5, 189–90
Haymarket Affair (1886), 16–17, 162
Hegel, Georg Wilhelm Friedrich, 86, 106, 131
Herzen, Alexander, 64
Herzen, Natalie, 65
historical anarchism, 22, 34, 40–1, 200
history
    anarchist philosophy, 201–2
    and geography, 92–3, 98–9
    materialist doctrine, 129, 169, 199
    and mutual aid, 31–2, 91
    and revolution, 121, 168–9
    see also evolution
Hobbes, Thomas, 145–6, 148, 149
Hobsbawm, Eric, 23
Honeywell, Carissa, 14, 40
Hopkins, John Baker, 65
Horowitz, Irving, 201
How We Shall Bring about the Revolution (Pataud
    and Pouget), 172
Howard, Ebenezer, 20
Hulse, James, 28
humanism, 91, 129
Huntington, Ellsworth, 97–8
Huxley, Thomas H., 55, 138, 147, 148, 189
Hyndman, Henry M., 71, 176

idealism, 49, 52, 62, 114
Ideals and Realities in Russian Literature (Kropotkin),
    55, 60, 62

and mutual aid, 38, 189–90
and nihilism, 75, 76, 106
and violence, 17
'The materialistic doctrine of history' (Bax), 169
means–ends doctrine, 165–8; *see also* prefiguration
Memoirs (Kropotkin), 27, 51, 61–2, 66, 67–8, 76, 79, 92, 109, 120, 131
Men against the State (Martin), 10
Mendeleev, Dmitri I., 144–5
Message of a Wise Kabouter (Duyn), 21
Michel, Louise, 134, 163
Miething, Dominique F., 105
Milan general strike (1904), 174, 175
militarism, 180, 181–3, 198–9
Mill, John Stuart, 112, 150, 151
Miller, David, 31–2, 185
Miller, Martin A., 26, 49, 50, 51–2, 109
minorities, 160–1
Modern Science and Anarchism (Kropotkin), 106–7, 113, 131, 133, 140, 144, 146
morality
and justice, 150–1, 158–9
and mutual aid, 21, 31, 38, 55, 148–50, 189
and Nietzscheanism, 58, 71, 128
and nihilism, 75–7, 151–2
and prefiguration, 39, 165–7
and prison, 190–1
and responsibility, 162–3, 192–3
sexual, 64–5, 69–71
and utopianism, 133
see also ethics
Morgan, Richard, 52
Morris, Brian, 12, 41–2, 91
Morris, William, 20, 128, 130, 135, 189, 202
movement politics
1960s, 22–3, 33–4, 35, 40
1990s, 25, 34–7, 40
categorisation, 3, 19–20
early twentieth century, 155–6
and Nietzscheanism, 57, 58
Russian, 50–2, 114–15
see also feminism; new anarchism; post-anarchism
Mukherjee, Subrata, 10–11
Mumford, Lewis, 20, 189
'Must we occupy ourselves with an examination of the ideal of a future system?' (Kropotkin), 49, 133, 139, 152
mutual aid
and contemporary politics, 40–1
and criminality, 192–3
and ethics, 55, 76
and evolution, 20–2, 127–8, 148, 189–90
and geographical science, 91–2
and overpopulation, 138
and political theory, 30–2
scientific value, 11–13, 38
significance, 10–11
and syndicalism, 171, 173
see also evolution; syndicalism
Mutual Aid (Kropotkin), 10–11, 27, 31, 93, 98–9, 137, 147, 149, 192
mutualism, 122, 131, 136, 140–1

nationalism, 83, 114–15, 180; *see also* internationalism
nationality, 94–5, 113, 136–7, 156
Nechaev, Sergei, 16, 64, 75
Nettlau, Max, 11, 13, 57, 107, 172, 201
new anarchism
description, 18–19

evolution and revolution, 21–3, 25, 31, 197
and historical relevance, 33
and movement politics, 20, 34–6
and small-a anarchism, 35–6, 39–40
theory and practice, 26, 200
Newman, Saul, 36–8, 40–1, 45, 105, 185
Nicholas I, Tsar of Russia, 83
Nietzscheanism
amorality, 56–7, 58, 60, 75, 150, 158
and bourgeois individualism, 42
and communism, 57–8
and nihilism, 52, 53, 55–6, 68–9, 71, 76–7
nihilism
and ethics, 71, 75–7, 127, 151–2, 158–9, 199
and feminism, 56, 63, 64–8, 69–71, 77, 105–6
influence on Kropotkin, 52–3, 71–2, 197
and literature, 60–3
and revolution, 68–9, 74, 97, 194
scepticism, 106–7
and terrorism, 16, 55–6, 63–4
Nineteenth Century (periodical), 27
Nouvelle Géographie Universelle (Reclus), 94

Oliver, Hermia, 18, 20
oppression
capitalist, 142–3
and complicity, 114–15, 158, 159
and elite power, 87–8, 110
and powerlessness, 72–3, 160
role of the state, 106, 177–8, 180–1, 182–3
and violence, 60
see also slavery
optimism, 16, 103, 157, 185, 186–7, 191
'Our most distinguished refugee' (Sellers), 17
Ouvrier, Prends la Machine! Prends La Terre, Paysan! (Reclus), 90
Owen, Robert, 20, 127, 131, 171

P. A. Kropotkin (ed. Miller), 49, 51–2
Padovan, Dario, 151
Paléologue, Maurice, 15
Pallás, Paulino, 59–60
Paris Commune (1793–4), 113, 122, 188
Paris Commune (1871)
anti-militarism, 182
defeat, 177, 179–80
food supply, 170
significance, 100–1, 194
and statism, 111–12, 115, 156
and utopianism, 133
'The Paris Commune and the idea of the state' (Bakunin), 100, 111
parliamentarism, 112, 122–5, 156, 175–7
Les Paroles d'un Révolté (Kropotkin), 52, 71–2, 86, 90, 95, 124–5, 158
Participation and Democratic Theory (Pateman), 200
Pataud, Emile, 172
Pateman, Carole, 114, 200
Peet, Richard, 91
Perovskaya, Sophia, 64, 71, 82, 151–2, 162, 163
'Peter Kropotkin and his vison of anarchist aesthetics' (Reszler), 160
'Peter Kropotkin' (Malatesta), 11–12
Pisarev, Dmitri, 60, 62, 63, 66
Pleckhanov, George, 130
Poland, 83, 84, 183
political theory
anarchism and liberalism, 29–31
anti-statism, 13–14, 93–4, 187, 198

EU Authorised Representative:

Easy Access System Europe Mustamäe tee 50, 10621 Tallinn, Estonia

gpsr.requests@easproject.com

Printed and bound by CPI Group (UK) Ltd, Croydon, CR0 4YY

14/07/2025

01915952-0005